CRITICAL REFLECTIONS ON THE PARANORMAL

SUNY Series in Religious Studies
Harold Coward, Editor

CRITICAL REFLECTIONS ON THE PARANORMAL

Edited by
Michael Stoeber
Hugo Meynell

State University of New York Press

Published by
State University of New York Press, Albany

For information, address State University of New York Press,
State University Plaza, Albany, N.Y., 12246

Production by Marilyn P. Semerad
Marketing by Dana E. Yanulavich

Library of Congress Cataloging-in-Publication Data

Critical reflections on the paranormal / edited by Michael Stoeber,
   Hugo Meynell.
      p.   cm. — (SUNY series in religious studies)
   Includes bibliographical references and index.
      ISBN 0-7914-3063-4 (hardcover : alk. paper). — ISBN 0-7914-3064-2
(pbk. : alk. paper)
      1. Parapsychology. I. Stoeber, Michael (Michael F.)
   II. Meynell, Hugo Anthony. III. Series.
   BF1031.C84 1996
   133—dc20   96-1517
                                                                      CIP

10 9 8 7 6 5 4 3 2 1

CONTENTS

ACKNOWLEDGMENTS

Support for this book came from the Social Sciences and Humanities Research Council of Canada, a University Research Grant from The Catholic University of America, and from the School of Religious Studies and the Department of Religion and Religious Education at CUA. We thank the Council, the Grant Committee, William Cenkner, Raymond Collins, John Ford, and Stephen Happel for providing the resources for us to bring the manuscript together. In this regard, we appreciate very much the help of David Dawson, who provided very skillful technical and editorial assistance.

In "Parapsychology: Merits and Limits," by Donald Evans, some excerpts from Donald Evans, *Spirituality and Human Nature* (Albany, N.Y.: State University of New York Press, 1993) are reprinted by permission of the publisher. Quotations from "Terms and Methods in Parapsychological Research, *The Journal of the American Society for Psychical Research* 82, 4 (1988), 353–57; Rhea A. White, "Exceptional Human Experiences: The Generic Connection," *ASPR Newsletter* 18, 3 (1994), 1–6; William G. Braud and Marilyn J. Schlitz, "Psychokinetic Influence on Electrodermal Activity," *The Journal of Parapsychology* 47 (1983), 95–119; and Ian Hacking, "Some Reasons for Not Taking Parapsychology Very Seriously," *Dialogue* 32, 3 (1993), 587–94, are reprinted by permission of the publisher. "Reflections on Incorporeal Agency," is a development and expansion by Terence Penelhum of some arguments from "Divine Action and Human Action," in *Antropolgia e Filosofia della Religione*, ed. Albino Babolin (Perugia: Benucci, 1982). By permission of the editor. In "Postmortem Survival: The State of the Debate," by Stephen E. Braude, quotations from Ian Stevenson, "Birthmarks and Birth Defects Corresponding to Wounds on Deceased Persons," *Journal of Scientific Exploration* 7 (1993), 403–16, are reprinted by permission of the publisher.

1

CRITICAL REFLECTIONS ON THE PARANORMAL: AN INTRODUCTION

Michael Stoeber

Since the founding of the Society for Psychical Research in London in 1882 and its American counterpart in 1885, the paranormal has become the subject of serious academic enquiry. Led by philosophers such as A. J. Balfour, Henri Bergson, C. D. Broad, William James, and Henry Sidgwick, it has come to be regarded as a legitimate, though controversial area of study. Most facets of paranormal phenomena, those at least that seem to pertain to human states and powers, have come to be included within the distinctive discipline of psychical research or *parapsychology*, a term coined by J. B. Rhine.[1] The subject matter is abbreviated as *psi*: apparent "parapsychological factors or faculties collectively."[2] Formal experimental work was pioneered by people like Rhine at Duke University, S. G. Soal at London University, and W. Carrington at Cambridge University.[3] The *Journal of the American Society for Psychical Research* began circulation over eighty years ago, and today various refereed journals publish extensively on it.[4]

The paranormal has come to include in its field of reference a rather wide variety of apparent anomalies that involve states and powers that are ostensibly not explicable in terms of normal theories of perception and mechanical causation. Traditionally, it has been associated with extrasensory perception (ESP), within which are included telepathy, clairvoyance, precognition, psychokinesis (PK) or telekenesis, and mediumistic communications.[5] However, in an attempt to systematize intelligibly these and related phenomena, a helpful distinction might be made between (1) receptive-psi, signifying the psi which focusses on the receiving subject; and (2) expressive-psi, signifying the psi which focusses on the agent. A further distinction will also be made regarding

(3) otherworldly-psi, which posits the possibility of discarnate phenomena involved in various kinds of psi-reception and psi-expression.[6]

Receptive-psi includes (a) telepathy (where information or influence originates from another mind, rather than through normal sensory modes); (b) clairvoyance or remote viewing, clairaudience, and psychometry (where seen or heard information or influence originates from a physical object or event, rather than through normal sensory modes); (c) precognition (where information or influence occurs about the future); (d) postcognition (where past events are known without normal sensory means); (e) super-psi (exceptional psi-abilities); and (f) animal-psi (anpsi) (involving telepathy, clairvoyance, and clairaudience with respect to animals, including, for example, psi-trailing, homing, and healing).

Expressive-psi includes psychokinesis (where people, animals, and objects are directly influenced by a mind without normal sensory modes), which includes: (a) teleportation (movement of objects by PK), (b) hypnotism, (c) psychic healing and psychic stimulation, (d) levitation (where the subject elevates without normal means), (e) materialization (where objects are materialized from nowhere), and (f) apportation (where objects disappear and reappear in another location).

The field of study is further expanded and complicated by the inclusion of the possibilities of the influence of discarnate spirits or forms of disembodied existence in explaining certain paranormal phenomena.[7] In such contexts, psi events would involve realities beyond or distinct from that of this natural world. This obviously moves the paranormal beyond the discipline of parapsychology proper, and leads Donald Evans, for example, to distinguish between the possibilities of "this-worldly paranormal" (1 and 2 above) and "otherworldy paranormal."[8] Although otherworldly paranormal phenomena might possibly be explicable solely in terms given for (1) psi-reception and (2) psi-expression,[9] it is not clear that they are subcategories of these types, and they are usually described initially in terms of otherworldly reference. For systematic clarity I include them under a separate type, labelled "otherworldly-psi."

Otherworldly-psi includes (a) mediumistic communications (involving telepathy, clairvoyance, clairaudience, and automatic writing or speaking), (b) apparitions and poltergeists, (c) angelology, (d) spirit-possession, (e) out of body experiences or astral projection, (e) near-death experiences, and (g) past-life phenomena associated with rebirth or reincarnation claims.

The complexity of the subject and the advances made in the area naturally pose immense difficulties in coming to understand these phenomena and assessing their status. For example, isolating specific forms of receptive-psi and distinguishing in particular cases between receptive-psi and expressive-psi are notorious problems. Moreover, much specialization has occurred in the context of an ongoing accumulation of data. Experimental techniques have been refined and there has been much significant research done on the role of variables in the experimental dynamic.[10] For example, besides experimental methods and materials, various distinctive attitudes of the subjects clearly affect the data.[11] But there are wide-ranging variables pertaining to experimenter expectations and attitudes which also affect the experimental climate, ranging from fatigue to sexual attraction towards the subject.[12] As a consequence of the appreciation of the various physical, personal, and social factors surrounding the experimental climate of psi experiments, there is much controversy over the validity of specific research.[13]

But the popular appeal of the paranormal compounds the difficulties in studying and assessing the phenomena. The literature pertaining to it is vast but uneven in critical scope. Its treatment ranges from popular overviews to rigorous technical analyses, both sympathetic and disparaging of the various specific or general phenomena.

A cursory survey of the current publications reveals a wide variety of reaction to this complex area, from naively accepting the veracity of all the purported happenings to fiercely resisting the truth of any of it. It is a very controversial field in that it holds powerful emotional appeal, both positive and negative, for all segments of society. This is because its nature and status has significant implications for religious/atheistic, philosophical, and scientific attitudes and beliefs. It is a sensitive topic; it is intimately related, one way or the other, with fundamental experiences, attitudes, and worldviews.

Indeed, recent surveys would indicate that at least some paranormal experiences are not that uncommon. George Hansen notes "that over half the population in the U.S. have had psychic experiences and believe in the reality of the phenomena."[14] Since the 1970s there has been a significant rise in interest in the paranormal, including the development of the New Age movement as well as a more general popular openness to various forms of spiritualism, angelology, and paradeath phenomena and afterlife possibilities.[15]

On the other hand, there are those who are deeply skeptical of paranormal possibilities. One example is the Committee for the Scientific Investigation of Claims of the Paranormal (CSICOP), whose magazine, *The Skeptical Inquirer*, includes over 35,000 subscribers. This group is very media-proactive and influential, especially amongst the highly educated, despite the fact that it has largely abandoned scientific study and generally disregards the serious research of refereed journals of parapsychology. CSICOP focusses upon an "ongoing, organized debunking of the paranormal," which it considers to be characterized "by irrationalism, subjectivism, and obscurantism."[16]

The point of this volume is to examine critically such sweeping claims—to attempt to clarify the rational status of various distinctive facets of the paranormal in terms of recent studies and developments. In light of the radical divergence between its supporters and detractors, as well as the immense complexity of the topic, it seems crucial to bring some critical perspective to it. The essays in *Critical Reflections on the Paranormal* examine honestly and judiciously various aspects of the nature and implications of the paranormal, in light of contemporary treatments given by partisans, skeptics, and neutral observers of the phenomena. They involve reflections on assumptions, support, and criticism of various paranormal phenomena that have been generated by past and contemporary researchers and commentators on the field.

Hugo Meynell begins the focus in chapter 2, "On Investigation of the So-Called Paranormal," by distinguishing between three possible kinds of skeptical attitudes towards the paranormal. *Pseudoskepticism* assumes that all significant data that is gathered in support of various paranormal realities are the consequence of deception or lies on the part of relevant participants. This form is contrasted with legitimate skepticisms: *Skepticism-a* is the application of every paranormal claim, including those of their very possibility or impossibility, to appropriate measures of testing. These he adapts from Bernard Lonergan's epistemological framework: one ought to establish the nature of the phenomena, explore the various possible modes of its explanation, and tentatively determine that which is "the most convincing and economical," including an openness to evidence which would falsify such a judgment. *Skepticism-b* is the view that might follow from the application of the methods of scepticism-a: that no genuine paranormal events actually happen with respect to specific classes of the phenomena. Meynell considers both scepticism-a and -b to be legitimate attitudes, though he does not think that the application of scepticism-a in some areas of the paranormal will justify scepticism-b. The specific paranormal phenomena which he begins to examine in terms of the methodology of scepticism-a are cases of precognition, mediumistic phenomena, and afterlife possibilities.

Meynell uses his discussion of the research of J. B. Rhine and S. G. Soal as a springboard to raise the problems of fraud, natural law, experimenter variables, and replication. Fraud, a charge raised in the case of Soal's experiments, is always a possibility in paranormal activity and research, but Meynell insists that one ought not to subscribe to this explanation in cases where the evidence does not warrant it. For one thing, it is not clear that evidence against paranormal realities is always initially stronger than that which favors them. Perhaps paranormal powers and realities are not beyond the laws of nature; moreover, sometimes the evidence appears just as strongly in support of paranormal phenomena as other evidence tends to support particular natural laws. This kind of cumulative evidence means that one should not confidently *assume* the infallibility of scientific laws, nor presume deception at the outset.

Meynell also notes how skeptical attitudes might very well affect negatively parapsychological experiments. Performance proficiency in fields other than the paranormal is clearly affected by the attitudes of colleagues or observers, be they supportive or hostile. Meynell sees no reason why civility and encouragement on the part of the investigators is not compatible with critical acumen, especially since the expectation of fraudulence is unjustified as an assumption.

But even positive experimenter attitudes do not ensure successful replication of significant results. Productive participants of experiments often cannot even repeat their own performances, let alone other participants repeating successfully the same experiment. The issue is compounded by the "file drawer" theory, which supposes the existence of many unsuccessful experiments that go unreported. The database then remains incomplete, and the favorable results of those reported experiments are misleadingly distorted. But Meynell argues that recent research suggests that this problem is exaggerated, and in a number of cases reasonable file drawer estimates have not adversely affected the success of experiments.

Replication in the area of mediumistic performances is currently hindered by the apparent reluctance of contemporary practitioners to subject themselves to laboratory analyses. Although Meynell does not propose possible reasons for this reluctance, he constructively relates mediumistic accounts to afterlife issues. On its own, mediumistic evidence for afterlife possibilities is not very persuasive. But in combination with near-death accounts, as well as the many documented instances of automatic writing, clairvoyance, and astral projection, Meynell argues that the case for an afterlife becomes very strong indeed. This body of evidence in support of afterlife possibilities is further bolstered by recent work in support of past-life memories. Meynell argues that the cumulative strength of the source material is quite strong, "about the same order of evidential support as the theory of evolution." One must either agree that the case is quite formidable or postulate a massive, independent fraudulence or hallucination. Moreover, he closes his essay by suggesting a general account of personal identity in these contexts. He speaks of "quasi memories," with which one might identify psychologically and physically in various ways, and by which one can coherently suppose she is the same conscious subject with that of previous occurrences.

Like Hugo Meynell, Donald Evans is concerned in chapter 3 with the skeptical attitudes and assumptions brought to bear upon paranormal phenomena. In "Parapsychology: Merits and Limits," he focuses on the influence of positivistic scientific methodologies in parapsychological studies. Early in this chapter, Evans distinguishes between "causal mechanism" approaches to the paranormal and "psi-abilities." Causal mechanistic understandings arise from positivistic assumptions which insist on accounting for phenomena solely in terms of physical mechanisms. This approach demands proof that anomalies associated with the paranormal are not merely coincidental phenomena and seeks to explain them in terms of a scientific account of causal mechanisms. But this rules out the very possibility of psi-abilities involving influence without physical intervention (PK) or perception without the physical senses (ESP); in this view these labels signify anomalous events, not possible realities or abilities. On the other hand, the psi-abilities approach involves an assumption that agents can be causes ("*John* moves the billiard cue") even where we do not know what mechanical causation involving local contact is at work. This applies whether the human abilities be ordinary (moving a cue) or psi (PK).

Positivists assume that the only way to come to know reality is through the scientific method, insofar as it illuminates hidden causal mechanisms in terms of the principles of isolation, repeatability, quantifiability, and theoretical plausibility. Evans summarizes these principles, then discusses some of their limitations within the positivistic framework. Causal mechanisms cannot explain how mental activities might initiate physical changes, and there is evidence to suggest that consciousness can and does affect changes in the brain. Moreover, positivism assumes that the scientist is an agent who can apply at will the principles of science; it presupposes agent causality. Although clearly not all agent causality involves action of the mind upon matter, the positivist scientist herself assumes agent causality in her actions. Evans uses these arguments to support his view that human reality is more than what scientific methodology can uncover and explain.

This does not mean that scientific principles have no relevance to parapsychology. Not only do scientific experiments have a positive bearing upon attempts to prove or disprove the reality of psi-abilities, they also can illuminate the specific conditions within which various psi-abilities might obtain. Evans begins to illustrate these two points through an examination of the official statement of the Parapsychological Association. This statement calls for explanatory causal mechanisms to account for apparent anomalies. But to ignore statistically significant data until specific physical mechanisms are established is an unwarranted dogma. So too is the requirement to eliminate all alternative explanations, if the demand excludes the possibility of a psi-abilities explanation altogether.

Evans goes on to cite some of the difficulties mentioned by Meynell regarding replication in parapsychology, and responds to the issue optimistically. Perhaps psychic ability is not restricted only to certain gifted individuals and improves with practice. Moreover, although there are certain subjective and circumstantial factors involved in significant experiments, these can be replicated, even if the replication is not of an "impersonal" scientific nature.

Evans illustrates his views in reference to a series of apparently statistically significant psychokinetic experiments performed by William Braud and Marilyn Schlitz. The experiments, involving primarily nongifted psychics, focused not on uncovering causal mechanisms but rather on agent-causality as this might pertain to the practical application of psychic healing. Braud and Schlitz took careful measures to rule out placebo-explanations and fraud, as well as seven other possible nonkinetic explanations, including other paranormal powers. Although it is likely the experiments required positive openness and motivation towards success, these kinds of conditions are consistent with a variety of other human capabilities and their replication possibilities are not restricted to gifted psychics.

But also in reference to replication, Evans suggests that direct access to paranormal phenomena might be beyond the limits of strict science. Postivistic methodological assumptions restrict experience possibilities to those that can be impersonally verified. But if certain energies, powers, or events involve private experiences which arise only through a relevant process of personal change, positivistic perspectives cannot judge such truth claims, for these are not publicly observable phenomena, though some of the effects of these experiences might be. Evans says "the *meaning* of many statements is intrinsically linked with the *experiences* on which they are partly or entirely based and . . . many of these experiences are not accessible to people, or are only partly accessible, unless they undergo the appropriate *process* of personal change." So Evans argues both that it is rational to question impersonalist scientific dogma which insists we can only come to know reality through scientific methods, and that one should take seriously certain cases of alleged paranormal happenings. Even a single case, if it is adequately detailed, can provide reason for an individual to regard paranormal powers or cognitions as veridical. Citing unusual experiences arising in informal meditative settings, he suggests that the most effective ground from which to judge these happenings "is one's own personal experience of one's own psi-abilities."

David Ray Griffin further elaborates upon elements discussed by Evans, focusing in chapter 4 on the history and nature of mechanical causation, the various attitudes towards the paranormal, and the implications for the philosophy of religion and theology should certain paranormal powers come to be accepted. In "Why Critical Reflection on the Paranormal is so Important—and so Difficult," Griffin acknowledges the prevalence of the kind of pseudoskepticism cited by Hugo Meynell, and stresses the importance of an open-minded treatment of the evidence. The hostile and contemptuous a priori attitude on the part of many scientists and philosophers is explained by Griffin in terms of the serious threat parapsychology poses for the assumed basis of modern science—mechanical causation.

Parapsychology brings into question the assumption that all causation is a matter of direct contiguous action of one physical particle upon another. Griffin gives a brief account of paranormal events within the framework of the general categories of extrasensory perception and psychokinesis. These paranormal powers all seem to involve action at a distance or a nonmaterial causal influence, in contrast to the local contact associated with mechanical causation. Griffin suggests that historically the idea of action at a distance, or noncontiguous causation, was rejected over time in response to religious concerns that miracles might be interpreted in terms of natural influences, and because of worries that witchcraft might be theoretically grounded in such a perspective. Then interpretations of the theory of gravitation, dualistic perspectives, and even cosmological arguments all contributed to a belief that by the early modern period held that noncontiguous causal influence only occurred in supernatural intervention, a possibility which itself was eventually generally denied as materialism displaced dualism in the late modern period.

Griffin argues that a number of factors have contributed to the assumption by most contemporary scientists and philosophers of the impossibility of noncontiguous causal influence. The most important of these is the element of wishful thinking that influences two distinctive methodological orientations—the rational and the empirical. The rational is a methodology guided by paradigms, where prior beliefs frame the interpretation, and the empirical is the data-led, where data determines belief. Empirical evidence and rational argument favorable to parapsychology is regularly overlooked by both data-led empiricists and paradigmatic rationalists because of hopes and fears which include the potential frustration of scientific progress, the undermining of the authority and prestige of science, the presumed dangerous powers of parapsychics, the subversion of the supernatural claims of Christianity, and the revisions of science that parapsychological realities would entail.

But Griffin suggests that such revisions implicit to the acceptance of the paranormal, though significant, are not radically extreme. They would involve the inclusion of a second form of efficient causation—noncontiguous causal influence—which implies a mind-matter distinction (not an ontological dualism), but this feature can fit coherently into the current scientific worldview. Moreover, the hypothesis of this "action at distance" helps to provide an intelligible and coherent account of freedom, physical realism, and time, all of which are assumed phenomena that a solely sensationist theory of perception cannot explain.

From a religious, theological standpoint, the reality of parapsychology has significant implications. Noncontiguous causal influence explains how miracles might be perceived as no different from other forms of divine causation, and suggests that psychokinetic powers in the cases of extraordinary healing might be understood in terms of a divine-human cooperation. This would counter charges of divine impassibility or arbitrariness. More importantly, agent-causality provides an analogy within which one might conceive of divine activity in the world. If true, it also helps to support claims of religious experience, which in a strictly sensationist doctrine of perception are impossible. The paranormal thus might provide a credible analogue that gives claims of religious experience plausibility, including the possibility of the experience of nonphysical values as "one dimension of the constant experience of God." Moreover, postmortem afterlife possibilities of a disembodied nature are given intelligibility and plausibility in this paranormal perspective, in terms of ESP and PK. Out-of-body experiences, near-death accounts, past-life memories, and mediumistic phenomena can then be interpreted as evidence in support of afterlife possibilities.

In "Reflections on Incorporeal Agency," Terence Penelhum extends this discussion about the relevance of paranormal perspectives for religious beliefs, focusing specifically in chapter 5 on the possibility of noncontiguous causal influence. He provides an analysis of the nature of the activity of an incorporeal personal being, and develops the implications of such human spirit agency for the idea of divine agency.

The idea of spirit agency involves an effective action on an object external to the agent's body. Penelhum refers to a Cartesian model of normal human agency in order to illustrate spirit agency. This begins with a mental stage, involving choice or volition, which precedes both the body's movement and the actual movement of the object in question. Spirit agency would eliminate the body movement that occurs in normal processes of agency. In such cases either the judgment or intention directly affects the object (psychokinesis) or the object takes the role of the agent's body—where the object is "animated" by the agent's mind (animation).

In discussing these possibilities, Penelhum stresses the distinction between merely thinking or wishing a deed and the actual doing of a deed. He argues from this crucial dynamic that spirit agency involves the postulation of a mind-body dualism because it requires that the location of the efficacy of the intention, and not just its conception, be somewhere other than the body. There seem to be two possibilities: the intention is to be found either in the mental stage (PK) or in the object which acts as the body in the animation theory.

Penelhum analyzes both possible options of spirit agency. In the context of dualistic perspectives it has been suggested that PK is a power that is manifested in all normal mind-body interactions. In this view the movement of external objects is not an extraordinary claim—it is simply an extension of a power we exhibit in our normal unconscious body movement. But Penelhum points out that PK cannot be associated with the normal mental control of one's own body. Indeed, this unmediated control over one's own body is one of the conditions of it being one's own body; typical PK claims do not characterize the moved object as an aspect of the agent in question, and they moreover require conscious mental volition on the part of the subject.

On the other hand, the animation theory is sometimes perceived as more economical than PK for it appears not to involve the inner mental act. Penelhum questions this opinion. Although the animation theory involves the idea that the spirit temporarily occupies the moved object, the process is not "equivalent to the object's moving itself." As in the understanding of PK, volitional features of the animation process must be mental in nature in order to speak legitimately in terms of animation of spirit agency rather than those of the self-movement of an object. Though the animation theory suggests that the object plays a role similar to the spiritual agent's body, it must postulate, like the PK model, mental acts associated with the volitional agency of the spirit.

These considerations of both PK and animation do not illuminate the nature of the powers postulated in moving external objects through noncontiguous contact, nor do they clarify controversial issues of personal identity that are normally settled with reference to bodies, such as the processes of disembodied spirit-individuation or agent-identity through time. But Penelhum's reflections do have relevance to theological questions. Although the idea of incorporeality is sometimes cited as crucial in avoiding anthropocentric conceptions of God, Penelhum thinks that it suggests with respect to spirit agency that the mental life of God be "in some respects rather like ours."

Even if PK is suggested as a plausible account of divine activity, we still need to postulate a mental act prior to the movement in order to secure the distinction between God and the objects of divine activity. But this requirement of an effect mediated by an inner act would appear to impinge upon the notion of divine omnipotence. Moreover, to suggest an account of quasi-embodied animation does not solve the issue. Even if we propose an unmediated agent-control on the part of the Divine, likened somewhat to a person's mind-control over her own body, we must still postulate some kind of inner mental act distinct from the movement in order to maintain the distinction between the divine spirit and the object of activity, and thereby avoid the charge of pantheism.

There are of course significant differences between human intentions and the idea of divine intentions: God does not attempt and fail in action, nor does the Divine have conflicts or changes of intention, as humans do. Although these differences accentuate the necessity of analogy in human reference to divine intentions, Penelhum nevertheless insists "there would seem to be a logical requirement that there be some feature of the divine mental life that performs the same role or function that inner expressions of intention play in our case, and in that of finite spirits, if there are any."

In chapter 6, Susan Armstrong also relates issues in paranormal phenomena to religious questions, though she focuses specifically on the question of the postmortem survival of animals. In "Souls in Process: A Theoretical Inquiry into Animal Psi," she suggests with David Griffin that psi supports afterlife possibilities. She develops her argument in the context of an overview of the varied evidence of animal psi. Like Donald Evans, who stresses the significance of single instances of alleged paranormal happenings, she affirms the importance of spontaneous psi phenomena, generally referred to as anecdotal evidence. Although the weaknesses in such an approach are many, including distorted accounting, lack of replication, and sampling and investigative biases, they avoid the difficulties of sterile experimental settings which can inhibit performance, and they can have some bearing upon the more careful and systematic analysis of the other two kinds of evidence, the formal experimental or semi-experimental.

Armstrong goes on to illustrate a wide variety of all three kinds of evidence that has accumulated over the last sixty years with respect to animal psi. Although she acknowledges the various difficulties in testing both human and animal psi, as well as the questions and limitations of some of the experiments, she judges the data of the varied studies to be significant. It "suggests that individual animals of many species exhibit some degree of psi functioning," but typically as psi recipients rather than givers.

In attempting to account for these phenomena, she proposes A. N. Whitehead's "process thought." In Whitehead's metaphysics, ultimate reality is depicted in terms of "actual occasions" or momentary events. The defining characteristics of things are a result of a sequence "of occasions of experience" which vary in complexity according to the arrangement of the "situation" or world within which they are positioned. Past actual occasions contribute to an actual occasion through the feeling or "prehending" of these previous occasions into the actual, which gives it form. In this way it becomes an enduring entity of either an aggregate form, with no dominant member, or a form with a dominant entity, which can be called a "dominant occasion." In the latter type, the dominant member consolidates not only subordinate entities but also subordinate societies of past and actual occasions. The human psyche is an example of a very complicated and centrally organized dominant occasion, intimately connected to a vast array of past and actual occasions which play a significant role in its development and constitution, as various prehensions integrate these into momentary experiences.

It is with respect to the experiences of these actual occasions that the paranormal becomes prominent. Normal sensory experience involves a presentational immediacy through temporal events that are linked contiguously together. Its immediate nature gives it a general clarity and consciousness of perception that is not typical of paranormal perception via the "mode of causal efficacy." This second, nonsensory, mode of perception is grounded in the metaphysical relation of occasions of experience, where feeling or intuition of past and other occasions discloses reality directly, "without other actual occasions in between." The transmission of these intuitive prehensions is immediate, bypassing typical contiguous chains through atemporal forms which link various occasions together at subtle levels. Armstrong speaks of "hybrid physical prehension," wherein earlier occasions feel themselves in the context of the actual occasion. This means that usually this immediate conceptual prehension is unconscious, hidden by the contiguous consciousness of the present actual occasion. Sensory consciousness mediates psi activities by its very attention to present circumstances. But occasionally an immediate prehension becomes a conscious phenomenon, thereby revealing this noncontiguous mode of perception to consciousness.

Although animal psi is primarily receptive, rather than expressive, it nevertheless suggests that animals are constituted by distinctive psyches. Armstrong argues that because evidence would suggest that animals participate in hybrid physical prehension, they must have minds like, though simpler than, humans. Insofar as one maintains human postmortem survival on the grounds of the nature of the psyche, one should extend this belief to animals. She points to evidence of animal apparitions to bolster her argument, and closes her paper with a summary of religious perspectives on animal immortality, including four kinds of arguments to support the possibility: divine justice, an extension of the idea of spirituality beyond that of human rationality, universal salvation, and divine love.

Extending the focus on this theme of afterlife possibilities, Heather Botting examines paradeath phenomena, or near-death experiences in chapter 7. In "Medico-scientific Assumptions Regarding Paradeath Phenomena: Explanation or Obfuscation?" she outlines in the context of various illustrations two possible kinds of explanations of the phenomena. Standard physiological accounts depict such experiences as the consequence of drugs or anesthetics, or brain trauma or dysfunction, wherein anoxia leads to a disruption of the temporal lobe, releasing endorphins into the bloodstream. These in turn lead to deluded visions and feelings of euphoria displacing the intense fear involved in the physical trauma. The other option centers the cause in the mind rather than the brain, suggesting a sentient and conscious disembodied existence to account for the phenomena of paradeath experiences.

Botting cites the work of Karlis Osis, which speaks against the physiological accounts of paradeath experiences, and she goes on to argue that temporary disembodiment accounts do not trivialize the pain and suffering normally associated with death, as some critics have argued. Moreover, critics who point towards unpleasant paradeath experiences and cases of no paradeath experiences in criticizing afterlife possibilities fail to appreciate that such phenomena count just as strongly against physiological accounts. How can innate physiology explain both positive *and* negative near-death experiences? And why does such an innate response not occur in some cases?

Moreover, physiology cannot explain paradeath experiences that are conscious—the "peak-in-Darien" phenomena which involve conscious visions. Nor does it account for factual knowledge claims that could not arise through normal sensory experiences, when near-death victims claim to recognize people and events beyond their sensory range. Even ESP on the part of people present with the paradead person cannot account for this phenomenon in cases when the facts remain as yet unknown.

Botting notes the kind of dogmatic defiance exuded by certain positivists, as Donald Evans illustrates in his essay, and goes on to show the limitations of wish fulfillment and delusion in treating the paradeath phenomena of peak-in-Darien experiences and various kinds of apparitions. Moreover, physiological accounts have yet to provide a thorough explanation of these and other specific elements of the paradeath phenomenon. Like David Griffin, she suggests that the general resistance to paradeath and other paranormal events in general is not because of effective objective scientific reasons but rather "a matter of personal belief and explanation."

She too questions the effectiveness of mechanistic-materialist paradigms in accounting for paradeath phenomena, and criticizes the insensitive mistreatment and disparagement of those people who experience or study phenomena that fail to fit the established scientific framework. Botting suggests that the hostile attitudes of some skeptics might be grounded in the very inability of socioscientific models to account intelligibly for paradeath phenomena. Evidence continues to bring the system into question, but the deep resistance to scientific revolution forces the anomalies to be treated as deviant—a consequence of physiological defects or pathologies on the part of the subjects. Like Donald Evans, she argues that mechanistic-materialist models might not be the sole means for knowing reality, and calls for one which can conform to the various dimensions of experience.

In chapter 8, Stephen Braude further pursues the question of the relevance of the paranormal in supporting afterlife possibilities, though he takes a contrasting position from that of Heather Botting with respect to the possibility of ESP as a plausible explanation. In "Postmortem Survival: The State of the Debate," he focuses primarily upon the research concerning ostensive past-life memories that some people have considered to support rebirth or reincarnation claims. Rather than proposing survivalist hypotheses, Braude proposes the possibility of "super-psi" to account for the phenomena. He suggests that cases of knowledge of or other characteristics related to a past life might be adequately explained by reference to super-psi—an unusually refined and high degree of psychic functioning on the part of living subjects—rather than by associating a past life with the subject in question.

Much of the resistance to such a possibility on the part of researchers, argues Braude, is unwarranted, and by neglecting the super-psi hypothesis the survival literature is to some extent limited and misdirected in its approach. He argues that the extent of posited psi in such cases is neither radically excessive nor different from typical psi functioning. The possibility of such a high level of psi functioning is supported by mediumistic phenomena, certain PK experiments, and ostensible precognition. But crucial to its plausibility is the recognition that psi in this context would be "motivated": Braude "posits the operation of psychic abilities in the service of some agent's genuine or perceived real-life needs and interests." Moreover, the relationship between psi and normal human demands and concerns very likely extends to unconscious—and therefore often hidden—desires and motivations.

But the survival literature generally ignores the psychological nuances that would be associated with the operation of psi in terms of covert and inconspicuous interests or needs. Various forms of personality dissociation, for example, evidence strikingly similar phenomena to that of mediumship cases, and seem relevant to certain reincarnation cases. It "appears that dissociation liberates or permits the development of abilities that would presumably not have manifested in normal waking states." In cases involving reincarnation claims, personality dissociation would combine with the psi functioning of living subjects to explain the phenomena.

Braude begins to illustrate the deficiencies of research in this regard by examining the hypothesis of parental influence in explaining purported past-life memories of children. This hypothesis has been proposed and rejected by some researchers, on the grounds that parents in certain cases have no prior detailed knowledge of the deceased person who is associated with their child's alleged memories, nor knowledge of other reincarnation cases. But Braude argues that other cases are irrelevant to the specific instance; and, more importantly, such a focus does not address the crucial questions of possible parental motives for desiring a child's association with any, or a specific, previous personality. What is important in such cases, and would provide information pertinent to the super-psi hypothesis, is "the personal meaning *behind* the detail." In what ways might the past-life connection of the child be significant to the parent? This information requires a depth-psychological probing on the part of the researcher that is generally lacking in alleged rebirth cases.

Braude goes on in his essay to respond specifically to critical issues raised for the super-psi hypothesis, including an exploration of the relevance of out-of-body experiences (OBEs) as evidence for survival. In cases of OBEs, he suggests a two-stage ESP process wherein the subject first interacts with another mental (telepathically) or physical (clairvoyantly) state of affairs, followed by an interpretive context wherein the subject filters the material "according to their own psychological idiosyncracies, prevailing moods, needs, concerns, etc." Such an account, argues Braude, suggests how OBEs might be "a particularly vivid (or imagery rich) form of veridical ESP," one which accounts through the second (interpretive) stage for the wide variations in accuracy and depth and degree of images of subjects, and without the need to postulate the actual presence of the subject at the location in question.

But Braude's specific responses to critical issues facing the hypothesis of super-psi are bolstered by an overriding and crucial concern: further depth-psychological analyses of individuals relevant to specific cases are required in order to assess properly not only the super-psi hypothesis but also the survivalist explanation that is opposed to it. And this demand applies not only to cases of ostensible rebirth, but extends also to other survival research.

Despite his resistance to survivalist accounts of alleged past-life memories and out of body phenomena, Braude feels that research pertaining to postmortem survival is significant enough to rule out "malobservation, misreporting, and fraud" in a substantial body of cases. Hugo Meynell agrees in his essay on this point, but not all scholars share this view. Heather Botting acknowledges the negative attitude evinced by certain skeptics towards both subjects of near-death experiences and parapsychologists who are sympathetic to them. With reference to paranormal phenomena in general, David Griffin mentions Henry Sidgwick's observation about the "absolute disdain on a priori grounds" of some skeptics towards various aspects of the paranormal. Often this critical attitude takes the form of moral denunciation, questioning the character of both subjects and parapsychologists. Both Donald Evans and Hugo Meynell mention the problem of fraud in this regard. Meynell labels as "pseudo-skepticism" the extreme position that all significant evidence supporting paranormal phenomena is a result of deception or lies, and argues that it ought not be assumed at the outset in evaluating paranormal claims. Evans suggests that paranormal powers might very well be within the grasp of most people and might even improve with practice. By focusing experiments away from gifted psychics towards these neophytes, the parapsychologist can better secure against the charge of fraud.

In chapter 9, "Morality and Parapsychology," James Horne draws this question of fraud into the larger issue of the moral status of the paranormal. He focuses primarily on parapsychology, the study of the paranormal, and frames the moral issue within the question of its status as a practice: "Is it a cooperative human activity that tends to produce and extend human good, or does it tend to do the opposite?" He then goes on to answer this question by responding to three standard charges raised against parapsychology.

Parapsychology has been accused of wasting human resources, of being fraught with morally culpable human errors, and of having a corrupting influence upon both subjects and experimenters. Against the first charge, that it is an indulgence that squanders time and resources, Horne notes J. S. Mill's observations about the importance of a "mixed life" which includes recreational pursuits within the framework of more useful or pragmatic ideals. To include parapsychology as a respectable activity of such a mixed life, however, requires that it be a morally and intellectually acceptable field of endeavor. This relates to the second and third charges.

On the question of fraud, Horne notes that the moral character of the founders of parapsychology has generally not been in doubt, but rather their methodologies have been questioned. One must distinguish between the fraudulent character of the experimenters and weak experimental designs that leave open the possibility of deception on the part of subjects. It is important to maintain the distinction between parapsychologists who investigate paranormal claims, and the subjects of their experiments, some of whom have been disreputable. The cases of proven fraudulence on the part of scientists, even in contemporary studies, are relatively rare, hardly endemic as some critics have charged. Rather, Horne cites the similarities in character and results between parapsychologists and scientists of more respectable fields, which also include their share of fraudulence. Moreover, there have been limited positive results in paranormal experimentation for a variety of reasons: weak experimental designs, the difficulties in isolating paranormal events, and problems of replication. But these limitations do not speak against the morality of the practice.

Rather, the morality of the practice is brought into question given the nature of the examined phenomena. As Donald Evans points out in his paper, the subject matter of parapsychology is private, not open to the public verification that is associated with the "hard" sciences. Horne notes the similar difficulties facing psychologists of religion, and goes on to discuss the significance of empathy on the part of parapsychologists towards their subjects as well as the characteristic state of mind associated with successful performances. Participants are most effective when they are interested, calm, and hopeful about the results. Moreover, subjects and experimenters both must be subjectively involved in the process in order to secure the best results.

This, indeed, raises concerns about parapsychology as a science. However, this "sheep-goat effect," as Horne describes it in reference to the work of Gertrude Schmeidler, is found also in social psychology, in terms of the Rosenthal effect. Experimental climate is a crucial element for both parapsychology and psychology. Moreover, he cites instances in anthropology which also involved experimenter involvement in understanding certain phenomena. Both parapsychology and the practice of magic occur in situations of chance and involve unverifiable beliefs. Both hold that experience can be transformed beneficially in the context of outstanding coincidences, when a positive attitude is brought to bear upon particular circumstances. Linking magic to parapsychology, Horne suggests "that successful parapsychologists not only study magic but on occasion participate in it."

Horne cautiously defends such practices, even though he associates the patterns of imagination and attitude of both subjects and experimenters of parapsychology with the orientation of gamblers. Indeed, the morality of gambling has been challenged much in the manner that Horne questions parapsychology in his essay. The charges of wastefulness, foolishness, fraudulence, and obsession have been raised against gambling by its critics. But these condemnations are not decisive. There may be some benefits associated with gambling. It only becomes clearly destructive in extreme cases involving abuses, corruption, and addiction.

Nevertheless, the serious dangers gambling poses to addictive personalities parallels and illustrates the moral perils associated with parapsychology. The paranormal can become an addictive and destructive obsession for some people. Horne concludes that there are real moral risks associated with parapsychology. But there is no more reason to disapprove of it than there is to object to gambling or certain religious practices.

∽⌇∾

Despite major differences in focus, approach, and position of the various authors of this volume, there are common or related concerns weaving through the chapters. James Horne addresses specifically an issue raised both directly and indirectly in many of the chapters, arguing that in and of itself parapsychology is not an immoral practice. A number of the authors address fundamental methodological issues, especially as these pertain to extreme skepticism towards paranormal phenomena. Heather Botting points out weaknesses in physicalist accounts of paradeath experiences, calling for further reflection on mechanistic-materialist paradigms of inquiry. This latter opinion is echoed by both David Griffin and Donald Evans. Griffin explores possible reasons behind the resistance towards such methodological revision, and notes some of the implications of a scientific model that would include the possibility of noncontiguous causal influence. Evans illustrates the limitations of positivist scientific methodologies, elucidates a psi-abilities approach, and stresses the significance of further paranormal research even in the absence of causal mechanistic understandings of apparent paranormal powers and realities.

Some of the authors, directly or indirectly, discuss issues associated with various otherworldly psi. Like David Griffin and Donald Evans, Hugo Meynell criticizes extreme skepticism associated with various paranormal phenomena and discusses specifically questions associated with research and experimentation. Both Meynell and Griffin suggest the relevance of receptive-psi and expressive-psi for issues pertaining to postmortem survival. Terence Penelhum explores the nature and implications of certain paranormal powers as they apply to spirit agency, and evaluates their relevance for questions surrounding divine agency. Heather Botting clarifies elements surrounding near-death experiences, while Susan Armstrong evaluates in the context of process thought the status of animal psi, and develops its implications for afterlife possibilities. Finally, Stephen Braude stresses the importance of depth psychology in illuminating cases of past-life memory, and defends in this context super-psi as a plausible explanation of the postmortem survival phenomena.

But the most common, general thrust of the diverse contributions of this book is found in the approach to and regard for the subject. Certain paranormal phenomena do not warrant attitudes of extreme and dogmatic skepticism, but rather invite the kind of serious and critical attention on the part of both empirical researchers and philosophers that is evidenced by the authors of this volume.

NOTES

1. G. R. Schmeidler, *Parapsychology and Psychology: Matches and Mismatches*, (Jefferson, North Carolina: McFarland, 1988), 7.

2. J. B. Sykes, *The Concise Oxford Dictionary*, 7th ed. (Oxford: Clarendon, 1982).

3. Regarding the controversies surrounding S. G. Soal, see the chapters by Hugo Meynell and James Horne in this volume.

4. For example, *Journal for the American Society for Psychical Research, Journal of Parapsychology, International Journal of Parapsychology, European Journal of Parapsychology, Journal of the Society for Psychical Research, Journal of Scientific Exploration.*

5. C. W. K. Mundle, "ESP Phenomena, Philosophical Implications of," *The Encyclopedia of Philosophy*, vol. 3, ed. Paul Edwards (New York: Macmillan, 1967), 49–58.

6. This schematic is influenced very much by the chapters in this volume by David Ray Griffin, Susan Armstrong, and Donald Evans. See also David Ray Griffin, "Parapsychology and Philosophy: A Whiteheadian Postmodern Perspective," *Journal of the American Society for Psychical Research* 87, no. 3 (1993), 217–88. Although extraterrestrial phenomena, astrology, and palmistry are sometimes included as paranormal phenomena, it is not clear how they are related to the major categories. I do not attempt to draw them into this general schematic.

7. For example, besides the postulation by some thinkers of real, creative, and autonomous disembodied entities in attempts to account for certain mediumistic communications, C. D. Broad postulated the possibility merely of a temporary psychic factor which includes certain experiential modifications or memory traces of the deceased individual with which the medium links.

8. See Donald Evans's chapter in this volume.

9. See, for example, the chapter by Stephen Braude in this volume, which proposes various forms of psi as an explanation for certain postmortem paranormal phenomena.

10. For a good summary of the research pertaining to experimental variables, see G. R. Schmeidler, *Parapsychology and Psychology*, especially 29–92. She also provides a significant bibliography concerning relevant past and recent reseach in this area.

11. For example, M. T. Orne has distinguished subjects in terms of the common types of "antagonistic," "apprehensive," "good," and "faithful." See "On the Social Psychology of the Psychological Experiment: With Particular Reference to Demand Characteristics and Their Implications," *American Psychologist* 17 (1962), 776–83. See Schmeidler, *Parapsychology and Psychology*, 32–33, for a summary of the problem.

12. See R. Rosenthal, *Experimenter Effects in Behavioral Research*, (New York: Appleton-Century-Crofts, 1966).

13. See the chapters by Susan Armstrong, Hugo Meynell, Donald Evans, and James Horne in this volume.

14. G. P. Hansen, "CSICOP and the Skeptics: An Overview," *Journal of the American Society for Psychical Research* 85 (1992), 51. Hansen cites on this infor-

mation A. Greeley "Mysticism Goes Mainstream," *American Health* 6 (1987), 47–49, and E. Haraldsson and J. M. Houtkooper, "Psychic Experiences in the Multinational Human Values Study: Who Reports Them?" *Journal of the American Society for Psychical Research* 85 (1991), 145–65.

15. See the chapters by Heather Botting, Hugo Meynell, and Stephen Braude in this volume.

16. Hansen, "CSICOP and the Sceptics," 19, 22, 41–42.

2

ON INVESTIGATION OF THE SO-CALLED PARANORMAL

Hugo Meynell

In this chapter I intend to do two things: (1) to consider what is the proper way of investigating those actual or alleged phenomena which are often labeled "paranormal"; and (2) to inquire about the bearing of such phenomena on the question of life after death.[1]

It may seem quite unnecessary to make the point that the proper aim of investigating any phenomenon whatever is discovery of the truth behind it. But unfortunately, as a recent book about physical mediumship laments,[2] such a motive is by no means to be taken for granted in this area. Investigators seem much too ready to assume the mantle of lawyer, either for the prosecution or for the defense. Sir Karl Popper's admirable maxim, that one should always be on the look-out for evidence which would tend to falsify one's hypothesis,[3] should be borne in mind at least as much in this as in other areas of human concern.

The basic questions to be asked with regard to the paranormal are whether phenomena of certain types occur, and if they do, what are the most satisfactory explanations of them. I do not think it is useful to purport to dispose of these questions a priori by distinguishing between "scientific" and "magical" views of the world, and then stating or insinuating that anyone who does not reject out of hand belief in the reality of any kind of paranormal phenomenon hankers after the "magical" way of thinking.[4] In general, we have two kinds of explanation for phenomena; the physical kind best exemplified by natural science, and that involving appeal to conscious agents. It is by no means clear that the latter kind of explanation is dispensable, or that it can even in principle be reduced to or replaced by explanation of the former kind. Indeed, there are good reasons, as I shall argue briefly below, to the effect that it is neither dispensable nor so reducible or replaceable. Many paranormal phenomena seem to demand an extension of agent-type explanations beyond the range where they would ordinarily seem to be applicable; as when someone appears to possess information which they could not have acquired by the normal means, or to be able to influence the course of events without the ordinary kinds of bodily contact. In other cases, like mediumistic "communications" and some poltergeist phenomena, there seems to be a question of agents who either are bodiless or possess bodies of a rarefied kind.

It is easy to say that the right way of investigating these matters is the strictly scientific one. But it is strongly disputed just what it is for an investigation to be scientific, and over how great a range of problems scientific method should be applied. How, if at all, does one adapt "scientific" inquiry, for example, to the treatment of ethical, metaphysical, or religious questions? Are the methods of the natural sciences to be extended without modification to what are sometimes called the human sciences? If they are not, what types of modification are needed, and why? Questions like these can hardly be avoided if one is going to consider applying "scientific" methods to the matters in which we are interested here.

Actually, I believe that there *is* a very general method adapted to finding out the truth about any matter of fact whatever;[5] I do not intend to be sidetracked into the interminable ramifications of the question whether this is or is not in all respects identical with "scientific" method, though I think it can be shown quite easily that all inquiries worth dignifying with the honorific title "scientific" in fact follow it. This consists roughly of three parts: (1) establishing what the relevant phenomena are; (2) thinking up a range of ways in which they might be accounted for; and (3) judging tentatively that that one is the most liable to be the case which explains the phenomena in the most convincing and economical way. Attempts to tamper with the phenomena, or to rule out possible explanations on the basis of metaphysics (including materialist metaphysics) or of sheer prejudice, should be avoided like the plague; unfortunately, neither abuse seems to be exceptional or even uncommon in this line of inquiry.

The expression "materialist metaphysics" is regarded as an oxymoron in some circles. Yet it has been stated that the essence of "scientific" explanation is that it should be materialistic.[6] This is a metaphysical dogma which seems to be falsified by the very existence of science itself—unless indeed it is to be conceded that there are some kinds of inquiry into the truth about things where "scientific" method is not appropriate. Science in a broad sense is a matter of attending to data, constructing hypotheses, and affirming provisionally as true those hypotheses which seem best corroborated by the data. But to make a judgment *because* it is corroborated by data is at first sight at least incompatible with being caused by any sort of mechanism to make that judgment. Recent philosophy is littered with attempts to make it appear that this incompatibility is only apparent; if many of them do credit to the ingenuity of their proponents, they all appear to be unsuccessful.[7] But how is acting for reasons related to being influenced by causes? We are all physical organisms, and so presumably subject to physical and chemical laws; yet if we could not also act and speak for reasons, science itself, which in accordance with a strict metaphysical materialism eliminates acting for reasons in favor of determination by physical causes, would be impossible. It is sometimes complained, in the context of investigations of the paranormal, that no one has ever shown how a mind could directly influence what is external to its body; as though how a mind could directly influence what is *internal* to its body were not equally obscure. But if minds can exert no such influence, as I have just briefly argued, then science itself lies in ruins.

Since it seems to me that the word *skeptic* and its cognates (*skeptical, skepticism*) are often abused in this connection, I would like to distinguish various uses of the term. The kind of extreme philosophical skepticism which doubts, or purports to doubt, whether knowledge is available to us on any matter whatever, will not be at issue. I propose the label *"skepticism,"* or *pseudo-skepticism*, for the attitude which assumes from the start that all reports of paranormal phenomena are due to error or downright lies, before they have even been considered; and then deals with them accordingly. *Skepticism-a* is the attitude which treats every claim whatever as subject to testing at the bar of the relevant evidence, whether it is the claim that some paranormal event has occurred, or that it has not occurred, or that no paranormal event ever occurs, or that such events sometimes do occur.[8] This attitude *may* result in what I shall call *skepticism-b*, which is the considered opinion that no paranormal events ever occur; but that it *must* do so cannot be taken for granted by the skeptical-a investigator.

"Skepticism" or pseudo-skepticism is to be deplored in investigations of any kind, but is unfortunately particularly common in this one; "skeptics" are not always above subjecting to public contempt and ridicule those who sincerely report evidence which is not to their liking.[9] Skepticism-a, on the contrary, is the attitude which ought to be cultivated by investigators of any matter whatever. The skeptic-a is characterized by cultivation of the Popperian disposition which I have already mentioned; she is always particularly on the look-out for evidence *against* the theory which she happens to favor. Skepticism-b is a position worthy of the utmost respect, whether one happens to occupy it or not. When I refer to skepticism without qualification in what follows, the reader may assume that I am referring to skepticism-b; that is to say, to the belief that honest and impartial scrutiny of the relevant evidence tends to indicate that paranormal phenomena never occur. (Of course, one may be a skeptic-b with respect to some classes of paranormal phenomena, though not to others.)

The differences between skepticism-a or -b on the one hand, and "skepticism" or pseudo-skepticism on the other, may be illustrated by an anecdote from my own experience. A case was reported which achieved some notoriety in the 1950s: an American housewife named Virginia Tighe had, or claimed to have had, "memories" of the life of Bridey Murphy, an Irishwoman who lived in the early part of the nineteenth century. A friend of mine who is interested in such reports told me what a scandal it was that this case was taken so seriously by many people, when it had been so conclusively disposed of as due to error or fraud. Now I at the time knew only the barest outline of the case, and could make no informed judgment about it. However, I did know of two persons who were likely to know much more about it than I did,[10] so I got in touch with both of them and repeated what my friend had said. Their reactions were immediate and indignant; and both, independently of one another, referred me to the discussion of the matter in C. J. Ducasse's book *The Belief in a Life After Death*.[11]

There I read what is surely a classic example of the "debunking" of a "'debunking.'" The "exposers" were exposed as gratuitously assuming from the start that memories of a past incarnation could not be the explanation of Mrs. Tighe's statements; as plainly ignorant of some of the facts that were unearthed in Ireland; and as having resorted to the old and shabby trick of explaining away the data by animadversions on the motives of those who had reported or publicized them. The point is not that the claim that Mrs. Tighe was the reincarnated Bridey Murphy was vindicated, but that a particular claim to discredit it was exposed as intellectually and evidentially worthless. The moral to be drawn from this affair, I think, is that neither the believer nor the skeptic is to be absolved from the obligation of being critical of the arguments of those on her own side of the question. Both should remember that admirable practice of Charles Darwin, who kept a notebook in which he jotted down all the data he came across that told against his own theories. The fact is that "skepticism" or pseudo-skepticism is really a kind of credulousness—in the infallibility of common sense or of scientific laws as known at present—but less respectable than other kinds in that it is apt to be fuelled by contempt for one's fellow human beings, who are supposed so foolishly to be bamboozled into believing such absurd falsehoods as the actual occurrence of paranormal events. "Debunking" is a practice which is wholeheartedly to be commended, when it is a matter of arrival at skepticism-b by way of skepticism-a—in other words, when it is honest and impartial. But much of what goes under the name of debunking appears to be neither.

Systematic investigation of alleged paranormal events of a kind which is "scientific," in however broad or narrow a sense, may be said to have begun with the foundation of the (British) Society for Psychical Research in 1882. The history of this kind of investigation since then has been amply chronicled elsewhere,[12] and there is no point in going over it again here. But it does have some remarkable features which are very much relevant to our concerns. One might have expected that more than a century of intensive research would have established some kind of broad consensus among scientists and the educated community about the status of these phenomena. But this is not the case at all. Now, just as in the late nineteenth century, a large proportion of the scientific community regards serious investigation of these phenomena with contempt, assuming that all reports of them can be attributed to a combination of credulity and chicanery. But a remarkable number of scientists who in other respects at least seem first-rate—Sir William Crookes, Alfred Russel Wallace, Robert Hare, Charles Richet, Sir Oliver Lodge—have become convinced by the weight of the evidence of the genuineness of some paranormal phenomena, sometimes when they had previously been very skeptical.

During the first half-century or so of these investigations, attention was devoted to study of spontaneous manifestations of apparently paranormal powers in persons who seemed to be specially gifted in this respect. There was an important development in the subject in 1929, when Joseph Banks Rhine began to conduct his famous card-guessing experiments at Duke University in North Carolina. Rhine's work seemed to give promise for the first time of subjecting these elusive phenomena to experimental control. The results at first seemed to be quite sensational; Hubert Pearce, Rhine's most talented subject, once achieved results of which the chances against explanation by normal means was 5 to the 25th—a number of the order of 300 quadrillions—to one. Appeal was made to the American Mathematical Association to discredit Rhine's use of statistics; unfortunately, that august body found that it was unable thus to oblige the skeptics. However, other laboratories were unable to replicate Rhine's results, and plausible suggestions were not lacking as to how there might have been fraud or unconscious contamination of the data by Rhine or his subjects. (It should be mentioned that no charge of fraud was ever substantiated against Rhine.)

For several decades the experiments of S. G. Soal, which were carried out at the University of London in the late 1930s and the 1940s, appeared to constitute a major component of the database for a science of parapsychology. The story of Soal is so depressingly typical of this field that it is worth giving a summary of it here.[13] Soal had tried unsuccessfully for some time to replicate Rhine's results. But someone made the suggestion that there might be a displacement effect in his data. Soal needed a great deal of prodding to submit himself to the tedium of going over the records of his experiments again; but when he did so, he came out with strikingly positive results when he attended to the correlation between the guesses of his experimental subjects and the card *after* the target card. However, Soal actually must have cheated in the course of his experiments, as was finally discovered in 1978 through a remarkable combination of ingenuity and good luck, by Betty Markwick.[14] Now that so important a part of the database of parapsychology has been discovered, largely as a result of chance, to be due to fraud, is it not only too plausible, the skeptic asks, to assume that the rest could be explained by a mixture of fraud and honest error if only the truth were known?[15] It is perhaps worth mentioning that Markwick's own conclusions about the affair are hardly such as to oblige the skeptic, let alone the "skeptic." She thought that Soal might have initially got some positive results, which he then proceeded to bolster by chicanery. If he had been disposed to cheat all along, it is rather difficult to account for his initial lack of results, or his reluctance to accept the proposal that he should go through his records again.[16] But certainly his results are rendered in general quite worthless by the discovery of his fraud.

Rhine himself, followed recently by the physicist John Hasted, claimed that an attitude of enthusiastic helpfulness on the part of the experimenter, and a disposition to treat the experimental subject as a collaborating colleague rather than an object of suspicion, tends to promote the production of positive results. It has been objected on the other side that it is this very attitude which encourages experimental subjects to cheat, and enables them to get away with doing so.[17] For myself, I find it rather surprising to assume that it is not possible for investigators at once to be civil and encouraging *and* to be on the look-out for sharp practice. In fact, it seems to me that such an assumption—that *either* one must treat experimental subjects in a suspicious and discouraging manner, *or* one is leaving the way wide open for cheating—is essentially appropriate to a lawyer; it assumes that the experimenter must be out to make a case either for the prosecution or for the defense. The genuine seeker for truth will surely be open to both possibilities, and will adjust her behavior towards her experimental subjects accordingly.

Certainly, that a negative attitude on the part of an experimenter is liable adversely to affect a subject's performance can seem a lame excuse, and not only if one is a "skeptic." But is it really a hypothesis that can be dismissed a priori? Are not the performances of actors, lecturers, concert performers, and others notoriously liable to be affected positively by the enthusiasm of their audiences, and adversely by their suspicion or hostility? Why should not the same apply to a person's proficiency in telepathy, psychokinesis, precognition, or whatever?[18]

In relation to paranormal phenomena, many people appear to have an attitude of a kind which finds classical expression in David Hume's argument against miracles.[19] Some indeed have explicitly appealed to Hume in this context.[20] His argument, briefly expressed, goes as follows. A miracle is a violation of a law of nature, which is to say that human experience is uniformly against it—laws of nature being nothing other than the correlations between phenomena which are confirmed by uniform human experience. But it is by no means a law of nature that human beings never lie, or are never deceived. Unless we assume that laws of nature hold uniformly, moreover, there is no way in which we can establish any matter of fact whatever by appeal to evidence, as the connection between any matter of fact and the evidence for it depends on the holding of such laws. Consequently, the evidence *against* any alleged miracle having happened is always and quite systematically greater than the evidence *for* it.

As applied to paranormal phenomena at least, Hume's argument seems to me to make at least one unjustified assumption—that such phenomena, if they occurred, would *not* be in accordance with natural laws of some kind. Much evidence suggests that they would be—for example, the association of poltergeist phenomena with psychologically disturbed adolescents, of "precognitive" experiences and hunches with disasters, of vivid "apparitions" of persons with the death of those persons, or of telepathic *rapport* with close family relationships.[21] Surely the spectacular changes in physics during the present century should make the thoughtful person somewhat skeptical of the view that we know, or are even close to knowing, all the laws of nature that there are; and consequently that we are always justified in rejecting out of hand reports of events which appear incompatible with the "laws of nature" as we now believe them to be. Furthermore, as I have already briefly argued, science itself depends on what amounts to something of a scientific anomaly; the operation of "mind" upon "matter," the occurrence of autonomous human thought, speech, and agency in a world which operates according to physical laws.

Henry Sidgwick, who was a moral philosopher of the first rank as well as a pioneer in psychical research, made the following remark in the course of his presidential address to the first general meeting of the British Society for Psychical Research in 1882: "We must drive the objector into the position of being forced either to admit the phenomena as inexplicable, at least by him, or to accuse the investigators either of lying or cheating or a blindness or forgetfulness incompatible with any intellectual condition except absolute idiocy."[22] I think the point that he makes in such a provocative way is an important one, and fully worthy of a philosopher of his eminence, though it is sometimes contested. Thus Ray Hyman points out, in opposition to Sidgwick, that eminent scientists can be deceived, and that they are usually by no means qualified to detect a conjuror at his tricks. His point is a fair one so far as it goes, but it does not really amount to a satisfactory answer to Sidgwick, who implies merely that lying may be far the most plausible hypothesis when some person or persons report what would seem to be overwhelming evidence that an event of some kind has occurred, when one is absolutely convinced that it could not have done so.

As Hyman sees it, "Sidgwick does not allow for the possibility that an investigator could be competent, honest, sane, intelligent and still wrongly report what he believes to be 'conclusive' evidence for the paranormal."[23] Hyman for his part, I believe, does not adequately take account of the fact that in some conceivable cases, and indeed in my view as in Sidgwick's in not a few real instances, the sum of the relevant evidence may be such as to render such a mistake extremely unlikely. In such circumstances, the skeptic-a may well ask herself how she can be so sure that a paranormal event could not have occurred, when the evidence for it is so strong. To adapt a point of Hume's in a way in which that philosopher would not much have approved—if I say that an event is contrary to the laws of nature, on what do I base my belief as to what such laws are, except evidence? But may not the evidence that some peculiar event has occurred be as strong as the evidence for the proposition that the supposed law of nature both obtains, and is incompatible with the occurrence of the event in question? Sidgwick is surely correct that evidence could conceivably build up in such a way, though one might quarrel with his own belief that it sometimes actually does so. Hyman is right that it is also quite likely that any individual witness, however eminent, may have been deceived on any particular occasion. But surely circumstances might render such deception over a large range of cases extremely unlikely.

In connection with the issue of methodology, it seems worth mentioning a dispute between Hyman and Charles Honorton, who appears to have been one of the most resourceful contemporary workers in the field of parapsychology. Hyman pointed out some flaws in ganzfeld[24] experiments conducted by Honorton, and Honorton admitted them to be such but challenged Hyman to state how the flaws accounted for the findings. Hyman in turn charged Honorton with "a confusion between supplying plausible alternatives and achieving scientific acceptability"; Honorton's counter-challenge, he said, "shifts the burden upon the wrong party."[25] I agree with Hyman that Honorton would do better to perform experiments without technical flaws, but I think that Hyman ought to concede that it at least counts somewhat against his own views if they are incompatible with Honorton's results as they stand. Here again the contrast between the lawyer out to make a case and the genuine seeker for truth seems pertinent. In criminal law, it is a good thing that certain safeguards are in place; but the result of these is that occasionally persons who are clearly guilty get off on a technicality. That he has a good case against his opponents, but that they have got off on a technicality, I take to be Honorton's contention on this matter.

Parapsychological research in the laboratory has been dogged by the problem that experimenters are apparently unable to replicate results; it is not just that X, Y, and Z are unable to repeat the results claimed by A, B, and C; but that A, B, and C are unable to repeat their own results on subsequent occasions. Matters are made worse by the so-called file-drawer problem. Most unknown studies presumably have produced negative results; skeptics may very sensibly suggest that, if all these results were added to the database, it would reduce to what is easily compatible with chance. However, it may be of interest to note "just how large that file-drawer would have to be to bring the observed result below the level of significance." It may further be noted that, in a small field like parapsychology, the content of the file-drawers cannot be all that extensive.[26]

In 1985, the *Journal of Psychology* arranged a debate between Hyman and Honorton, during which Hyman raised the file-drawer objection in relation to ganzfeld studies. It has been suggested that the file-drawer estimate should be at least five times the known number of studies to rule it out as a potential problem. Honorton showed that, if the results were to be reduced to chance, there would have to be fifteen unsuccessful studies for every successful one. "Instead of there being 28 direct-hit[27] ganzfeld studies, there would have to have been 451, only parapsychologists would have never heard about 423 of them. Given that parapsychology is such a small field and the ganzfeld is a very time-consuming experiment, this is an absurdly high figure."[28] Similar analysis of the psychokinesis of random number generators also appears encouraging; the alternative to the reality of these effects appears to be either "wholesale collusion among more than sixty experimenters," or on "a methodological artifact common to nearly six hundred experiments conducted over nearly three decades."[29] Investigation of the historical record going back to the 1930s, on precognition[30] and psychokinesis with dice,[31] also appeared to yield very positive results.

One important result of this debate was agreement by Hyman and Honorton about standards which should be met by subsequent studies. In 1989, Honorton carried out tests according to the agreed guidelines, and the overall success rate, in a test identifying a correct target out of four possibilities, was 34 percent, 7 percent more than what would have been predicted by chance. The odds against such an outcome being due to chance are higher than 20,000 to 1. It is remarkable that these results "are consistent across experiments and experimenters. . . . While it would be rash to say that anyone can run a successful ganzfeld experiment, there can be no doubt that *in the hands of a competent experimenter* the ganzfeld ESP is a repeatable experiment."[32] The reader will observe that the quotations in this paragraph and the last two are from the work of a believer; skeptics-b will no doubt be able to provide alternative accounts without unduly taxing their ingenuity.

I myself, in common with some authorities who have studied the subject in a great deal more depth than I have,[33] think that consideration of the performances of the most notable physical mediums still constitutes the best basis for making an informed judgment on these matters; and that such considerations are quite liable rationally, albeit perhaps tentatively, to come down on the side of the believers. Eusapia Palladino seems not to have been at her best on a famous occasion in Cambridge in 1895, and her American tour of 1910–11 was something of a disaster. But provided one is not a lawyer in the skeptical interest, one will not concentrate one's attention exclusively on the episodes just mentioned, but will also ponder what seems by all accounts to have been her most impressive achievement, the sittings at Naples in 1908. Not only scientists were present, but first-rate conjurors as well; it has been well said that the process by which these came to be convinced, against their will, of the genuineness of Palladino's phenomena should be compulsory reading for all skeptics.[34] The fact that the era of the great physical mediums seems to have come to an end in about 1930, however, ought to give pause to believers. Why are these wonders not seen today? They should also take note of the apparent failure of any practitioner to accept recent challenges to produce paranormal phenomena under laboratory conditions.

The first investigators of these matters were especially preoccupied with the problem of life after death. Unfortunately, this problem seems to be at least as resistant to solution as any other in this area. One important reason for this is well expressed in a classic paper by E. R. Dodds.[35] Dodds argues that all the evidence which may appear to tell in favor of life after death for human beings can be accounted for in at least as satisfactory a manner by other means, normal or paranormal. Suppose my uncle George has recently died, and I visit a medium, who appears to go into a trance, and then tells me that I have a recently deceased uncle named George who wishes to make contact with me. A "spirit" then appears to "take over" the medium, and talks to me in just the manner that I would expect of my deceased uncle. To confirm the genuineness of his communication, "Uncle George" goes on to inform me that a King Charles guinea is lying at the bottom of the middle drawer of the chest in his bedroom. It might seem that, if I actually find the guinea in the place specified, this will be strong evidence that my Uncle George, or perhaps rather his soul, has survived bodily death. Dodds would maintain that such an inference is quite erroneous. The medium may have had clairvoyant knowledge to that effect; or she may have been picking up telepathically the contents of my unconscious mind, which could after all have contained the information even if my conscious mind was ignorant of it. It will be objected, of course, that these alternative hypotheses are somewhat extravagant. But surely, the skeptic will reply, no more so than that my disembodied Uncle George "lives on" and is trying to make contact with me.

It is sometimes suggested that such considerations amount to an impermeable barrier to the progress of knowledge about whether we can expect any life after our bodily death, whether reincarnated or in the form of a disembodied soul or a resurrected body. Contemporary philosophers have raised other objections which make such beliefs appear to be incoherent in the last analysis, so that they would not be worthy of belief *whatever* the apparent evidence in favor of them.[36] How, they would ask, do we learn our concept of a person? By interaction with visible, tangible, and audible beings of flesh and blood. These are what persons essentially are. It might be claimed that the identity of a "disembodied person," or of a reincarnated person with one previously embodied, could be a matter of continuity of memory. But this, it is argued, is to overlook a crucial fact: that continuity of memory *presupposes* personal continuity, and so cannot possibly be used to *establish* it.[37] However vivid and subjectively convincing the images that come into my mind of the Battle of Waterloo, and however impressively they check out historically (even when I have had no access to the relevant documents and so on), I cannot properly be said to remember the Battle of Waterloo unless my body was physically present there. And suppose something looking, sounding, and feeling exactly like me, and sharing all my "memories," came into existence twenty years, or several thousand years, after my death. It could at best be a remarkable replica of me; the complete annihilation of me, that is to say of my body, during the intervening period, would always be a fatal objection to its actually being identical with me. As to "disembodied persons," to destroy a certain kind of body of flesh and blood is to destroy a person. To talk of the "survival" of "disembodied persons," when their bodies have decomposed, is like saying of a glass ashtray that the ashtray as such continues to exist when the glass of which it consists has been shattered, melted, or ground to powder. Death is not lived through; and if it were, it would not really be death.

Over the last twenty years or so, a good deal of publicity has been given to the phenomenon of "near-death experiences," which are often held to provide evidence of an afterlife, and in fact do appear to decrease the fear of death in many of those who undergo them.[38] People who recover from close brushes with death often report a selection from a list of about fifteen experiences (a noise, going through a dark tunnel, meeting others, encountering a Being of Light, undergoing a review of one's past life, coming up against a kind of barrier, and so on). Two kinds of objections are apt to be made to the use of such data as these to support the hypothesis that conscious subjects may survive bodily death.[39] The first is based on the principle that it is of the very essence of death to be irreversible, and that death is an all-or-nothing affair. The fact that those who report near-death experiences have actually *recovered*, it is maintained, is as much proof as can possibly be imagined that they never really *died*. Therefore these reports, whatever interest they may have in other respects, are totally irrelevant to the question of whether consciousness continues to exist after bodily death.

I believe that this argument neglects the fact that, owing to the advances of modern medicine, death is no longer quite such an "all-or-nothing" affair as it once was, and that the concept of death has as a result become somewhat "open-textured." The beating of the heart, the expansion and contraction of the lungs, and the presence of electrical activity in the brain are all criteria of continuation of life, and their cessation of its termination. Certainly, when heart, lungs, and brain have all ceased to function, and this state of affairs is irreversible, one may say confidently and unequivocally that the patient is dead. But to make such irreversibility the sole and absolute criterion of death would appear to be somewhat arbitrary, a matter of stipulative definition. Rather than insisting that all human individuals are either definitely alive or definitely dead, it would seem less misleading to say of a certain sort of case: "Well, in that breathing and heartbeat had stopped, the patient was dead; but it happened that her attending physicians were so skillful as to be able to reverse the process, so in *that* sense she did *not* die." At this rate, is it wholly unreasonable to suggest that experiences enjoyed by patients who are physically dead in some respects but not in others have a bearing on the possibility of experiences being enjoyed by those who have entirely and in every sense undergone physical death?

Arguments of a second kind appear, to me at least, to be of rather more weight. Given the structure and chemical composition of the brain, which are common to human beings, it is surely only to be expected that they would give rise to very similar experiences, if consciousness depends ineluctably on the brain's functioning, when it is about to disappear forever due to the cessation of such functioning. Is it not more economical to account for near-death experiences in such a manner as this, than to conclude that they actually represent the threshold of an afterlife? It seems that near-death experiences could only properly be taken as evidence of an afterlife if their content could somehow be corroborated from an independent source. And, it might reasonably be wondered, what such source could possibly be available to us?

As a matter of fact, there does appear to be such corroboration, as we shall see in a moment. The philosopher Henri Bergson, supported by the physicist Sir Oliver Lodge, suggested a method by which one might resolve the central difficulty pointed out by Dodds—that alternative hypotheses, normal or paranormal, which may seem at least as plausible as "survival," can never be ruled out as alternative ways of accounting for the relevant phenomena. They suggested that what purported to be accounts of the future life could be treated like travelers' tales, and assessed in relation to one another in terms of their mutual consistency.[40] The putative Uncle George, for example, might be asked for, or spontaneously volunteer, information about what his immediate postmortem experiences were like, and his offerings could be compared with other material of a similar kind. The suggestion of Bergson and Lodge, which was made in the early years of the twentieth century, was not taken up for many years, until Robert Crookall, a distinguished British geologist, decided to devote the years of his retirement to it. The initial results of his investigations appeared in *The Supreme Adventure*, a book first published in 1961 and so far little known, but which I believe to be of greatly underestimated importance. In examining the evidence for the reality of postmortem survival, Crookall deliberately turns his attention away from phenomena which invite direct testing of the kind exemplified by the case of Uncle George, and sifts the enormous pile of available documentation—records of mediumistic trances, samples of "automatic writing," statements by "clairvoyants" and "astral projectors," accounts of visions by the dying and those who care for them, reports of those who have had a close call with death, and so on—to answer the single relatively manageable question: what would appear to be the experiences in the immediate aftermath of death by those of more or less average character and spiritual development?

By dint of piecing together material of this nature, but only accepting evidence which is multiply attested, Crookall arrives at conclusions which, so far as I can see, there would be no good reason to suppose a priori. Conspicuous among them are the following: Those who die naturally tend to remain in a comatose state for about three days, while those who die by violence are fully conscious immediately afterwards, and often do not know that they have died. Victims of explosion constitute yet a third category. The quasi-cinematographic run-through of one's past life, which turns up in many near-death experiences, appears to be a regular feature of the after-death experience as well; another common element is "meetings" with dead friends and relatives. Of more existential concern is a second run-through, which Crookall calls "the judgment," in which one is made aware of the effects of one's actions on other people; it is apparently avoidance of this dreadful event which makes it impossible for some souls to progress, and keeps them "earthbound" and so liable to haunt the places where they lived.

But I do not wish to emphasize the details of Crookall's account of the immediate afterlife, which I am quite aware will excite the disbelief and indeed the ridicule of many readers. What I do wish to stress is the method which he follows to establish and confirm his conclusions. Each of his claims is supported by a corpus of references to sources of the kind which I have mentioned, sources which individually would carry very little weight indeed, but in combination with one another should, I think, be impressive to any reasonable person. (I would not go quite so far as to say that every reasonable person would be convinced by them.) The deeply held opinions and assumptions of many people will, of course, be violently opposed to Crookall's line of argument. But opinions which were just as deeply entrenched were equally opposed to claims made by the pioneers of natural science in the early seventeenth century, which since that time have been abundantly vindicated. The skeptic may fairly be asked, I think, how she would account for what is to be read in Crookall's book. Is the author lying, or deceived by his sources? The first possibility can easily be checked by following up his copious references; and also by a nodding acquaintance with the vast corpus of other literature, most of it not favored much in cultured circles, which deals with these matters. The second possibility seems scarcely compatible with the fact that so many witnesses agree with one another, in circumstances where collusion seems impossible or at best extremely unlikely. Crookall remarks that, on the basis of the data which he has collected, the hypothesis that people in some sense survive bodily death has about the same order of evidential support as the theory of evolution. This seems to me a reasonable judgment if one has actually read the book, and takes seriously T. H. Huxley's often-quoted maxim, that one ought to sit down before the facts like a little child.

Another point to be made in favor of Crookall's conclusions is that they do not fit very neatly with any conventional religious view. The popular Christian notion that we are to expect to see Jesus immediately after we die, and the common Protestant view that we are bound directly either for an eternal heaven or an eternal hell, find no support in Crookall's data. They provide still less warrant for the belief that we are to expect no afterlife at all until the resurrection of our bodies at the second coming of Christ. Catholics may perhaps take some comfort from the apparent corroboration of their doctrine of purgatory—which is to the effect that most people at least, even if they are ultimately bound for the vision of God in heaven, have to go through a great many trials after death before they attain it; and from the strong vindication of the practice of prayer for the dead. (*The Supreme Adventure* contains an appendix in which the value for the dead, and especially the recently dead, of our prayers for them, is confirmed over and over again.[41])

I have in the last few paragraphs stated my belief that there are substantial grounds for opinions which will seem silly or monstrous to many of my readers. What is the point of my doing so, it may be asked, when they could only be supported by the adducing and critical discussion of a huge amount of actual or alleged evidence? Fortunately this is not so, since the basic point I am making is methodological, and in essence very simple; it is virtually the same as the one attributed to Sidgwick earlier in the paper. One must conclude either that Crookall or the authors whom he cites are behaving in a manner of which it is very difficult to give a remotely plausible explanation, or that the case they present is a formidable one. That so many should, apparently to a great extent independently of one another, lie, hallucinate, or be deceived to such a similar effect is surely somewhat difficult for the genuinely rational person to swallow. Nor is it rational, for all that so many who would regard themselves as rational have behaved in this manner, simply to avoid attending to the relevant evidence. It is not profitable to be side-tracked by the distracting and confusing question of what, if anything, those who have adduced this material have "proved." What is at issue is provision of the best hypothesis to account for a range of data; skeptics-b and "skeptics" may reasonably be asked how they explain what is reported in Crookall's book. Nothing is easier than to poke fun at particular samples of the material that he cites, but there is no excuse for serious researchers into this matter to overlook its cumulative effect.

One might regard Crookall's work as a bridgehead, from which further advances may profitably be made into the territory of more or less confirmed speculation about the afterlife. Many writings on this topic, which otherwise would seem obviously absurd or merely fantastic, serve to confirm and supplement Crookall's account. Among the more impressive of these, in my view, are some that support the doctrine of reincarnation—a fact which ought to be of some concern to orthodox Christians. After all, reincarnation has been considered heretical by most representative Christian authorities—though some, notably the great Origen, have defended the doctrine. But those who reject it out of hand, I think, can fairly be asked how they explain what is to be read in books like Ian Stevenson's *Twenty Cases Suggestive of Reincarnation*,[42] Hans Ten Dam's *Concerning Reincarnation*,[43] and Joel L. Whitton's *Life Between Life*.[44] In Stevenson's work one finds case after case of small children with "memories" of previous lives and deaths that check out in detail when carefully followed through. Whitton surveys many examples, from the author's own psychotherapeutic practice, of "memories," recovered through hypnotic trance, of traumas apparently undergone and decisions taken in previous lives, the reactivation of which seems both to account for and to cure severe psychological and physical disorders, just as recovery of memories of the present life often appears to do.

What, in the light of such evidence as this, is to be done with the a priori objections of the philosophers? It has to be acknowledged that, if a claim makes no sense in the last analysis, then no amount of evidence really supports it. But the evidence cited by the authors to whose works I have just been referring, and the most obvious and natural way of accounting for this evidence, do at first sight make obvious sense, however repugnant and implausible they may appear to the common sense of the average intellectual of our time. But do they break down conceptually at a deeper level of analysis? The subject is rather a complex one; I will try as well as I can in a brief compass to set out why I find the standard philosophical objections to be of very little weight. I suggest that the proper way to construct a theory of personal identity is not to proceed a priori, and then impose the result on the data, however recalcitrant; but rather to attend to the data, and then see what account of personal identity yields the most satisfactory explanation of them. It is very easy to construct in one's imagination circumstances in which "I seem to be conscious after the death of my body," or "So-and-so who recently died seems to be trying to get in touch with us," would at first sight at least be the appropriate conclusion to draw. The literature to which I have been alluding abounds with such examples, of course; the point which I am making at present is not that the examples are descriptive of real occurrences, but merely that they make sense as accounts of conceivable ones. For example, however bizarre may be the claim of many people that they have had the experience of seeing their body from a position a few feet above it, it is merely pedantic to argue that it makes no sense. The most well-documented cases have of course "returned to their physical bodies" to tell the tale; but is it not conceivable, and would it not even be plausible if there were somehow enough corroborative evidence to this effect, that there are some cases at least where the "soul," or whatever it is, has not thus returned after the experience? Similarly, I can clearly imagine my pen wandering all by itself to a sheet of paper, and inscribing a message, in writing just like that of someone recently dead, and purporting to be written by her, asking me to carry out her wishes in relation to a certain matter with which I know her to have been concerned. Would not the most natural thing to say in this case be that either the "soul of" the person concerned, or the person who had previously been embodied but was now disembodied, still existed and was attempting to communicate with me? If one hesitates to use the word "person" of such an entity, one might call it a "conscious subject."

The most natural interpretation of a large and rapidly growing body of data which has been accumulating since the 1970s is that conscious subjects (if one prefers this way of speaking) inhabit a series of bodies, and also enjoy an existence (disembodied or with a rarefied kind of body) in between. The criteria for identity between conscious subjects inhabiting different bodies are not very obscure in principle, though one can conceive of cases that were systematically ambiguous. (One can also imagine cases where two or more individuals, in the present embodiment, were identical with a past individual, which would be systematically ambiguous as well.) Suppose that you recover in trance quasi-memories (to use a phrase which seems as little question-begging as possible) of a past life which "check out" in quite a large number of particulars; and some of these quasi-memories, when recovered, have a profound effect on your psychological and even on your physical state, just as memories repressed within one physical lifetime have been known to do since the classical researches conducted by Sigmund Freud.[45] Then it seems appropriate, at least if you are just one of a large number of rather similar cases, to say that you are the identical conscious subject with the one who lived that particular physical life, and different from your brother in this life and your husband in that one (who might well, it appears, be the same conscious subject). Let us concede to philosophers that there is one sense in which an individual's identity begins and ends with the present body (we may label this kind of identity "identity-a"). But suppose that the kind of phenomena to which I have been alluding really occur with considerable frequency. In that case there is another sense in which human identity need not be thus circumscribed, and in which an identical conscious subject can and probably does in the course of time inhabit a series of different individual bodies. The fact at the present time is, I believe, that to insist that human identity is exclusively and ineluctably identity-a is mere stipulation, and misleading stipulation at that, if a large and ever increasing pile of reports is to be taken into account.

One can of course at a pinch produce "normal" explanations (coincidence, cryptomnesia, outright deception, and so on) of even the most striking instances of supposed "past-life memory" when taken by themselves. But such explanations have an increasingly labored air about them, reminiscent of the epicycles which preserved Ptolemaic astronomy in the face of recalcitrant data, when the sheer quantity of the available evidence is taken into account. Those who make polemical moves on behalf of "normality" are apt to commit what one might call the Heap of Coal fallacy, whereby the most natural interpretation of a large body of evidence is contested by the more or less ingenious interpretation of a few instances in terms of a more palatable theory. Cumulative arguments should not be confused with arguments depending on a chain of inferences. While it is true that a chain is no stronger than its weakest link, it is certainly not the case that a heap of coal is no heavier than its two or three largest pieces. Plausible interpretation of a few apparent memories of past incarnations in terms of coincidence, fraud, or cryptomnesia begin to ring rather hollow when thousands of such cases are at issue.

I conclude that the case for the reality of a large proportion of the classes of events usually termed *paranormal* is very strong; and that some of these, in spite of the popularity of the counterarguments, provide substantial grounds for belief in life after death for human beings.[46]

NOTES

1. The term *paranormal* is in many ways misleading, as there is an open question about how common some of these phenomena are, if indeed they occur at all. Thus, one may be impressed with the sheer abundance of reports suggesting telepathy, precognition, the activity of poltergeists, or contact with the recently dead. But the term will have to do for want of one which is obviously better.

2. S. E. Braude, *The Limits of Influence: Psychokinesis and the Philosophy of Science* (New York: Routledge and Kegan Paul, 1986), ix–x. There is a depressingly up-to-date ring about the complaints made by Alfred Russell Wallace, over a century ago, about W. C. Carpenter's aspersions against table-turning and spiritualism: "There is hardly any attempt to deal with the evidence. Instead we have irrelevant matters put prominently forward, backed up by sneers against believers, and false or unproved assertions against mediums" (Ray Hyman, "A Critical Historical Overview of Parapsychology," in *A Skeptic's Handbook of Parapsychology*, ed. Paul Kurtz [Buffalo, N.Y.: Prometheus, 1985], 17). If, as is sometimes claimed, positive findings in this field would not have wide-ranging consequences for science in general (cf. Martin Johnson, as cited by John Beloff, "What is Your Counter-Explanation? A Plea to Skeptics to Think Again," in Kurtz, *Skeptic's Handbook*, 90), it is difficult to explain the frequency or violence of these reactions.

3. Cf. *The Logic of Scientific Discovery* (London: Hutchinson, 1959); *Objective Knowledge* (Oxford: Clarendon, 1972).

4. Cf. L. Zusne, "Magical Thinking and Parapsychology," in Kurtz, *Skeptic's Handbook*.

5. For the most convincing and sophisticated defense of this position known to me, see Bernard Lonergan, *Insight: A Study of Human Understanding* (Toronto: University of Toronto Press, 1992); *Method in Theology* (London: Darton, Longman and Todd, 1972), ch. 1.

6. See James E. Alcock, "Parapsychology as a 'Spiritual' Science," in Kurtz, *Skeptic's Handbook*, 562.

7. See, for example, John Beversluis, *C. S. Lewis and the Case for Rational Religion* (Grand Rapids, Mich.: Eerdmans, 1985), 73f. For a recent account of unsuccessful attempts over the last few years to explain the phenomena of mind in terms which are "scientific" in the restricted sense, see William Lyons, "Modern Work on Intentionality," in *Faith, Skepticism and Personal Identity: Essays in Honour of Terence Penelhum*, ed. J. J. MacIntosh and H. A. Meynell (Calgary, Alberta: University of Calgary Press, 1994).

8. Paul Kurtz expresses this attitude very well when he says: "An experimenter should play the role of neither a sheep (believer) nor a goat (disbe-

liever), but more appropriately should be a fox committed to careful and critical scrutiny of the hypotheses and the evidence" (Kurtz, "Introduction," *Skeptic's Handbook*, xxi). As to "goats," the investigator of these matters is not "entitled to assume," in the absence of any evidence to this effect, that the famous "physical medium" D. D. Home was "a practiced conjuror" (thus F. Podmore in 1902, as cited by Ray Hyman, "A Critical Historical Overview of Parapsychology," in Kurtz, *Skeptic's Handbook*, 27); she is only qualified to point out that this is one hypothesis, itself subject to testing by evidence, which might account for Home's alleged feats. Just the same objection may be made to such "skeptical" remarks as the following by Martin Gardner: "The reason D. D. Home was never caught cheating was that Home took extreme precautions to perform miracles only in the presence of persons he knew to be untrained in magic. . . . Randi and I will happily tell anyone how Nina Kulagina uses invisible threads to move matches and float table-tennis balls" ("Magicians in the Psi Lab," in Kurtz, *Skeptic's Handbook*, 354, 356). With regard to Home at least, such categorical statements seem quite improper, in view of the fact that no charge of fraud was ever substantiated against him (Braude, *Limits of Influence*, 72).

9. For a particularly gross instance of "skepticism" of this kind, on the part of an astronomer, see the description by J. Allen Hynek, *The UFO Experience* (New York: Ballantine, 1972), app. 2. Hynek himself may be commended as a remarkable example of a skeptic-a. Whether his inquiries led him to skepticism-b or not, I shall leave my reader to determine by consulting his excellent book.

10. Peter Preuss has written a book entitled *Reincarnation: A Philosophical and Practical Analysis* (Queenston, Ontario: Edwin Mellen, 1989); while Terence Penelhum is the author of *Survival and Disembodied Existence* (London: Routledge and Kegan Paul, 1970).

11. Springfield, Ill.: Charles C. Thomas, 1961; see chapter 25.

12. An excellent summary is to be had, from a skeptical-b viewpoint, in Ray Hyman, "Critical Historical Overview."

13. It ought to be borne in mind, however, that the history of science in general is replete with instances not only of unconscious distortion of one's work through passionately held conviction, but of outright fakery. Cf. Martin Gardner, *Science: Good, Bad and Bogus* (Buffalo, N.Y.: Prometheus, 1981), 123; cited by Betty Markwick, "The Establishment of Data Manipulation in the Soal-Shackleton Experiments," in Kurtz, *Skeptic's Handbook*, 306. "Cheating and self-deception are greater in parapsychology than in most sciences, especially the physical sciences, but not by much" (Gardner, *Science*, 130; quoted D. M. Stokes, "Parapsychology and its Critics," in Kurtz, *Skeptic's Handbook*, 410).

14. Markwick's own account of her investigation and its results ("Establishment of Data Manipulation") is conveniently provided in Kurtz, *Skeptic's Handbook*.

15. Cf. Simon Newcomb: "If we admit the existence of gifted individuals having such abnormal powers as these, why not equally admit the existence of men having the faculty of seeing, or thinking they remember having seen, the nonexistent? The latter certainly seems much easier to suppose than does the former" ("Modern Occultism," in Kurtz, *Skeptic's Handbook*, 158).

16. Again, as Markwick says, "it is difficult to reconcile the null series of 1954–58 (with university students) with the hypothesis that Soal was wholly fraudulent. Why did he persist for so long without falsifying that series?" ("Establishment of Data Manipulation," 303).

17. Hyman, "Critical Historical Overview," 32.

18. Cf. Mark 6:5–6.

19. David Hume, *Enquiry Concerning Human Understanding* (Oxford: Clarendon Press, 1902), Section X.

20. E.g., George R. Price, in "Science and the Supernatural" (*Science*, 26 August 1955; cited in Hyman, "Critical Historical Overview," 52–54). Hyman rightly remarks that this attitude smacks rather of dogmatism than of skepticism properly speaking.

21. Braude does well to draw attention to the *consistency* of reports of certain types of paranormal phenomenon, especially of poltergeists, apparitions, and hauntings: "Non-experimental case reports frequently agree on peculiar and unexpected details, despite the fact that the reports are made independently of one another and often under quite different social and cultural conditions." Among these details are, in the case of poltergeists, "the slow and gentle trajectories of airborne objects, the apparent passage of levitated objects through walls and closed doors, and . . . bombardment with human excrement." Victims have usually been unfamiliar with such literature as exists on the subject. As to apparitions, it may be remarked that they are strikingly different from accounts of ghosts in popular fiction (Braude, *Limits of Influence*, 27–28).

22. Cited in Hyman, "Critical Historical Overview," 35–36.

23. Hyman, "Critical Historical Overview," 35–36.

24. A *ganzfeld* is a completely homogeneous visual field; this is thought by some to be specially conducive to extrasensory perception.

25. Hyman, "Critical Historical Overview," 82–83.

26. See Richard S. Broughton, *Parapsychology: The Controversial Science* (New York: Ballantine, 1991), 280, 284. I am grateful to my colleague George Fritz for having referred me to this work.

27. "The most typical scoring procedure classifies the outcome as a 'hit' if the percipient correctly judges the actual target as closest to the ganzfeld impressions" (Hyman, "Critical Historical Overview," 78).

28. Broughton, *Parapsychology*, 285–86.

29. Ibid., 289–91.

30. Ibid., 292–94. Honorton and Diane Ferrari were astonished at the amount of research which was available; in the studies that they retrieved, "over 50,000 subjects" had "participated in nearly 2 million trials. . . . Thirty percent of the studies were statistically significant (where 5 percent is expected by chance). The odds of this result happening by chance are about one-in-10 to the 24th."

31. Ibid., 294–96.

32. Ibid., 288. Italics in the original.

33. Cf. Beloff, "Counter-Explanation." See also Braude, *Limits of Influence*.

34. See Beloff, "Counter-Explanation," 371. Beloff provides quite a detailed account of this episode, as does Braude (*Limits of Influence*, 130–33).

35. "Why I Do Not Believe in Survival" (*Proceedings of the Society for Psychical Research*, 1934; cited in A. G. N. Flew, *God, Freedom and Immortality* (Buffalo, N.Y.: Prometheus, 1984), 118.

36. For the arguments of the present paragraph, see especially Flew, *God, Freedom and Immortality*, chs. 8–11.

37. See Penelhum, *Survival and Disembodied Existence*, 55–67.

38. See R. Moody, *Life After Life* (New York: Bantam, 1975), and *Reflections on Life After Life* (New York: Bantam, 1977); and M. Rawlings, *Beyond Death's Door* (Nashville: Nelson, 1978).

39. For a useful rehearsal and defense of these objections, see Gerd H. Hovelmann, "Evidence for Survival from Near-Death Experiences? A Critical Appraisal," in Kurtz, *Skeptic's Handbook*.

40. Cf. R. Crookall, *The Supreme Adventure* (Cambridge: James Clarke, 1974). Crookall well exemplifies what is at issue in the following shrewd remark by Braude: "We need . . . fewer technicians and more parapsychological naturalists, people with an eye for regularities and connections" (*Limits of Influence*, 255). Hans Holzer, in *The Psychic Side of Dreams* (St. Paul, Minn.: Llewellyn, 1992), applies similar methods. Crookall himself provided more material to corroborate his findings in *The Next World—And the Next* (London: Theosophical Publishing House, 1966); *What Happens When You Die* (Gerrards Cross: Colin Smythe, 1978); and several other publications.

41. *The Supreme Adventure*, 234–41.

42. Charlottesville: University Press of Virginia, 1974.

43. London: Penguin Books, 1990.

44. Garden City, N.Y.: Doubleday, 1986.

45. Whitton, *Life Between Life*, includes detailed descriptions of several such cases.

46. I have to thank Elizabeth Anderson for a great deal of stimulating discussion on the topic of this paper.

3

PARAPSYCHOLOGY:
MERITS AND LIMITS*

Donald Evans

In *Spirituality and Human Nature* (1993)[1] I argued that there are nonscientific yet rational bases for believing in the reality of some paranormal phenomena. Two central arguments can be mentioned here. First, I challenged impersonalism, which I defined as "the dogmatic rejection of any truth-claim that requires personal transformation to be adequately understood and appraised" (101). The dogma that the only truth possible is truth that can be known impersonally is prominent in positivism,[2] a species of impersonalism. Positivists hold that scientific method (a prominent impersonal method) is the only way to knowledge of reality. There are, however, many kinds of truth-claim, including some pertaining to the paranormal, which require personal changes in order to be adequately understood and verified experientially. I argued that the requirements of personal change are intelligible and plausible, and cannot be easily dismissed. Second, I showed how belief in the reality of a particular paranormal phenomenon can be rationally justified if the particular case is sufficiently impressive in its details. One case can be enough, even if it can not be replicated scientifically.

If some paranormal claims cannot be tested by anyone who has the appropriate scientific training, but require a prior process of personal change, and if one case can sometimes suffice, this has implications for parapsychology, the application of scientific method to the paranormal: nonscientific approaches are also possible. At the end of

* This chapter has benefited greatly from comments by George P. Hansen, Peter Hess, and James Wheatley. Their insightful criticisms, coming from perspectives differing in ways from my own, were very helpful in revising the chapter. I am also grateful to Michael Stoeber and Jessica Utts for technical advice.

this chapter I will return to these approaches. The chapter itself, however, is devoted to parapsychology, which seems to me to deserve very serious consideration. Although in *Spirituality and Human Nature* I criticized impersonalism as a dogma, I readily acknowledged the importance of impersonal methods, especially scientific method. Science has achieved universal or nearly universal agreement concerning many matters, thereby transcending profound personal and ideological differences among human beings. And science has had amazing success in enabling us to transform our world. So it is important to see whether anything can be established scientifically concerning the paranormal. In my book I stressed the difficulty in finding people who can allegedly repeat psychic feats *at will*, which seems necessary if experiments are to be repeatable. I now think that I exaggerated this difficulty, for psi-ability seems to be present to some extent in many ordinary people who can be recruited for experiments, and statistically significant results can be obtained using them, even if they fall short of a 100 percent success-rate.

In my book I also failed to distinguish between two very different approaches to the paranormal, which I will call the "causal mechanism" and the "psi-ability."[3]

1. *Causal mechanism*: The first approach considers the paranormal in terms of apparently *anomalous* events which cannot be explained by reference to *causal mechanisms* now known to science. The task of parapsychology is, accordingly, (i) to establish that there actually is an anomaly requiring scientific explanation, rather than merely a coincidence deserving no further consideration; and (ii) to provide a scientific explanation in terms of causal mechanisms—either now, which is extremely difficult, if not impossible, or eventually, which may be possible if scientific theory can be radically revised.

This first approach arises from positivist assumptions. I have already described positivism as the dogma that scientific method is the *only* way to knowledge of reality, ruling out all nonscientific truth-claims. Positivism also claims that the only real explanations are scientific explanations. Hence, any explanations by reference to agent causality (for example, "the billiard cue moved because Jones moved it") must always be replaced or replaceable by scientific explanations in terms of mechanical causality. Agent causality has to do with voluntary actions involving human abilities. Although explanations by reference to agent causality served humankind very well for centuries preceding the scientific era, and continue to do so, for a positivist they must all eventually be replaced by mechanical-causal explanations.

In contrast with such a view, Richard Taylor (1966), an advocate of agent causality, says, "If it is really and unmetaphorically true, as I believe it to be, that I sometimes cause something to happen, this would seem to entail that it is *false* that any event, process or state not identical with myself should be the real cause of it" (111). If an explanation in terms of agent causality is thus primary, any mechanical-causal explanation will at best supplement and fill in the agent-causality account. (In section II of this chapter, I will note that even though scientific method tries to ignore agent causality, and positivism rejects it, scientific method paradoxically presupposes such causality when it requires that experiments be repeatable *at will*.)

2. *Psi-abilities.* The second approach to the paranormal focuses on alleged psi-abilities—for example, the ability to alter the state of an object by mental influence alone without any apparent physical intervention, or the ability to perceive changes in an object or in another's consciousness independently of the senses. These two abilities are often called "psychokinesis" (PK) and "extra-sensory perception" (ESP), respectively. Although this second approach is strictly scientific in many respects, it does not accept the positivist rejection of causal agency as an explanation. The experimenter will still demand very strong evidence, including a virtual elimination of plausible alternative accounts, whether commonsensical or scientific, but will *not* require (i) scientific proof that an anomaly requiring scientific explanation exists or (ii) a scientific explanation in terms of hidden causal mechanisms.

Whereas on the causal-mechanism approach the *only* alternative to "It's merely a coincidence" is a scientific explanation, on the second psi-ability approach there is another alternative: "It's a human ability whose workings we may or may not be able to explain adequately in scientific terms." Scientists are beginning to understand how I can move my arm, but such understanding is not necessary in order to establish that I do indeed move my arm. Similarly in the case of alleged psi-abilities.

On the causal-mechanism approach, no psi-abilities could ever be established, since the reality of human causal agency in general is denied. At best all that could be established is the reality of some previously unknown causal mechanisms linking a human organism with other organisms or things. Such a discovery would, of course, be important, not only for positivists but also for scientists committed to a psi-ability approach, for whom the discovery would fill in their causal-agency account. The psi-ability approach as such, however, involves an investigative context that is subtly and critically different in that scientific evidence can in principle establish the reality of a psi-ability. Moreover, experiments can be devised so as to shed light concerning what subjective and circumstantial conditions best facilitate the exercise of an alleged psi-ability, rather than focusing solely on attempting to prove its reality to positivist critics.

One objection to an approach to the paranormal in terms of psi-abilities is that only a very few people allegedly have such abilities, allegedly performing feats of PK and/or ESP *at will*. There are three reasons, however, for focusing on alleged psi-abilities in parapsychology:

First, there is a fine line between involuntary and minimally voluntary behaviors, and the latter can sometimes become more and more voluntary through practice. The first flailing-about movements of a baby gradually become movements towards crawling. Similarly the first vague discernments of a blind person whose sight is returning gradually become more and more accurate perceptions. And similarly a minimal voluntary control in matters of PK or ESP can apparently improve through practice.

Second, even if subjects have only a minimal control in matters of PK or ESP, experiments where subjects are "trying" can yield statistically significant, though unspectacular, results.

Third, we typically distinguish "paranormal" from other exceptional human happenings by reference to their apparent similarity with exercises of the *human abilities to perceive or to move something*. Indeed, we will see in section III that even on a causal-mechanism approach in parapsychology some such criterion of selection seems to be implicitly at work. Not all scientific anomalies are regarded by such parapsychologists as "paranormal." Even if they regard such terms as "PK" and "ESP" as misleading because they purport to provide an explanation when only causal mechanisms can provide explanations, the parapsychologists' initial delimiting of the range of phenomena to be investigated requires some such terms or others which resemble them.[4]

There is thus much to be said in favor of a psi-ability approach in parapsychology. Indeed, the merits of this approach will be demonstrated in section IV of this chapter, where I outline an experiment by Braud and Schlitz (1983). Before that, however, I will sketch in the first section four principles of scientific method that are pertinent to parapsychology. Then I will consider in section II some issues concerning scientific method and human agency, and in section III I will scrutinize a rather positivist official description of parapsychology by the Parapsychological Association (1988). After reflecting on Braud and Schlitz in section V, I will conclude with a brief summary of the chapter's findings. Then I will outline two nonscientific bases for belief in the paranormal which I presented more fully in my book: First, direct experiential access is possible to such alleged paranormal phenomena as healing energies and spirits, but this typically requires non-scientific "training" or transformation. Second, all we need is *one* impressively detailed case for it to be rational to believe that ESP has occurred.

I. FOUR PRINCIPLES OF SCIENTIFIC METHOD

There are various versions of scientific method, each one differing slightly from the others. A thorough study would note not only these variations but also the complexities which arise for scientific investigators in various fields. For the purposes of this essay it seems appropriate to offer a brief and simplified account of scientific method which would find broad acceptance among both parapsychologists and their critics,[5] though the account would not be acceptable to scientists who refuse to restrict science to *experimental science*. Four main principles are prominent:

(1) *Isolation*:	Isolate genuine causal factors by using control groups.
(2) *Repeatability*:	Devise an experiment which anyone can repeat, and accumulate data on the basis of which one can establish
either	(i) Invariant Laws: whenever anyone produces A, there is B.
or	(ii) Statistical Correlations: whenever anyone produces A, there is such-and-such a probability of B.
(3) *Quantifiability*:	If possible, describe A and B in terms of measurable units rather than in purely qualitative terms.
(4) *Theoretical Plausibility*:	Relate your investigation to, or create, a theoretical framework which (i) brings together many Laws or Correlations concerning observables,
and perhaps	(ii) refers to nonobservable theoretical entities that help to explain the Laws or Correlations.

Let us consider each principle in turn. *Isolation* can be easily illustrated in medical research. If a new drug is being tested for its efficacy in treating cancer, there might be three groups, X, Y, and Z, all of whom consist of people who have the same kind of cancer at the same stage. Group X would be injected with the drug, group Y would be injected with a saline solution, and group Z would receive no treatment. Groups Y and Z are "control" groups. It they improve as much as group X, this indicates that the new drug is not shown to be the source of any improvement in group X. Improvement may come equally in groups X and Y because the injection of anything which the patient thinks might help is a "placebo" for the patient, inducing a confidence which itself brings improvement. Improvement may come equally in groups X and Z because the particular kind of cancer common to both groups is open to spontaneous remissions, independent of any treatment. If, however, group X's rate of improvement is significantly better than group Y's or groups Z's (or if Y and Z both get worse), the new drug is genuinely a causal factor in group X. And more important, if the researchers had used no control groups, but simply injected X with the new drug, any improvement in group X would not be attributed scientifically to the drug, for maybe the change occurred because the injection acted as a placebo, or maybe the change would have occurred without any treatment. In testing drugs the main concerns are the placebo effect and spontaneous remissions. But the more rigorous the attempt towards ruling out *all* possible alternative explanations, the more precautions might be taken while conducting the experiment. For example, perhaps the technician giving the injections might unwittingly convey to the recipient a suggestion concerning whether the recipient was receiving the drug or the saline solution. In order to prevent this from happening, the technician could be precluded from knowing, and the recipient could be prevented from having contact with any person who does know. Another possible precaution would be that the results of the experiment would have to be registered by a computer or by someone who does not know which group is which, so that no subjective bias for or against the drug could distort the account of the results. I do not know how frequently such "double-blind" procedures are used in research on drugs, but they have become standard requirements in many parapsychological experiments (see Reinsel, 1982: 158.)

In my presentation of the principle of isolation, I have depicted scientific method as an attempt to identify *causes*. This is an oversimplification. Sometimes scientists are satisfied even though they cannot establish a causal connection, provided that they can establish a significant correlation which enables them to make reliable predictions. What more is being claimed when someone claims not only a significant correlation but also a causal connection? Especially since David Hume[6] posed this question, it has evoked much controversy in philosophy of science and in metaphysics. It is not appropriate to explore this here. What I want to stress here is that there seem to be two main paradigms of causality:

mechanical causality (a billiard cue hitting a billiard ball which then hits another ball) and *agent causality* (my purposively moving my arm, which holds the billiard cue). The second paradigm, agent causality, is not what scientific method usually refers to in explaining events (though later we will see that scientific method has to presuppose it). When a scientist claims to establish a mechanical causality, two kinds of consideration seem to be relevant. The first consideration is whether the investigation fulfills the principles of isolation and repeatability. The second consideration is whether the items in the evidence itself (e.g., billiard balls) or the entities in the relevant theoretical framework (for example, molecules) are collected mechanically: that is, by local impact or at least by some contact analogous to local contact.[7]

As the essay proceeds, the contrast between agent causality and mechanical causality will become increasingly important, but here my main point is simply that the scientific principle of isolation aspires towards identifying (mechanical) causes, though it will accept significant correlations.

Repeatability has been depicted by me in its ideal form, where a scientist does not merely observe A and then B, but herself *produces* A and then observes B, in an experiment which she and anyone else who has the appropriate training can repeat. In a less ideal version of the principle, the scientist makes observations which are repeatable both by her and by others—for example, observing that such-and-such cloud formations and changes in barometric pressure are frequently followed by rain. Such scientific compilations at best enable us to *predict* rain but not to *produce* it. Both kinds of repeatability provide bases for universal intersubjective agreement concerning truth-claims, but experimental repeatability provides bases for techniques for control, for knowledge as power-over. Where the experimental repeatability yields only significant correlations rather than invariant laws, the degree of control is correspondingly less, but it is nevertheless very important.

What statistical correlations count as significant? This is a very technical and complex issue concerning which scientists sometimes disagree, especially if the question is posed pragmatically: "How high must the statistical correlation be for us to *apply* the findings (e.g., to use the new drug in treatments)?"

Quantifiability is in one sense a part of the principle of repeatability. What one produces or observes must be an item (A) which is repeated for such-and-such a *number* of times, with such-and-such a *number* of instances of B following. The principle of quantifiability which I am noting here, however, goes beyond this numerical feature. In its most rigorous form this principle insists that both A and B must themselves be described in terms of measurable units rather than in purely qualitative terms. For example, if water is described not merely as "very cold" but as "at 0 degrees centigrade," then the generalization "At 0 degrees centigrade water freezes" involves *one* quantified variable. The concept of freezing, however, remains purely qualitative. Since there is minimal possibility of disagreement among observers concerning what counts as freezing (in contrast with the possibility concerning what counts as "very cold"), the generalization is acceptable to most scientists. Some scientists, however, aspire towards a science which includes only generalizations where both A and B are describable numerically. For example, in some research concerning sexual orgasm, personal testimony concerning experienced satisfaction tends to be replaced by data concerning measurable physiological changes or, less radically, people are asked to rate their satisfaction on a scale of one to ten. Since only the quantifiable aspects of an event can be included, some qualitative aspects are either ignored or artificially construed.

Quantifiability is not universally required by scientists, though it remains as an ideal for many. The move towards it seems to arise from three distinguishable considerations. First, as I have already noted, quantifiability tends to reduce the possibility of disagreement concerning what counts as A and B. Second, there is increased scope for the application of mathematics and computers if all the items are measurable units. Third, some scientists are convinced metaphysically that reality has an underlying mathematical structure.

Theoretical plausibility is the scientific principle that gives rise to most disagreement among scientists; and the more remote the theories are from particular empirical observations, the more disagreement there tends to be. In this aspect of science the creative intuitions of individual scientists are most evident. Sometimes the scientist devises a new theory (involving higher-order laws) that is simpler, more consistent, more comprehensive or more elegant than existing theories. Sometimes he devises crucial experiments whose outcome decisively shows the superiority of one rival theory over another. The creative intuitions are not themselves produced simply by applying scientific procedures, but eventually they must be tested scientifically.

My listing of theoretical plausibility with the first three principles of scientific method is potentially misleading, for science sometimes proceeds in the absence of any relevant explanatory theory. Sometimes scientists can bring about changes or predict changes on the basis of observed correlations without citing any theory. But although scientists can get by without being able to invoke theories as they carry on some of their investigations, the absence of an adequate theoretical framework can nevertheless often be a serious drawback, and an intrinsic part of scientific method seems to be the commitment to provide, eventually, such an explanatory framework. Often such frameworks designate hidden causal mechanisms, for example, those in physiological psychology.

Some scientists and philosophers of science, however, especially in the field of physics, are not concerned to explain regularities mainly by reference to hidden causal mechanisms. Rather, scientific explanation consists mainly of discovering or devising higher-order laws which bring together many lower-order regularities into a coherent, comprehensive system. On such a scientific approach, abstract theory has a very prominent place, and the main reservation concerning parapsychology is not so much the inadequacy or absence of explanatory causal mechanisms but rather the absence of a theoretical framework within which alleged paranormal regularities could be coherently included. Most parapsychologists and critics of parapsychology, however, do not seem to have such a conception of scientific explanation mainly in mind. Instead, they focus on experiments involving isolation, repeatability, and quantifiability, and on explanation by reference to causal mechanisms. Whatever the conception of "scientific method," however, an approach is positivist if an assumption is made that scientific method is the *only* way to knowledge of reality, so that explanations by reference to agent causality are not genuine explanations.

In section III we will consider parapsychology in relation to scientific method by reference to an official statement of the Parapsychological Association. Before that, however, we need to note some problems which arise not only in parapsychology but also in *any* application of scientific method to human agency.

II. SCIENTIFIC METHOD AND HUMAN AGENCY

The insistence that scientific tests must be repeatable *at will* if causal connections are to be shown involves scientists in a contradiction unless willed human behavior is assumed to be outside deterministic causal connections. On the one hand there is a sense of oneself as an independent will, as the origin of one's own decisions and actions, as an agent who causes events. When I move my arm voluntarily, *I* cause it to move. When I repeat an experiment, *I* cause the initial event(s) in the experiment. On the other hand, there is the scientific view of oneself as a material body conditioned by physical stimuli in a deterministic way. When I move my arm, some external stimulus causes a brain-change which in turn causes the arm movement. When I initiate the experiment it is not really I, but some physical stimulus. Since our culture's common sense includes both a libertarian insistence on *agent*-causality and a scientific emphasis on *mechanical*-causality, and since science itself presupposes agent causality in its methodology, a serious problem arises. Usually we "deal" with it by not facing it.[8] Instead, we alternate the perspectives. When I am pondering a choice between alternatives and then choose one and enact it, I cannot at the same time be viewing myself as totally determined; so I forget about science then. But on other occasions I ignore the fact that I am making decisions and acting on them—for example, while investigating causes. This is much easier if the focus is not on myself, but on someone else or something else. To view *myself* deterministically I have to be considering my past or future behavior, not what I am doing right now.

If, as positivists claim, scientific method is the *only* way to knowledge of human reality, human beings consist only of whatever patterns of behavior, together with their internal and/or external causes, that are accessible to scientific method. Not all social scientists, however, are positivist. Some have told me that although very strict in their application of scientific principles of isolation, repeatability, and quantifiability when they are doing science, they regard science as only one resource among many in the study of human beings. Others—for example, some anthropologists—either disclaim the label "social *scientist*" or, retaining it, insist that its meaning should be broadened so as to include their own empirical studies, which do not conform strictly to scientific method. Where the studies are most remote from science it is clear that their goal is not (as in behavioristic psychology) to explain human behavior in mechanical-causal ways so as to become able to control it, but rather (as in some anthropology) to understand the rationale for the actions of other human beings by seeing their world and interpreting their causal agency from their perspective.

Although scientific explanations can thus be distinguished from explanations by reference to agent causality, sometimes there are scientific investigations into the mechanisms associated with this agency—for example, what happens to my brain when I move my arm. Another investigation might explore what mechanisms are at work when electrical activity on my skin changes because I have learned how to produce such changes and am deliberately doing this now. Or, as in a typical instance of placebo effect, what endorphins or other substances are released when I think confidently of the "treatment" which I am receiving for my arthritis. In all three cases, scientists eventually may be able to trace extensively the brain changes which initiate other bodily changes which culminate in the arm movement, skin change, or reduced arthritis. What cannot, in principle, be explained in this way is *how* the initial mental change initiates a brain change. If one is a materialist, one can either deny the reality of consciousness or insist that for every change in consciousness (e.g., deciding to move my arm) there is allegedly a brain change which not only accompanies it but actually causes it. Since it can be shown that some changes in consciousness are produced by changes in the brain, this might seem plausible. There is, however, also evidence that changes in consciousness cause changes in the brain, both specifically and also, overall, in the placebo effect which is so emphasized by scientists! The placebo effect is itself very striking evidence for mind-over-matter causation!

Such mind-over-matter causation is not necessarily identical with agent causality. That is, when changes in consciousness cause changes in the body this is not always an instance of agent causality. The change in consciousness must itself be caused by the agent rather than by another agent or by a mental or physical change beyond the first agent's control. For example, even if it were true that my muscles relax because a chemical (or a psychic healer) first affects my consciousness and *thereby* affects my body, such mind-over-matter causality is not in itself an instance of agent causality. If, on the other hand, I relax my muscles by using a silent meditative technique, this *is* an instance of agent causality because my inner monologue is caused by me.

I am not claiming that agent causality always involves a specific, introspectible mental event or state that causes a physical change. Typically when I raise my arm I am not thinking about doing so. If someone asks me to raise my arm, however, I do think about it, and my conscious intention as I do it is linked closely with my sense of personal agency: "*I* am doing this." If, unknown to me, my arm is paralyzed, and I *try* unsuccessfully to move it, my trying is a specific introspectible mental event. So, also, is my trying at a distance to reduce stress in someone as I participate in a PK-healing experiment. All these examples tend to blur the distinction between agent causality and mind-over-matter causation, but it is intelligible for someone to reject the former while accepting the latter. That is, someone could reject explanations by reference to agents as causes while granting that sometimes mental events cause physical events. On such a view, the mental events would themselves have been caused by other events, either mental or physical. Such an approach, however, would be very difficult to apply experimentally in accordance with the principles of scientific method outlined in this essay. There are three reasons for this: the mental events are not publicly observable, they are often elusive, and they are not readily producible by the experimenter. If on the other hand they are produced by the experimental subject, the experiment directly involves agent causality.

In this chapter my explorations of psi-abilities involves *agent causality*, with a particular focus on *mental acts* by agents who, for example, are trying to influence the electrical activity on someone else's skin where there is no known mediating physical contact with that person. Their trying is not publicly observable, and one must rely on the honesty of their testimony in this regard, but it is not elusive and it is produced by them. Such psi causal agency differs from examples of mental influences on one's own body, where we do have some clues concerning how brain changes can initiate some pertinent gross-bodily changes. The cases are similar, however, in that whether I am causing skin-changes in myself or psychically in another person, the mind-to-body causality is in itself mysterious. Perhaps some day some of the mechanisms of psychic influence will be discovered; but perhaps not, for if I can directly cause changes in my own brain perhaps I can also directly cause changes in other parts of my body and in various parts of someone else's body.

Already, of course, some parapsychologists have been trying to establish whether current scientific theory can shed some light on what mechanisms or contributing factors are at work in PK and ESP. For example, Reinsel (1982) notes one experiment where the rate of enzyme catalysis was increased both by a healer's hands and by a high-intensity magnetic field; but the healer's hands displayed no unusual magnetic field. She also notes that tests with Faraday cages have ruled out most of the frequencies of the electromagnetic spectrum as "carriers" of psi processes (162, 165). More recently Persinger (1987) has compiled evidence which may indicate that low geomagnetic activity may facilitate ESP.

But I have digressed. My main interest in this section is not in parapsychology but in the application of scientific method to human beings generally. In some very strictly scientific approaches, not only human agency but even human consciousness as cognition is either eliminated or treated merely as a useful postulate, leaving only behavior as real. Such a treatment of consciousness, however, if applied to oneself, contradicts the one crucial way in which a positivist scientist limits her reductionism. That is, even if all the other human beings whom the scientist studies are seen merely as patterns of physical behavior, the scientist is also real to herself as a conscious being: "I think scientifically, therefore I am." Indeed, "I think and behave scientifically, and this activity results in truth." Hence, human reality is not, after all, restricted to what scientists can investigate. Although the scientist is viewed by herself and other scientists as someone who (like everyone else) is determined causally in her behavior, the same scientist is also viewed as someone who can repeat experiments at will, a causal agent who *acts according to the principles of scientific reason* rather than being merely conditioned in her behavior.

The contradiction disappears if human nature is not limited to what scientists can investigate and if determinism is viewed as merely a methodological assumption that can be modified or set aside in various contexts. A nonpositivist scientist can affirm a freely chosen commitment to scientific method, while acknowledging the legitimacy of various nonscientific approaches in the study of human beings such as those which explain events by reference to agent causality. Positivism, however, is caught up in a very awkward contradiction. Some positivists try to evade it. They may claim that when they say that they repeat experiments "at will" this involves only a postulating of their own free agency as a useful fiction. They may claim that somehow they have become conditioned so as to behave "in accordance with" scientific reason. They may claim that their own consciousness is merely a postulate, similar to what can be ascribed to a very intelligent computer. Such intellectual ploys require not only considerable ingenuity but also fantastic abstraction. A thoroughgoing, fanatical positivism is difficult to *think*. And if one is actually going to *live* it, one must cultivate, or fall into, a schizoid state similar to that of a psychotic who thinks that he is a machine, or wishes that he were. Indeed, I once heard a psychology professor call on those of us at a conference who were involved in projects to reduce the risk of global war to shift our focus of concern to the preservation of artificial intelligences. "These might survive the inevitable end of mankind, which is doomed because it is not simply a reasoning machine, but has inherited from its evolutionary history various emotions which unfortunately cannot be eliminated."

When I quoted this psychologist to a colleague who is a computer scientist, he protested, "Don't blame us for him!" Not all positivists are fanatical positivists, and some scientists, such as my colleague, are not positivists at all. They refuse to restrict other people to the devalued and constricted reality of what scientists can investigate. Many parapsychologists, however, and most critics of parapsychology, seem to be positivists. What they say seems to imply that parapsychology, provided that it is scientific, is the only possible way to knowledge concerning alleged paranormal phenomena. So the whole debate focuses on whether or not parapsychology satisfactorily fulfills the principles of scientific method. Such a debate is, of course, important. We should realize, however, that if positivism is mistaken, the outcome of the debate is not decisive.

Let us now consider how parapsychology attempts to conform to the principles of scientific method that I have discussed in the first and second sections, bearing in mind the contrast between two approaches: positivist explanations of scientific anomalies in terms of causal mechanisms, and nonpositivist explanations in terms of psi-abilities.

III. PARAPSYCHOLOGY AND LIMITS IMPOSED BY SCIENTIFIC METHOD

It seems appropriate to begin with an official statement by the Parapsychological Association (1988):

> Parapsychology studies apparent anomalies of behavior and experience which exist apart from currently known explanatory mechanisms which account for organism-environment and organism-organism information and influence flow. When an event is classified as a psi phenomenon, it is claimed that all known channels for the apparent interaction have been eliminated. Thus it is clear that labelling an event as a psi phenomenon does not constitute an explanation for that event, but only indicates an event for which a scientific explanation needs to be sought. Phenomena occurring under these conditions are said to have occurred under *psi-task conditions*. Labels such as "extra-sensory perception" (ESP) and "psychokinesis" (PK) refer to the apparent direction of information or influence. ESP refers to situations in which, under psi-task conditions, an organism behaves as if it has information about the physical environment (as in "clairvoyance"), another organism's mental processes (as in "telepathy") or a future event (as in "precognition"). PK refers to situations in which, under psi-task conditions, an organism's physical environment changes in a way that appears to be related to the organism's mental or physiological processes. Many parapsychologists dislike such terms as "ESP" and "clairvoyance" because they do not constitute an explanation and carry implicit theoretical loadings which may not be justified. (353–54)

Early in this essay I noted that even a positivist, causal-mechanist approach in parapsychology requires an initial selection of allegedly paranormal phenomena by reference to terms such as "ESP" and "PK," even though these terms are for them misleading. The official statement confirms this claim and refers implicitly to psi-abilities when it speaks of "psi-*task* conditions." There are four other features of this statement that I will now discuss.

Explanatory Mechanisms

The statement speaks of "currently known *explanatory mechanisms* which account for organism-environment and organism-organism information and influence flow" (my italics). The emphasis on the absence of, and need for, explanatory mechanisms is linked with an insistence that labels such as "ESP" and "PK" provide no explanation whatsoever, but merely describe an anomalous event for which a scientific explanation must be sought. This scientific explanation would be in terms of mechanisms which are currently unknown. Until such physical[9] mechanisms are set forth, even ideal evidence would show at best that there definitely is a scientific anomaly requiring scientific explanation. For example, suppose that not merely 60 percent of the time but *every* time a psychic healer can bring about an intended change in another person's skin electrical activity. We would still have to wait for someone to propose a plausible account of the mechanisms, which would involve presenting a new or radically revised scientific theory, involving references to theoretical entities and/or energies. Meanwhile, however, parapsychologists concerned with psi-abilities might be piling up statistically significant evidence concerning, say, psychic healing, including evidence concerning maximal conditions for success. Even if the accumulated evidence were to provide as reliable a basis for *application* as typical evidence in pharmaceutical research, the evidence would allegedly still only point towards an anomaly from the perspective of a positivist. On such a narrow approach, the reality of psychic healing (a species of PK which is a species of agent causality) would not be established until someone shows that physical mechanisms intervene between the conscious intentions of the healer and the change in the other's skin electrical activity. Clearly it is worthwhile to look for such mechanisms, which may exist. But perhaps they do not, and the healer acts directly on the other person's body as he somehow does on his own. In either case, if the evidence warrants it, it seems to me dogmatic to exclude agent causality (psychic healing) as an explanation.

Elimination of All Alternatives

Note that, according to the official statement, only if "all known channels for the apparent interaction have been eliminated" is there any need to seek a scientific explanation. The stringency of this requirement varies in accordance with the views of whoever sets it forth. At one extreme, the claim that all have been eliminated is utterly impossible to prove to a dogmatic unbeliever. Consider Galen Pletcher (1982): "Someone who *does not believe* that there is any kind of underlying order of the sort parapsychologists seeks will look at these experiments as evidence of some other misleading factor, just as I look at the fact that a woman *seems* to be sawed in two and then to be whole again as evidence that some other hidden feature(s) of the situation *must* exist" (175, first and last italics mine). Pletcher goes on to cite various alternatives, such as fraud, unconscious recording errors, and faulty experimental design.

If, as in the case of the particular conjuror's trick, some alternative non-paranormal explanation *must* exist, then no matter how scrupulous and careful a parapsychologist is in conducting an experiment, skeptics such as Pletcher would not be convinced that all alternatives have been eliminated. Parapsychologists have nevertheless taken up the challenge to try to eliminate all alternatives. As a result, this science tends to impose on itself requirements that are more rigorous than those imposed by other sciences. In one way this self-defensive rigor is very appropriate, for psi-phenomena, if not mere coincidences, challenge much of contemporary scientific theory and assumptions. In another way, however, the rigor is inappropriate, insofar as it is a futile attempt to persuade scientific fundamentalists whose dogmatism precludes any change of belief on the basis of evidence.

The most notorious such demand came from C. E. M. Hansel (1980) in relation to fraud: "If the result *could* have arisen through a trick, the experiment must be considered unsatisfactory proof of ESP, *whether or not it is finally decided that such a trick was in fact used*" (18, my italics). According to Hansel, such dogmatism is required because, in his words, "If their [parapsychologists'] claims are justified, a complete revision in contemporary scientific thought is required at least comparable to that made necessary in biology by Darwin and in physics by Einstein" (7–8). Fortunately the critics of Darwin and Einstein did not successfully put the onus on Darwin or Einstein to disprove charges of fraud concerning every claim they made![10] (Later I will note, however, that concern about fraud, especially by psychics with big reputations who have trained as magicians, is sometimes extremely appropriate.)

Repeatability/Replication

Although this requirement is not explicitly mentioned in the association's official statement, it almost certainly would not be rejected, for it is a basic principle in scientific method. According to one veteran parapsychologist, Charles Honorton (1993), there have been many successful replications of parapsychological experiments (199). Indeed, whereas "replication research is neither strongly encouraged nor highly valued in mainstream science" (202, where Honorton cites studies of attitudes and practices in journals for social and behavioral science), parapsychology "has long recognized the importance of replication and of reporting nonsignificant results" (203). Such results include unsuccessful attempted replications. To the best of his knowledge, the Parapsychological Association is "the only professional scientific organization that has adopted an official policy against selective reporting of 'positive' results" (203).

Critics such as Pletcher hold that "demand for repeatability is demand for one of the criteria that we ask a phenomenon to meet before it is considered other than a coincidence" (176). This requirement, in contrast with his version of the need to eliminate all alternative accounts, is in principle possible to fulfill. If, however, causal agency, including the exercise of a psi-ability, is a genuine alternative to coincidence, then replications can shift from being merely a preliminary attempt to show that a scientific investigation of mechanisms is needed. Instead, replications themselves can help to show the reality of a particular alleged psi-ability.

One difficulty in trying to replicate experiments concerning psi-abilities is that no significant statistical results in support can occur unless the psychic(s) being studied can to some extent repeat their feats at will. A scientist can only repeat a (successful) experiment if she finds psychics who can repeat it. This reduces the possible scope of parapsychological inquiry, since many or most allegedly paranormal events either occur involuntarily (spontaneously and unexpectedly) or voluntarily but rarely and not by utilizing an ongoing, reliable ability. If, however, psychic ability like musical ability is not confined to a few geniuses but is present in varying degrees among human beings, this problem is not insuperable. And significant results can fall well short of 100 percent success.

Another difficulty in replicating experiments concerning psi-abilities is that these seem to be linked both positively and negatively to various subjective and circumstantial factors which can themselves be detected. This is, indeed, what parapsychologists have found. According to Reinsel (1982), "Psi scores have been shown to be affected by the subject's personality, attitudes, mood and motivation, and the nature of the subject's social interaction with the experimenter and the testing situation. Experiments in which these variables are not taken into account generally show chance results" (159).[11] Moreover, both relaxation and mild sensory deprivation have been shown to be positive factors (see p. 160). Such results complicate the quest for replicability, as more motivational and circumstantial factors need to be replicated. But as we will see later, these difficulties in relation to exact replication may be worth the price in terms of increased success in establishing and exploring psi-abilities.

Statistical Significance

In the first section we saw that repeatability is linked in science with either invariant laws or statistical correlations. To the best of my knowledge, parapsychology has not aspired to invariant laws, but rather to significant statistical correlations. This less ambitious approach is not despised in other scientific contexts. As Hacking (1993) has pointed out, "A very large number of public decisions, especially in preventive medicine and agriculture, have long been made on the basis of detecting small but persistent effects" (590). According to Hacking, however, "If ever anything was refuted by statistics, it is the claims of parapsychology. . . . Every claim to persistent, subtle but statistically detectable psychic phenomena has been refuted" (591). Parapsychology should stay off statistics "because there are no phenomena, of the sort that can be detected by twentieth-century statistical analysis, that persist and are comparable to the phenomena of medicine or agriculture" (591). According to Hacking another reason for abandoning statistical trials in parapsychology is that "we have no idea what we are looking for" (590).

Since Hacking is an eminent philosopher of science with expertise in statistics, his sweeping allegation ("Every claim . . . refuted") cannot be ignored. Since it is unlikely that he has studied *every* claim, there may be some systematic reason for failure which he discerns—perhaps the alleged fact that "we have no idea what we are looking for," perhaps something more technically statistical. On the other hand, there are many statistically sophisticated parapsychologists who would not agree with Hacking's appraisal. (See, for example, Utts [1991].) Since I have no expertise in statistics, I can only draw the attention of readers to what Hacking and others say. Later I will venture the hypothesis that stringency in statistical requirements depends partly on *what kind of claim* is alleged and in relation to *what kind of world-view*.

Quantifiability

Although the official statement of the Parapsychological Association does not mention this principle, most parapsychology tries to fulfill it, and there does not seem to be much controversy concerning it. So I will not refer to it in the rest of the essay.

We now turn in sections IV and V to consider a particular experiment which not only raises questions about Hacking's view that paranormal studies yield no statistically significant data, but also shows how an appropriate application of scientific method can furnish important evidence relevant to psi-abilities and their application. Moreover, the experiment shows that the charge that "we have no idea what we are looking for" (while perhaps to some extent pertinent where the approach is positivist) is not pertinent where the approach focuses on psi-abilities.

IV. AN EXPERIMENT IN BIO-PK HEALING: BRAUD AND SCHLITZ (1983)

During the late 1970s and early 1980s, William Braud developed a series of experiments involving psychokinetic influences upon living systems. I quote from Braud's summary:

> The protocol for these bio-PK experiments is as follows. Some arbitrarily selected behavior or physiological activity of a freely responding target organism is monitored for a period of time. This period is divided into an equal number of influence and control periods. During the influence epochs, an influencer (beyond the sensory range of the target organism) attempts to psychically influence the ongoing activity of the organism in a predetermined direction. In all experiments conducted thus far, the influencer has received instantaneous and continuous analog feedback concerning the state of the target system. During the control epochs, no such psychokinetic attempts are made. The design is such that, in the absence of a psi influence, equal amounts of activity in the prescribed direction are expected to occur during control and influence epochs. A statistically significant excess of prescribed activity during the influence is evidence for a psi effect. Using this protocol, we have observed significant PK influences on the locomotor behavior of gerbils, the swimming orientation of electric knife fish and the electrodermal activity (EDA) of human volunteers. . . . The results do not seem to vary in any systematic way as a function of who serves as influencer. Results for the experimenter (W. B.), for a gifted psychic (Matthew Manning), and for unselected volunteer subjects are relatively comparable. (Braud and Schlitz, 1983: 96, 98)

Electrodermal activity (EDA) is electrical activity of sweat glands manifested in galvanic skin responses which can be monitored by a machine. High EDA levels indicate heightened activity of the sympathetic branch of the autonomic nervous system and hence heightened arousal, emotionality, and stress. Low levels of EDA indicate relaxation, the absence of stress, and physical and/or mental calmness. EDA experiments are specially promising because the electrodermal target system "seems to yield the strongest psi effect and because work with this system has the greatest likelihood of yielding findings relevant to a possible practical application in psychic healing" (98). Moreover, in the EDA experiment reported in 1983 by Braud and Schlitz, a further consideration was influential: "The use of experiments designed as psychic-healing analogs may provide a way of upgrading the meaningfulness of laboratory experimentation and optimizing the motivation of the participants. In psychic-healing experiments, there exists a definite *need* in the target organism, and a successful psi influence aids in the satisfaction of that need" (99). There is also a strong need in the influencer: "There exists a strong wish to *help* the ill or injured target organism; feelings of empathy with the target organism may also be present" (99). In the 1983 experiment, the need in the target organisms was not illness or injury, but the stress associated with continuously high EDA.

Braud and Schlitz (1983) present the following overview of the particular experimental design:

> Both of us (W. B. and M. S.) functioned as influencers in this study. Our goal was to psychically decrease the EDA of the target persons during only the influence periods, which were intermixed with control periods of no PK attempts. There were 32 sessions, one target person for each. Half of the target persons ($n = 16$) were persons with excessive EDA (active subjects); half of the target persons were individuals with normal or low levels of EDA (inactive subjects). For each of the 32 sessions, the target person's EDA (skin conductance reactions) was sampled and scored by computer during ten 30-second influence epochs and ten 30-second control epochs. Influencers watched a polygraph tracing of the target person's EDA throughout each session and therefore received instantaneous and continuous feedback about the effectiveness of their bio-PK attempts. The magnitude of the bio-PK effect was expressed as a percentage and was derived by dividing the EDA obtained during the influence (decrease) epochs by the total EDA of both epochs (the influence plus the control epochs). Mean change expectation (MCE) in the absence of psi effect was 50%. (100–101)

Prior to the session when bio-PK was attempted, each participant had sat for twenty 10-minute epochs hooked up to register EDA changes without any such attempts. This provided a way to distinguish subjects into relatively stressed ("active") and calm ("inactive") groups of 16. It also provided a first control session where no significant differences in EDA among epochs was in fact recorded—in contrast with the significant *10 percent difference* in the second session between the influence epochs and control epochs for "active" subjects.

Arrangements to set aside a placebo effect were complex. On the one hand, the subjects were told prior to the second session that "during certain parts of the session, the experimenter would attempt to psychically *calm* the subject, and that the subject should wish for and allow such calming effects to occur" (104). This by itself would seem to be an attempt to *increase*, rather than eliminate, any placebo effect. But the subjects were not told how many calming attempts were to be made, or when they would occur. "Indeed, at this point the experimenter was still unaware of the predetermined sequence of the calming versus control periods for that subject" (104). When the experimenter and subject went to their respective rooms (twenty meters apart), the experimenter opened an envelope which contained instructions for the influence versus the control epoch sequence for that particular session. "The envelopes had been prepared beforehand by another person, using a table of random numbers" (104). During each session no sensory clues were available to the subjects concerning when psychic influence was being attempted. Hence, overall, the expectation of subjects that they might be calmed cannot be used as an explanation of the significant difference between influence and control epochs.

Is it possible that the active subjects responded telepathically to the influencer so as to detect when the influencer was, or was not, attempting a calming influence? Braud and Schlitz concede that this is not only a vague possibility but, in some instances, a plausible hypothesis: "In these EDA experiments, subjects have spontaneously remarked that during certain periods within the session they actually *felt* that someone had entered the room to activate them (in the present study). They reported physical feelings of activation or quietude during specific periods of the session that could be correlated with activity seen in the polygraph records and with psychic influence attempts" (112). In such cases is it possible that the EDA changes were produced entirely by the subjects, so that instead of PK we have telepathy plus the placebo effect? Braud and Schlitz suspect that the 1983 experiment involved a mixture of PK and telepathy. One of the advantages of Braud's previous experiments with nonhuman targets (gerbils, fish) was that pure PK seems more likely, according to Braud and Schlitz. In an experiment reported in 1989, they tried to see whether influencers who had more opportunity to use ESP were more successful than those who lacked the opportunity. The former group could pick their own times to send healing, thus perhaps tuning in by ESP when the subject's EDA was beginning to increase. The former group scored no better.

Since the 1983 experiment raised the possibility that some subjects calmed themselves while responding telepathically to the influencer's attempts, Braud and Schlitz included a sequel experiment, which also has implications concerning the placebo effect. Braud and Schlitz had eliminated the plausibility of a placebo explanation (except if joined with telepathy). The sequel experiment was designed to "directly compare the magnitude of the psi effect obtained in the bio-PK/need experiment just described with the magnitude of a similar effect obtained through non-psychic means" (115) The experiment resembled the bio-PK/need experiment in crucial ways, so as to make possible a pertinent comparison of results, but some differences were of course necessary. High- or low-pitched sounds signalled to the subjects the beginning of control (no-influence) and influence epochs. The subjects, who were new to such attempts at calming themselves, varied considerably in their ability. Overall, their influence on themselves was slightly more significant statistically than that of Braud and Schlitz as PK-influencers on the other subjects.

I chose Braud and Schlitz because their experiments seem to me to be an example of parapsychology at its best. I have no doubt left some questions unanswered in my brief outline, so interested readers will need to consult their whole report. In the next section I will present some reflections concerning the experiment in relation to the first four aspects of parapsychology that we noted in section III.

V. PARAPSYCHOLOGY AS APPLIED BY BRAUD AND SCHLITZ

Explanatory Mechanisms

Braud and Schlitz do not even mention the issue of explanatory mechanisms. Obviously they do not think that they must wait until what is going on can be explained by reference to physical mechanisms before they can use the expression "psychic healing" as an explanation of their results—an explanation by reference to a kind of causal *agency*. Indeed, their main interest does not seem to be in trying to show that such a psi-ability exists (though the experiment does in my opinion provide some evidence in support of this) but rather to yield findings "relevant to a possible practical application in psychic healing" (98). This seems to me to be a legitimate approach. As I have noted, other experiments or investigations differ in approach, trying to find out known mechanisms such as electromagnetism or geomagnetism as factors in some paranormal phenomena. That, too, is a legitimate approach, but Braud and Schlitz do not have to wait for total success in such studies (plus new and plausible theorizing if previously unknown mechanisms must be postulated) before going on with their kind of research on psi-abilities, which explain events by reference to agent causality.

Sometimes issues concerning mechanical causality and agent causality become confused with questions concerning the "natural" and the "supernatural." Some thinkers imply that if an event can not be explained by reference to "natural" mechanisms, that is, physical mechanisms, this would make the event "supernatural." For example, Charles Honorton (1993) rejects the term *paranormal* because it "is usually used to imply that psi interactions must necessarily, if real, represent an order of reality outside the natural realm" (210). Instead, we should speak of "currently anomalous communication and energetic processes" (211), since what we are dealing with are "unexplained—anomalous , but not unexplainable—*natural* processes" (211, my italics). But this implies that if no physical mechanism can be found to explain, say, psychic healing, this psi-ability would be supernatural, "outside the natural realm." In fairness to Honorton, I should note that he explicitly rejects Newtonian physics (210) and cites such explanatory ideas in modern physics as "quantum nonlocality" (211), so his commitment is not to mechanisms but to physics. Indeed, some thinkers mean by *physical* "whatever is postulated by theories in physics," and this is typically very unlike billiard balls. But what if some elements in everyday agent causality are not explicable by physics? Surely they are still quite "natural." And likewise in the case of psi-abilities.

It seems clear to me that psi-abilities can be quite "natural" in a different sense. That is, their existence does not by itself imply the reality of another realm, for example, a realm in which discarnate spirits live. For this reason it has seemed important to me to distinguish the "this-worldly paranormal" from the "otherworldly paranormal." People who believe in the former often do not believe in the latter. Of course, if spirits do indeed exist and act then they, too, are part of the total world and in that sense part of "nature." Such discarnate spirits differ, however, from human beings and physical objects in that their existence is *by definition* nonphysical, whatever physics may mean by "physical."[12] In the "this-worldly" parapsychology which we have been considering, no such realm of spirits is implied. The alleged psi-abilities are all abilities of embodied agents.

From a positivist perspective, explanations by reference to everyday causal agency or to psi causal agency or to spirit causal agency all have in common the implication that explanations by reference to physical mechanism (or, more broadly, physics) do not suffice. All three alleged agencies are thus outside of "nature," outside of what is real. From a nonpositivist perspective, however, "nature" may include the first agency, the first and second, or the first, second and third—depending on one's worldview.

Elimination of All Alternatives

Braud and Schlitz list nine alternatives and show why it is plausible to reject them all. Indeed, the experiment was ingeniously set up so as to rule out various alternatives, as we have seen. For example, there was no non-psi way by which the subjects could know when the experimenters were attempting PK influence. I refer readers to their responses to all nine, especially the lengthy refutation of claims that the results are somehow due to fraud on the part of the subjects. Concerning the possible accusation of experimenter fraud, however, I shall quote part of their reply:

> No experiment, however sophisticated, can ever be absolutely safe from experimenter fraud. Even if an experiment were controlled by an outside panel of disinterested persons, a hostile critic could still argue that collusion was involved. The imagined extent of such a conspiracy would be limited only by the imagination (and degree of paranoia) of the critic. We can only state that we used a two-experimenter design so that one experimenter's portion of the experiment served as a kind of control for the other experimenter's portion. Only the successful replication of these findings by other investigators would reduce experimenter fraud to a non-issue. (110–11)

(I should note that if the "hostile critic" were Hansel, not even replication would make fraud a nonissue, for all the replications could be fraudulent!)

Perhaps there are other alternatives in addition to the nine considered by Braud and Schlitz. They do go on to consider some alternatives which involve some other psi accounts, for example, telepathy, but these are not what their critics would have in mind if the issue is whether any anomaly at all has been shown. Perhaps there are flaws in their responses to some of the proposed alternatives, flaws of which I am unaware because of my lack of experience and sophistication in parapsychology. Seemingly impressive experiments have been severely criticized not only by hostile external critics but also by fellow parapsychologists.[13]

What does seem clear to me as a philosopher is that the stringency of requirements for hypothetically possible alternatives is greater once one switches from a psi-ability approach to a conservative positivist approach. In the latter case, the experiment is intended to prove that at least one paranormal phenomenon is "real" in the sense that it is undeniably an anomaly which requires a (new) scientific explanation. The experiment then becomes, in every case, a test for one's conservative positivist worldview, which would be shattered if the experiment were successful. No wonder some people scrutinize experiments with a fanatical vigor and a fantastic imagination concocting hypothetical alternatives.[14]

Repeatability/Replication

To what extent would replication increase the credibility of the results of such an experiment as that of Braud and Schlitz? They themselves "encourage independent investigators to replicate the present experiment" (111), and they note that experiments very similar to some of Braud's earlier bio-PK experiments have been attempted by independent researchers—the major difference being that the others did not provide "immediate, trial-by-trial, analog feedback" (111). We have seen that for Braud and Schlitz replication can reduce the plausibility of the charge of experimenter fraud. Presumably replication also reduces the plausibility of other charges of flawed procedure. Does replication also improve statistical significance by enlarging the database? According to one parapsychologist-statistician, sometimes it does and sometimes it does not (Utts, 1988).

Is there a further reason for replication? In sciences other than parapsychology, the demand for replication arises mainly when the results claimed do not fit in easily with contemporary science, for example, a claim by some physicists to have achieved cold nuclear fusion. Otherwise, unless there is a need to build up the database, replication is not typically a big issue. Other scientists are willing to assume that the experiment can be replicated. Parapsychology, however, is different. Since every experiment involves a possible claim that at least one psi-ability is real, and since this, if true, would radically question much of contemporary science, replication seems to many psi-unbelievers a very legitimate requirement, especially if they are positivists, for whom the only possible rational basis for belief in psi-abilities is through parapsychology.

The issue of replication raises a crucial question: replication by whom? In science generally, the personal traits of the experimenter(s) should not matter. The experimental technique as set forth in the report of the experiment should be applicable by anyone who has the appropriate intelligence and scientific training, regardless of differences in personal attitudes concerning the results, personal motivations, or personal development of nonscientific abilities. Similarly, if the experiment involves human subjects, any relevant personal differences among them should either be effectively ruled out or specified in advance (unless the experiment is designed to identify these differences.) Braud and Schlitz, however, had "participated previously as successful bio-PK influencers" (101) and presumably had an expectation of a successful outcome in 1983. The subjects, moreover, had been encouraged by the experimenters to be open to positive effects. It seems likely that if the experimenters had been hostile skeptics, the experiment would not have been successful. Even a witnessing of the experiment by a hostile skeptic could have undermined morale and adversely affected the results. So the experiment is *not* replicable by an impersonal "anyone." Yet the limitation on replication is intelligible and justifiable.

Braud and Schlitz, however, have done much towards facilitating possible replication. Since psi-abilities vary greatly in accordance with various subjective and circumstantial factors, they devised the experiment in ways which would maximize positive factors. They maximized motivation by linking it with *need* and with *positive expectations*, both of which can occur again in a replication. Also, by focusing on EDA rather than some other alleged bodily change (e.g., levitation!), they selected a change which is relatively easy to affect. Replication is also helped by Braud and Schlitz in that they relied on themselves in 1983 rather than on someone with a reputation as a gifted psychic. More important, Braud had used twenty unselected volunteers as bio-PK influencers in previous experiments. The scores of these volunteers were not significantly inferior to those of Braud and a gifted psychic. Hence if psi-abilities exist among the general population, replication in various research settings is feasible without relying on a gifted psychic. There does seem to be a probable conflict, however, between easy replicability and higher scores if volunteers (or Braud and Schlitz themselves) can *improve* their psi-abilities through practice. Replication with neophytes seems more feasible than with participants who have varying degrees of past practice.

Perhaps it is impossible to replicate exactly the subjective or personal factors in Braud's experiments; also, verification by "anyone" is not attempted or attained; but such an approach seems to me very promising. Although quasi replications may not convert any skeptics, and although the skeptic himself is unlikely to be able to replicate the experiment even if he tried, parapsychology can best continue to accumulate evidence pertinent to psi-abilities by not trying to accommodate itself totally to the demands of positivists. Indeed, the assumptions that some psi-abilities may be real is not necessarily a distorting bias, and can be a "plus" in facilitating successful experiments. Even the assumption that some psi-abilities *are* real need not involve distortion if an experiment is as well designed as the one by Braud and Schlitz.

Braud did not use a gifted psychic as the only bio-PK influencer. Such an approach can sometimes be appropriate, where alleged psi-abilities are unlikely to be shown by neophyte volunteers and may be impressively demonstrated by a particular individual. On the other hand, if a gifted psychic has a big reputation at stake, so that there could be a motive to use conjuring tricks if psychic powers are non-existent or failing, additional precautions should be taken to try to rule this out. Such precautions are specially important if the psychic is known to have skills in magic, and in the absence of such one would not have to be a dogmatic skeptic like Hansel to have some reservations concerning the experimental results. Indeed, if one hopes to convince people by one striking experiment, high scores may be insufficient if precautions have been inadequate. Concerning this danger see Hansen (1990 and 1992c). But as can be seen from the responses to Hansen (1992c), scientists can and do differ concerning what precautions count as sufficient in such cases.

I have commended Braud's use of neophyte, positively motivated volunteers because of the potential for rough replication by other investigators. I also see an important "fringe benefit" in it: the introduction of these volunteers to a context where they can discover for themselves that some psi-abilities may be real. If one wants to convince more people in a rational way that some psi-abilities may be real, or even *are* real, the best way in my opinion is by helping them to discover their *own* psi-abilities. At the end of this essay I will say more about this.

Statistical Significance

Braud and Schlitz's statistics impress me, but I have no expertise in such matters, so perhaps I should be less impressed. In any case, what more interests me as a philosopher is the question, "*How* significant does the difference between figures for control epochs and influence epochs have to be to convince people who have such-and-such views of the world?" Clearly no statistical evidence whatsoever would convince someone who views such an experiment with the same kind of skepticism that she brings to a magician apparently sawing a woman in half and then restoring her to unity. Whatever the statistical evidence in an experiment, there must be an alternative, non-psi explanation. But what if a skeptic is open to the possibility that there might be anomalies requiring a scientific explanation by reference to mechanisms that are totally or partly unknown by contemporary science? Such a positivist skeptic would still insist that agent-causality terms such as "psychic healing" explain nothing, since the only real explanation would be one involving mechanical causality. And such a skeptic might, in varying degrees, be reluctant to question existing scientific theories; an ultra-conservative would require overwhelming statistical evidence.

Some parapsychologists, unlike Braud and Schlitz, seem to share such a positivist and scientifically conservative worldview with some critics of parapsychology. Perhaps differences in the stringency of statistical requirements vary according to the degree of tenacity with which such a worldview is held. Unlike the experiments in agriculture or medicine which Hacking (1993) cites, what is at stake is not primarily a pragmatic judgment concerning whether a particular fertilizer or drug will probably work effectively, assuming as obvious that fertilizers and drugs sometimes do work. What is at stake for positivist conservatives in a parapsychological experiment is what they see as the minimal likelihood that existing scientific frameworks could need to be revised so as to explain psi phenomena.

Beyond the issue concerning what evidence could prove that there is an *anomaly* requiring scientific explanation, there is the issue of what evidence could convince someone that *psi-abilities* are ever real. One positivist writer, William D. Gray (1991), has been very explicit about this: "It is very clear what would prove that ESP *does* exist. If a person consistently scored 99 percent on carefully controlled ESP tests for several years under conditions precluding the possibility of cheating and could perform for skeptics as well as believers, this would be convincing evidence of ESP" (87–88). Why would 90 percent, or even 80 percent, be insufficient for Gray? "It is a fundamental principle of science that if a phenomenon occurs once, it will occur again, if the conditions are the same" (88). But what if psi-abilities, like many other human abilities such as remembering or running or noting sensory clues, vary in accordance with many conditions, known and unknown, which cannot all be replicated? This might explain why only, say, an 80 percent success-rate can be consistently maintained; or perhaps only a lower success-rate. Gray's stringent requirements arise for him because the issue for him is whether ESP exists at all, and because he is a positivist conservative in his worldview. It seems likely to me that differences concerning statistical requirements arise not only from technical issues concerning which I am ignorant, but also from differences in worldview.[15]

VI. LIMITATIONS ON SCIENTIFIC INVESTIGATIONS OF THE PARANORMAL

In this necessarily brief and final section I will first summarize my findings in this essay concerning limits imposed on scientific investigations of the paranormal. Then I will note some limitations which emerged in my book *Spirituality and Human Nature*, which readers should consult for further details.

Parapsychology Cannot Satisfy the Demand of Some Skeptics

Parapsychological experiments concerning psi-abilities such as bio-K cannot convince anyone who:

(i) requires prior provision of a convincing explanation of how the psi-ability could work through a mechanical-causal sequence;

and/or (ii) requires that there must be a hidden non-paranormal factor at work in every experiment that seems to be successful;

and/or (iii) dismisses all forms of agent-causality as explanations of physical changes; or, while conceding that non-psi causal agency is real, dismisses all psi-abilities as unintelligible.

Parapsychologists should realize that it is futile to try to convince some of their skeptical opponents.[16]

Parapsychologists understandably differ, however, concerning the extent to which their experiments should attempt to meet the requirements of these opponents. If a parapsychologist is a positivist and/or a scientific conservative, these requirements will seem on the whole reasonable. If he is neither of these, and accepts explanations in terms of agent causality, and if in addition he believes already that some psi-abilities may be real, the skeptics will seem much less relevant.

Nevertheless, since each experiment does "double duty"—establishing a particular psi-ability and thereby the reality of at least one instance of psi, plus establishing a particular point concerning that ability—all parapsychologists should acknowledge a somewhat greater burden of proof than is generally required of scientists in other fields, unless the research of these scientists, like parapsychology, indicates a possible need for a revolution in scientific theories.

Direct Experiential Access Is Possible to Such Alleged Paranormal Phenomena as Healing Energies and Spirits

In my book I noted that scientific method can only deal with alleged paranormal access to normal phenomena, that is, publicly observable events. If science is to be involved, whatever is allegedly discerned psychically or changed psychokinetically has to be something open to observation in normal, nonpsychic ways. For example, when Bernard Grad (1976) investigated alleged psychic healing of mice and plants, he observed various changes in the mice and the plants, changes discernible to anyone else who can see. What about the healing energies that a spiritual healer says he can feel moving out from his fingers? The publicly observable evidence concerning mice and plants might lead a scientist to postulate some energies as unobservable theoretical entities. Or perhaps the presence of some energies, while not directly experienced by the scientist, could be detected if she were trained to use a scientific monitoring device. This would make the energies in a broad sense publicly observable. Indeed it would indicate that at least part of what the healer claims to experience directly can plausibly be identified as, say, electromagnetic energy. But the healer's conviction concerning the reality of the energies which he is feeling does not depend on such a scientific finding, and what he *means* by "healing energy" is intrinsically linked to his direct experience.

In another kind of case, if a psychic reports that a house is haunted by a discarnate spirit whom she has discerned, a parapsychologist has nothing whatsoever to investigate unless the "spook" is allegedly causing some publicly observable changes, which may or may not be the case. Perhaps some day, as in the "Ghostbusters" movie, scientific monitoring devices for detecting ghosts may be devised, but the psychic's conviction does not depend on such a scientific finding, and what she *means* by "ghost" is intrinsically linked to her direct experience.

In general, when people experience healing energies or spirits, what they *mean* by their report concerning this is intrinsically linked with the experience, and what they are experiencing may or may not be linked with publicly observable events. Hence, what they mean is similarly only contingently linked with any such events. Indeed, a typical experience of a discarnate spirit is like psychically experiencing the radiance and/or vibrations of a human being, except that there is no publicly observable physical body! And usually the spirit causes no publicly observable change. And not only are the experiences often subjectively convincing, they can also sometimes be verified by other psychics, whether neophyte or veteran.

If on the other hand all such experiences are delusions, then of course we must be grateful to science for discounting them. It is possible that most human beings in most prescientific cultures were deluded. It seems to me more rational, however, to question the impersonalist scientific dogma that a truth-claim cannot possibly be established unless *anyone* who has the appropriate intelligence and scientific training can test it. On the contrary, there have been many kinds of wisdom and truth which only become reliably accessible to the extent that people undergo a pertinent process of nonscientific personal change. In some instances, as with PK influence on electrodermal activity, the process may involve only a minimal shift in attitudes and motivations. In other instances, as in becoming aware of chi-energy through karate, undergoing psychoanalysis, becoming aware of one's own radical freedom, or becoming a saint indwelt by Jesus or Krishna, the process is more drastic and arduous. The crucial philosophical point here is that the *meaning* of many statements is intrinsically linked with the *experiences* on which they are partly or entirely based, and that many of these experiences are not accessible to people, or are only partly accessible, unless they undergo the appropriate *process* of personal change. Spontaneous, involuntary eruptions of experience do occur, but steady access usually requires involvement in such a process.

The links between experience, meaning, and processes of personal change is thus an important feature of paranormal access to *paranormal* phenomena such as energies or spirits. The same point also applies to paranormal access to *normal* phenomena, that is, to publicly observable events which are allegedly perceived by ESP or caused by PK. Consider, for example, a clairvoyant vision of someone's death or a PK-healing reduction of someone's stress: the death and the reduction are both publicly observable. When a person is exercising a psi-ability there is both an intended focus or outcome which can be confirmed by someone else and a *private experience*. What the person reports has a meaning which includes *all* of this. Note also that although spontaneous ESP or PK may occur, if there is to be an ongoing, reliable psi-ability, a process involving much practice and personal change is usually a prerequisite. Eventually the exercise of a psi-ability can become similar to using one's eyesight where keen attention is needed: only occasionally does it seem necessary to look again, or to ask someone else to check. In early stages of psi-development, confirmation from time to time is both prudent and reassuring, but gradually this need decreases, and what psi or PK mean is increasingly linked with characteristic experiences in exercising it. (For an exploration of varieties of such experience associated with psychic healing, see Cooperstein, 1992).

As I pointed out in *Spirituality and Human Nature* (145–46 and 162–63), the meaning of a statement is closely linked with its appropriate mode of verification. There are significant differences between verification by scientific method and verification by direct psychic experience, so we cannot and must not assume that what is meant is the same. The two meanings may be at most analogous, or overlapping. Insofar as we move from psychic experience into genuinely spiritual experience which requires and brings profound personal transformation, it becomes less and less clear to what extent *any* scientific investigations are appropriate, for without such transformation the scientist can only minimally *understand* what is being claimed, and *the scientist's methods dictate a different meaning.*

It Can Be Rational to Base a Specific Belief in the Paranormal on One Case

Henry Bergson (1975), in his presidential address to the Society for Psychical Research in London, argued that all one needs is *one* impressive case for it to be rational to believe that telepathy has occurred. The case under discussion (which I would call "clairvoyance") was one where the wife of an officer allegedly had a clear vision of her husband's death in battle at the time when it occurred. Bergson says that even if the woman had had thousands of false visions, he would be convinced concerning telepathy "if I could be sure that even the countenance of one soldier unknown to her, present at the scene, had appeared to her such as it was in reality" (85). Various other statistical concerns are presumably also irrelevant to Bergson—for example, the likelihood of the officer's death in battle, whether objectively or in his wife's expectations. What matters is detail. The more detailed the women's vision, and the more items included that she had no basis for including, the more impressive the case.

How much detail, and what kinds of detail, are required in a particular case for it to be rational to believe that a psi-ability was at work?

People obviously can and do differ concerning this. It seems clear to me, however, that some sort of fanatical dogmatism is present if someone is committed on principle to rejecting *any* appeal to a single case of alleged psi-ability, no matter how impressive the details. One source of such a dogmatism could be positivism, with its insistence that only a scientific study involving many cases could establish noncoincidence. A positivist would point out that, no matter what the odds, improbable events can and do happen, but only if they are repeated many times is there for him any evidence pointing towards an anomaly requiring scientific explanation.

Positivist dogma is irrelevant unless one is a positivist. But the point concerning improbable events happening is important. Even if one is not a positivist, one needs to have some rational initial way to distinguish among single cases that display remarkable patterns those which, however detailed, are merely coincidence or chance, and those which may be paranormal and hence require further investigation. According to P. W. Bridgman (1978), "the locus of chance is in ourselves, with strong elements of 'expectation' and 'surprise.' . . . There is little that is 'objective' about it" (194). In support of such a psychological account, Galen Pletcher (1982) argues that there seems to be no limit on the patterns of coincidence for which someone may, quite irrationally, demand an explanation. He constructs an ingenious example:

> A student sees the papers and sundry notes on my bulletin board and suddenly becomes very interested in their 'order,' as he calls it. I say, in response to the question, that they are in no particular order, but that I have tacked up various bulletins, memos, calendars and cartoons as seem to me noteworthy. He persists, and eventually it emerges that the colors on the bulletin board that are other than white are arranged alphabetically left to right. They are arranged, let us say, in the order of blue, gold, green, pink and yellow. He now presses me to explain how they got that way. (171)

Pletcher understandably rejects any need for an explanation of the pattern discerned by the student. He had various reasons for putting each item where he did. The alleged pattern is just a coincidence.

I agree that the alleged pattern does not require any explanation in terms of the paranormal (though a *psychological* explanation in terms of Pletcher's unconscious might not seem fantastic to some people.)[17] What Pletcher ignores is the fact that where psi-abilities such as ESP or PK are alleged, there is some subjective and objective similarity to standard, everyday instances of sense-perception or agent causality. The woman's vision cited by Bergson differed from Pletcher's example in that it was experienced by her as being subjectively similar in many ways to ordinary seeing. In both her everyday perceptions of people and in the vision there seems to be a cognitive element, as when she notes the facial features and expressions of a man standing beside her husband. Of course, many apparently cognitive visions turn out to be false. But if the details of her vision are independently corroborated, this confirms her subjective sense that cognition occurred. Clairvoyant visions are selected not from an infinite set of remarkable co-happenings, but from a particular sub-set which are prima facie candidates for explanation by reference to a psi-ability. For a positivist, however, such explanations cannot arise, so it is inappropriate to identify putative paranormal events in such a way; all selections of single remarkable cases as events requiring explanation seem equally arbitrary and subjective.

In my book I considered the rationality of one-case belief in the paranormal and I referred readers to several impressive cases from the Proceedings of the Society for Psychical Research selected by Broad (1962).[18] I also cited some examples which I had witnessed when I introduced a group of students to psychometry (telepathy and/or clairvoyance facilitated by holding in one's hand someone's personally significant possession such as a watch, necklace, ring, or wallet). The students, who worked in pairs, had not had any previous contact other than sitting in the same large class. Often, though not always, one student would intuit correctly a very detailed event in another's life. One "saw" the other receiving her necklace near a lifeboat on a pleasure-cruise from a dark-haired man with a beard. Another "saw" the other getting married across the ocean in a small English church on a sunny summer day. When the student has no reason to suspect that the fellow-student who confirms the vision is being dishonest, or that the information had been picked up unwittingly and forgotten, it is rational for him or her to believe, at least tentatively, that the convergence of vision and event was not merely a coincidence but was in some way a cognition. Where the case was less impressive in its detail, a response such as "Maybe there's something in it" usually seemed appropriate to the student involved. A few students were not persuaded at all, even by the most impressive cases; they wanted more detail. This seems to me very legitimate. People have to make up their own minds concerning such matters. And whatever the considerable merits of parapsychology, the best basis is one's own personal experience of one's own psi-abilities.

NOTES

1. When I began writing this essay, I thought at first that it would be essentially a revision and expansion of what I wrote in *Spirituality and Human Nature*. I soon realized that I wanted to do a substantial study of parapsychology. So I have only drawn on my book in my outline of scientific method (section 2) and in a few passages scattered through the essay. The excerpts and paraphrases are included by permission of State University of New York Press (copyright 1993).

2. The term *positivism* was coined in the mid–nineteenth century by Saint-Simon and Comte. When I use the term I do not restrict it to what in this century has been called *logical positivism*, a distinctive species of positivism which claims that any statement which is unverifiable has no meaning. It is possible to reject this claim while nevertheless insisting that scientific method is the only way to knowledge of reality.

3. A third approach, advocated by Rhea White (1994), moves in the direction of *transpersonal* psychology. Although this approach is in my opinion very significant, I will not be considering it in this essay. White's research and reflection concerning what she calls "exceptional human experiences" is a conscious shift on her part away from parapsychology: "I do not claim to be speaking today as a parapsychologist. . . . My approach to these experiences falls well outside the canon developed by the Parapsychological Association" (1). "I pursued the meaning of psi experiences rather than evidence for the existence of psi" (4). "*Exceptional human experience* is an umbrella term for many types of experience generally considered to be psychic, mystical, encounter-type experiences, death-related experiences, and experiences at the upper end of the normal range, such as creative inspiration, exceptional human performance, as in sports; literary and aesthetic experiences, and the experience of falling in love" (5). "Exceptional human experiences are those gifts life provides us that are meant to spearhead our lives—that can pull us out of boredom, disconnection, and anomie into a world of meaning and connection. We have to learn how to incorporate these experiences in our lives. I think that when a sufficient number of people do that, the larger story will emerge. Exceptional human experiences catapult us into a new paradigm" (6). My own perspective on exceptional human experiences and transpersonal psychology is presented in Evans (1993 and 1996).

4. Parapsychology, a branch of *psychology*, does not typically investigate apparent scientific anomalies which are in the domain of physics, unless human behaviors seem to be factors. The term *paranormal*, however, sometimes refers to anomalies which, if not explicable scientifically, allegedly point to interventions by extraterrestrials, spirits, and even God rather than by human beings. Such concerns, though perhaps legitimately part of what is called "psychical research," are beyond the scope of most parapsychology.

5. For a roughly similar account, see Mellow (1970). The principles which I list are not recipes for making scientific discoveries, but they do reflect testing procedures used by ordinary scientists in, for example, behavioral psychology, pharmaceutical research, and parapsychology.

6. Hume's claim that causality is simply "constant conjunction" is accepted by some contemporary philosophers of science and rejected by others.

7. I should note that some of the new physics seem to replace mechanical causality by a causality analogous to agent causality. See *Spirituality and Human Nature*, 137, 161–62.

8. Some philosophers deal with it by proposing ways in which freedom and determinism can allegedly be reconciled. Such a "compatibilist" thesis has serious flaws, especially in its rejection of the essential meaning of the crucial claim, "I could have done otherwise."

9. The official statement implies that the "mechanisms" are physical. In a previous sentence it referred to interactions "in which it appears that information or influence has occurred which cannot be explained through our current understanding of *sensorimotor channels*" (353, my italics). It is true the official statement as quoted does refer once to "experience" and twice to "mental processes," but it is unclear what place, if any, consciousness can have in the investigations. The statement does go on to say: "A commitment to the study of psi phenomena does not require assuming the reality of 'non-ordinary' factors or processes. Regardless of what form the final explanation may take, however, the study of these phenomena is likely to expand our understanding of the processes often referred to as 'consciousness' and 'mind'" (354). But if only physical-mechanical explanations are allowed, how could the "final explanation" expand our understanding of consciousness and mind unless these are reduced to physical phenomena? The official statement was written by a committee, so perhaps we should not be surprised if it involves some ambiguities, some hints towards a psi-ability approach in an otherwise positivist document.

10. For an extensive discussion by various people of issues concerning the requirement that parapsychologists disprove fraud, see Jan Ludwig (1978: 145–204).

11. Cf. Meehl and Scriven (1978): "ESP is a capacity like any other human capacity such as memory, in that it varies in strength and characteristics from individual to individual and in the one individual from one set of circumstances to another" (189).

12. On some worldviews such a definition rules out the possible existence of spirits. If spirits can cause changes in the physical world, however, such changes could, in principle, provide a basis for inferring the causal agency of the spirits.

13. See Hansen (1992b) concerning some experiments from the Princeton Engineering Anomalies Research (PEAR). The researchers replied in the same issue.

14. The Committee for the Scientific Investigation of Claims of the Paranormal (CSICOP) is committed to disproving all paranormal claims, including those made by parapsychologists. For a lengthy study of CSICOP see Hansen (1992a).

15. In a letter, Jessica Utts says: "You are noting that the amount of data one would require depends on one's a priori probability that psi exists. There is a whole area of statistical analysis, called Bayesian methods, that allows for the inclusion of a priori probabilities. The methods combine these subjective probabilities with the available data, and result in what are called *posterior probabilities*. If enough data are collected, eventually two people with very different prior probabilities will come to the same conclusion. The only case in which this would not happen is the extreme case where someone's prior probability of something is zero. In that case, no amount of data would change it. Unfortunately it is not straightforward to apply these methods to parapsychology, although you will notice some of the discussants of the enclosed paper [Utts, 1991] discuss the idea."

16. Not all skeptical opponents are appropriately ignored. Some, like internal critics within the parapsychological community, provide legitimate and helpful suggestions concerning important improvements in experimental design. For an appreciation of such an opponent, Ray Hyman, as well as a criticism of some of his biases, see Hansen (1991) and Honorton (1993:205–9).

17. Freud showed that at least some "coincidences" in everyday life are not merely coincidences, but arise from our unconscious mind. The pattern noted by the student could be given a Freudian explanation if there were other evidence that Pletcher already ascribed considerable symbolic significance to color arrangements and to alphabetical ordering. Such an explanation in the example given by Pletcher seems to me implausible. My point, however, is that sometimes explanations of an alleged or obvious pattern do plausibly refer to the unconscious, and that such explanations are often important *alternatives* to paranormal explanations. In my own view of the unconscious, explanations by reference to it are explanations by reference to (an unconscious) agent causality rather than by reference to physical mechanisms alone. Pletcher's concern about arbitrarily selected patterns thus raises issues concerning the unconscious as well as concerning the paranormal.

18. Broad (1962: 118–29). Broad argues that impressive cases, if well attested, together build up the argument for belief in the paranormal: "In the sporadic cases, the odds against chance-coincidence cannot be stated numerically. One can judge only that, in some cases, they are very great: that they are very much greater in this case than in that, and so on. Nevertheless, the ordinary

rules of probability hold. In judging the evidence for paranormal agency or for paranormal cognition, we must not, e.g. confine ourselves to this, that, or the other case, taken *severally*. What we have in the end to consider is the probability that *at least one* (no matter which) of all the numerous well attested sporadic cases really *did* happen as reported (and) was *not* a chance-coincidence" (115). It is not clear to me what Broad can mean by "probability" here. But I do agree with him that if there are 1,000 impressive cases, this does not make *all* of them more *plausible* than if there are only 100 and that, rather, this makes it more *plausible* that at least 1 of the 1,000 is genuinely paranormal. My central argument, however, is that *one* suitably-detailed case could suffice.

REFERENCES

Bergson, Henry. (1975). *Mind-Energy*. Westport, Conn.: Greenwood (reprint from New York: Henry Holt).

Braud, William G. (1990). "Distant Mental Influence on Rate of Hemolysis of Human Red Blood Cells." *Journal of the American Society for Psychical Research* 84, [January], 1–24.

Braud, William G., and Schlitz, Marilyn J. (1983). "Psychokinetic Influence on Electrodermal Activity." *Journal of Parapsychology* 47 (June), 95–119.

———. (1989). "Possible Role of Intuitive Data Sorting in Electrodermal Biological Psychokinesis (Bio-PK)." *Journal of the American Society for Psychical Research* 89 (October), 289–302.

Bridgman, P. W. (1978). "Probability, Logic and ESP." In Ludwig (1978).

Broad, C. D. (1962). *Lectures on Psychical Research*. London: Routledge.

Cooperstein, M. Allan. (1992). "The Myths of Healing: A Summary of Research Into Transpersonal Healing Experiences." *Journal of the American Society for Psychical Research* 86 (April), 99–133.

Evans, Donald. (1993). *Spirituality and Human Nature*. Albany: State University of New York Press.

———. (1996). "A Shamanic Christian Approach in Psychotherapy." In Seymour Boorstein, ed., *Transpersonal Psychotherapy*, rev. ed. Albany, N.Y.: State University of New York Press.

Grad, Bernard R. (1976). "The Biological Effects of the 'Laying on of Hands' on Animals and Plants: Implications for Biology." In Gertrude R. Schmeidler, ed., *Parapsychology, Its Relation to Physics, Biology, Psychology and Psychiatry*. Metuchen, N.J.: Scarecrow.

Gray, William D. (1991). *Thinking Critically About New Age Ideas*. Belmont, Calif.: Wadsworth.

Hacking, Ian. (1993). "Some Reasons for Not Taking Parapsychology Very Seriously." *Dialogue* 32, no. 3 (Summer), 587–94.

Hansel, C. E. M. (1980). *ESP and Parapsychology: A Scientific Reevaluation*. Albany, N.Y.: Prometheus.

Hansen, George P. (1990). "Deception by Subjects in Psi Research." *Journal of the American Society for Psychical Research* 84 (January), 25–80.

———. (1991). "The Elusive Agenda: Dissuading as Debunking in Ray Hyman's *The Elusive Quarry*." *Journal of the American Society for Psychical Research* 85 (April), 193–203.

———. (1992a). "CSICOP and the Skeptics: An Overview." *Journal of the American Society for Psychical Research* 86 (January), 19–63.

———. (1992b). With Jessica Utts and Betty Markwick. "Critique of the PEAR Remote-Viewing Experiments." *Journal of Parapsychology* 56 (June), 97–113.

———. (1992c). "The Research with B. D. and the Legacy of Magical Ignorance." *Journal of Parapsychology* 56 (December), 307–333. (Responses to Hansen are included in this issue.)

Honorton, Charles. (1993). "Rhetoric over Substance: The Impoverished State of Skepticism." *Journal of Parapsychology* 57 (June), 191–214.

Hume, David (1888). *A Treatise of Human Nature*. Oxford: Clarendon.

Ludwig, Jan, ed. (1978). *Philosophy and Parapsychology*. Buffalo, N.Y.: Prometheus.

Meehl, Paul E., and Scriven, Michael. (1978). "Compatibility of Science and ESP." In Ludwig (1978).

Mellow, E. L. (1970). *Methods of Science: An Introduction to Measuring and Testing for Laymen and Students*. New York: Universe.

Parapsychological Association. (1988). "Terms and Methods in Parapsychological Research." *Journal of the American Society for Psychical Research* 88 (October), 353–57.

Persinger, Michael A. (1987). "Spontaneous Telepathic Experiences from Phantasms of the Living and Low Global Geomagnetic Activity." *Journal of the American Society for Psychical Research* 81 (January), 23–36.

Pletcher, Galen. (1982). "Coincidence and Explanation." In Patrick Grim, ed. *Philosophy of Science and the Occult*. Albany: State University of New York Press.

Reinsel, Ruth. (1982). "Parapsychology: An Empirical Science." In Patrick Grim, ed. *Philosophy of Science and the Occult*. Albany: State University of New York Press.

Taylor, Richard. (1966). *Action and Purpose*. Englewood Cliffs, N.J.: Prentice-Hall.

Utts, Jessica. (1988). "Successful Replication Versus Statistical Significance." *Journal of Parapsychology* 52 (December), 305–320.

——. (1991). "Replication and Meta-analysis in Parapsychology." *Statistical Science* 6, no. 4, 363–403.

White, Rhea A. (1994). "Exceptional Human Experiences: The Generic Connection." *Journal of the American Society for Psychical Research Newsletter* 18, 3, 1–6.

4

WHY CRITICAL REFLECTION ON THE PARANORMAL IS SO IMPORTANT—AND SO DIFFICULT

David Ray Griffin

Critical reflection on the paranormal is important for a number of reasons. For example, almost exactly a century ago, William James paraphrased with approval the moral philosopher Henry Sidgwick's complaint, with regard to claims about the paranormal, that

> the divided state of public opinion on all these matters was a scandal to science,—absolute disdain on *a priori* grounds characterizing what may be called professional opinion, while indiscriminate credulity was too often found among those who pretended to have a first-hand acquaintance with the facts.[1]

The situation today is little changed. Scientists, philosophers, and theologians should, by engaging in reflection that is critical but open-minded, help overcome this division between "absolute disdain on *a priori* grounds" on the one hand, and "indiscriminate credulity" on the other, simply to discharge part of their public responsibility. But critical reflection on the paranormal is even more important because of another point mentioned by James:

> "The great field for new discoveries," said a scientific friend to me the other day, "is always the unclassified residuum." No part of the unclassified residuum has usually been treated with a more contemptuous scientific disregard than the mass of phenomena generally called *"Mystical"* [by which James meant phenomena now generally called *paranormal*].[2]

Today the "unclassified residuum" is called the "anomalous," and there has been much discussion of the idea that "paradigm changes" often come about through investigation of what the old paradigm had put aside as anomalies. Nevertheless, that body of data indicated as anomalous by its very name, the *paranormal*, is still treated, for the most part, with the same contemptuous disregard criticized by Sidgwick and James. Critical reflection about the paranormal is primarily important, I suggest, for the same reason that it has been so difficult: because it challenges the modern paradigm (with "paradigm" used in the broadest sense, to mean general worldview).

A few years ago, I struck up a conversation at a cocktail party with a well-known philosopher of science whose stance and background make him particularly interesting to talk with about the paranormal. On the one hand, he is an avowed materialist. On the other hand, he had, while a graduate student, been closely associated with C. D. Broad, one of the few major philosophers of the twentieth century to have devoted extensive attention to parapsychology, or psychical research[3] (which can be defined as scientific study of ostensible paranormal occurrences [the meaning of "paranormal" is discussed below]).[4] Having recently read an article arguing that, contrary to customary belief, materialism is not incompatible with belief in paranormal events, I asked my colleague if he agreed. He said no, adding that it belongs to the very meaning of materialism that paranormal events are deemed impossible. Given that unequivocal response, I asked how he regarded the fact that Broad had believed in the genuineness of certain types of paranormal phenomena, such as telepathy. Did he think Broad engaged in fraud? Absolutely not; Broad was a man of the highest integrity. Did he then suspect that Broad was a poor observer, or had been duped by fraudulent or careless psychical researchers? No, Broad was an extremely intelligent and circumspect individual. How, then, did this philosopher of science reconcile his knowledge that Broad accepted paranormal phenomena with his own belief that such phenomena are impossible? He didn't, he replied; he simply held his own beliefs and his knowledge of Broad's beliefs alongside each other.

In having a worldview that rules out the possibility of paranormal events a priori, this philosopher is not atypical. He is, in fact, unusual only in his acknowledgment that the data for paranormal events are sufficiently impressive to convince some reasonable thinkers. Intellectuals who share this philosopher's materialistic worldview more typically reject the evidence out of hand, either by refusing to examine it or by attacking the credibility of those reporting it—as typified by publications of the Committee for the Scientific Investigation of Claims for the Paranormal. As their acronym, CSICOP, suggests, they exist less to engage in scientific investigation of reports of the paranormal (sometimes called "psi") than to serve as thought-police, blowing the whistle on all claims for psi.

Whether evidence for the paranormal is rejected a priori, however, or simply set aside as anomalous, in neither case is there *critical reflection upon the paranormal*, by which I mean primarily two things: (1) examining the evidence for paranormal influence open-mindedly, and then, if the evidence is at all credible, (2) asking how the occurrence of paranormal influence might be compatible with those "normal" causal processes that have in modern times been assumed to rule them out. This latter question involves asking how, if the so-called paranormal were accepted as genuine, the modern worldview that had ruled them out would need to be revised.

Most intellectuals, however, cannot examine the evidence "open-mindedly" because they have minds that are *not* open, but chock-full, being filled with the modern worldview, which says that such things cannot happen. Having that prejudgment, they have little motivation to think through carefully what changes in the modern worldview the acceptance of paranormal influences would and would not imply. Besides seeing little point in considering a revised worldview that would allow for "paranormal" as well as "normal" influences, they furthermore often do not *want* such a revision made. Their prejudgment against the paranormal includes active hostility towards it.

In the first section of this essay, I discuss what would be distinctive about paranormal events, if they do occur, and why the modern worldview has created the presumption that they do not. In the second section, I discuss the way in which wishful (including fearful) thinking interacts with paradigms and empirical evidence to help account for the hostility involved in the prejudice against the paranormal. In the third section, I discuss some of the implications for a postmodern worldview in general, and for philosophy of religion in particular, if critical reflection upon the paranormal were to result in its acceptance.

I. THE PARANORMAL AND THE MODERN WORLDVIEW

One of the controversies about the paranormal is how to define it. Giving a complete definition, so that one has a "line of demarcation"—which excludes everything one wants excluded and includes everything one wants included—is extremely difficult. I will not attempt this, but will only hazard a statement as to what is distinctive of all those things intuitively classed as belonging to the paranormal: *apparent influence at a distance to and from minds*. The presupposition, obviously, is that "normal" causation occurs only between contiguous things, especially if minds are involved.

Most if not all types of paranormal events can be classified under the two major forms of paranormal interaction: extrasensory perception and psychokinesis.

Extrasensory perception (ESP) involves a mind's *reception* of influence from a distance. The two main forms of ESP are *telepathy* (which means "feeling at a distance"), in which one receives influence from inside another mind, and *clairvoyance* (sometimes now called "remote viewing"), in which one receives influences, sometimes resulting in sensory-like images, relating to the outer characteristics of things. (*Precognition* is sometimes classed as a third form of ESP, in which the "distance" from which the causal influence comes is the future; but this idea is of doubtful intelligibility. I discuss it briefly in the third section.) In either type of ESP, the mind receives influence that has not come through the body's sensory system, which is why "action at a distance" is involved. Perception by means of the sensory system, by contrast, involves chains of causal influence between contiguous events. For example, when I see the tree outside the window in my study, the tree-image results from a chain of photons travelling from the tree to my eye, then a chain of neurons from my eye to my brain. Extrasensory perception, if it occurs, is paranormal because it circumvents this system of contiguous causation. If I have a clairvoyant perception of the tree, the tree (evidently) exerts causal influence directly upon my mind. My mind, accordingly, has received causal influence from a distance.

Psychokinesis (PK) involves the *exertion* of causal influence at a distance by a mind. In what we consider "normal" human action on things beyond the body, by contrast, the mind or psyche influences its body, usually its motor-muscular system. (I ignore for now the view that equates the mind with the brain and hence with one part of the body.) The body then brings about an extrasomatic effect, such as picking up a match stick. The mind or psyche thereby brings about extrasomatic effects by means of a contiguous chain of cause-effect relations. In PK, however, this chain is circumvented, as the psyche brings about extrasomatic effects, such as moving a match stick, directly, without using the body. (The older term *telekinesis* better conveys the fact that it is causal influence at a distance that makes such an event paranormal.) The term *psychokinesis* most readily suggests events of this nature, in which locomotion is induced in a physical object. I am, however, using this term more broadly, as is commonly done, to include all forms of change directly induced by the psyche in noncontiguous things, such as psychic healing, psychic photography, levitation, and materialization and dematerialization.

The category of the *paranormal*, I suggest, consists of these two kinds of paranormal influence, in which influence at a distance is exerted *on* or *by* a mind (or both).

Quite often the category of the paranormal is said to include a third major type of alleged occurrence: the existence of a mind apart from a physical (biological) body, which would include out-of-body experiences (if taken literally) as well as life after bodily death. Adding this type would mean that we would need to speak not only of paranormal *influences*, but also of paranormal *states*. The evidence in question can, however, be subsumed under apparent influence at a distance in the light of two considerations. First, many of the types of phenomena that are taken as evidence for life after death, such as apparitions, involve apparent communications that do not come through ordinary sensory channels. Second, the very existence of a psyche apart from a physical body would probably involve extrasensory perception (and perhaps psychokinesis as well). In any case, I am, for the purposes of this essay, thinking of the paranormal as constituted by ESP and PK, therefore as involving a particular kind of causal influence.

The crucial question is why this kind of causal influence, involving influence at a distance to or from minds, should be so controversial. Why should modern minds be so convinced that it cannot occur? The answer, I suggest, is primarily that the distinctively modern worldview, sometimes called the "modern scientific worldview," not only excludes this kind of causal influence, but was in part *created to exclude it*. As Brian and Lynne Mackenzie say, the paranormal events studied by parapsychologists are not simply "anomalous" in the sense of being a "specifiable class of events which just happen to conflict with the scientific conception of the world." Rather,

> they were established as paranormal by the genesis of the scientific conception. . . . The "paranormal" was established as such by being ruled out of nature altogether. . . . The incompatibility of parapsychology with modern science is neither accidental nor recent, but is built into the assumptive base of modern science itself.[5]

This view, that the worldview associated with modern science was created in part to exclude what we now call the paranormal, is supported by sociologist of science Jerome Ravetz:

The "scientific revolution" itself becomes comprehensible if we
see it as a campaign for a reform of ideas *about* science. . . .
Scientific revolution was primarily and essentially about metaphysics; and the various technical studies were largely conceived
and received as corroborating statements of a challenging worldview. This consisted essentially of two Great Denials: the restric-
tion of ordinary faculties such as sympathy and intelligence to
humans and to a remote Deity; and *the relegation of extra-ordinary
faculties to the realms of the nonexistent or insignificant.*[6]

What was it about the new metaphysical worldview that ruled out what
is now called the paranormal? The Mackenzies point to the central issue
by quoting a statement made by scientist George Price in his attack on
parapsychology, "Science and the Supernatural" (which he later
retracted). "The essence of science," said Price, "is mechanism. The
essence of magic is animism."[7] The new metaphysics for science introduced in the seventeenth century was called, not coincidentally, the
"mechanical philosophy." Insofar as we are removed from the debates
of the time, we may assume that the chief point at issue in speaking of
"mechanism" was an exclusive focus on efficient causes, in distinction
from "final causation." The real bite of mechanism, we may suppose, is
that, by excluding all self-determination, it entails complete determinism. This was indeed one of the central issues, but not the only one.
An at least equally crucial meaning of the "mechanical philosophy"
was that action at a distance was proscribed.

Mary Hesse has pointed out, in her study of action at distance in
physics, that this idea lost favor through the introduction of the mechanical philosophy of nature, according to which its particles were purely
material, having no inner, hidden ("occult") qualities that could possibly exert or receive influence at a distance.[8] This philosophy implied
that all causation must be by contact. Other historians have added that
this implication was not simply an incidental side-effect of the mechanical philosophy, but a central plank. Richard Westfall says:

> All [mechanical philosophers] agreed on some form of dualism
> which excluded from nature the possibility of what they called
> pejoratively "occult agents." . . . All agreed that the program of
> natural philosophy lay in demonstrating that the phenomena of
> nature are produced by the mutual interplay of material particles
> which act on each other by direct contact alone.[9]

Westfall says that "the fundamental tenet of Descartes' mechanical philosophy of nature [was] that one body can act on another only by direct

contact."[10] Brian Easlea has in fact argued, in what is perhaps the best book on the origin of the "scientific revolution," that the desire to rule out the possibility of attraction at a distance was not simply one of many, but the *central* motivation behind the mechanical philosophers' denial of all hidden qualities within matter.[11]

The obvious objection to this portrayal is that many considered Isaac Newton the mechanical philosopher par excellence, and yet Newton, with his doctrine of universal gravitation, seems clearly to have been an advocate of action at a distance. Indeed, quite different from Descartes' *kinetic* mechanical philosophy, which mandated causation by contact exclusively, was Newton's *dynamic* mechanical philosophy, which portrayed the ultimate agent in nature as "a force acting between particles rather than a moving particle itself."[12] It was thereby open in principle to the idea of action at a distance. Newton's language of "attractions," in fact, created the suspicion that he affirmed it. Christiaan Huygens said about Newton: "I don't care that he's not a Cartesian as long as he doesn't serve us up conjectures such as attractions."[13]

The fact that the new worldview banned action at a distance is illustrated, however, not only by the comment of the Cartesian Huygens but also by Newton's own response to the controversy. It was with regard to gravitation that Newton made his famous positivistic reply that he did not "feign hypotheses" about the actual cause but only provided mathematical formulae.[14] In a well-known letter to Richard Bentley, Newton went even further, saying:

> Tis unconceivable that inanimate brute matter should (without the mediation of something else which is not material) operate upon and affect other matter without mutual contact. . . . That gravity should be innate and essential to matter so that one body may act upon another at a distance through a vacuum without the mediation of any thing else by and through which their action or force may be conveyed from one to another is to me so great an absurdity that I believe no man who has in philosophical matters any competent faculty of thinking can ever fall into it.[15]

In these disclaimers Newton may well, of course, have been hiding his true views. The point, however, is that Newton *as public philosopher* supported the rejection of causal influence at a distance. Furthermore, although the mechanistic worldview is nowadays often called "the Newtonian worldview," Robert Schofield in his study *Mechanism and Materialism* documents the extent to which Newton's ideas were assimilated as much as possible in the eighteenth and nineteenth centuries to the Cartesian form of mechanism.[16] (One manifestation of this development today may be the desire to find explanations of gravitation that do not involve attraction at a distance, such as curvature of space and "gravitons.") According to Richard Westfall, this development had already been anticipated by Newton himself: "In his final years, a growing philosophic caution led Newton to retreat somewhat toward more conventional mechanistic views."[17] In sum, the case of Newton does not significantly weaken the twofold claim that the mechanical philosophy with which science became associated in the latter half of the seventeenth century excluded action at a distance, and that this exclusion was one of the main reasons for its adoption.

Another objection might be that this discussion of physical theory is irrelevant to current attitudes toward the "paranormal" because the paranormal, as it is usually understood and as I have characterized it, involves causal influence at a distance exerted or received by *minds*, whereas the "mechanical philosophy" dealt exclusively with physical nature, from which all mental characteristics were excluded. There is truth in this objection: The dualism between mind and nature, which was adopted by Descartes, Newton, and all the other early leaders of the movement (except Hobbes), did indeed leave open the possibility that the human mind, said to be outside of nature, might be able to act and perceive at a distance; and a few thinkers, in fact, adopted this position.[18] The dominant position among these dualists, however, as articulated by the "empiricist" Locke as well as the "rationalist" Descartes, was that the mind could perceive and act upon the world only through its brain: The sensationist theory of perception said that the mind can perceive only by means of its physical sensory system; the corresponding theory of action said that the mind can act only through its motor-muscular system. Both perception and action, accordingly, occurred only through chains of contiguous causes.

In the dominant thinking of the time, the connection between the desire to exclude action at a distance in physics, on the one hand, and the desire to rule out all paranormal influence on and by human minds, on the other, was evidently something like this: Given the dualism between (spiritual) mind and (physical) nature, excluding action at a distance from nature did not, strictly speaking, rule out the possibility that human minds might either receive or exert causal influence at a distance. Nevertheless, a philosophy of nature in which all causal influence was by contact created a context in which the idea of causal influence at a distance to or from minds seemed unfitting. In this context, the stipulation (by a Descartes or a Locke) that the mind could not receive or exert any influence at a distance would not seem arbitrary (even though it was). It was for this reason, I suggest, that the issue of action at a distance in physics was so controversial.

In any case, a development unforeseen by these partisans removed the arbitrariness from their argument from nature to mind. Their dualism collapsed into a fully materialistic position. This development occurred in the latter half of the eighteenth century in France, and in the latter half of the nineteenth century in the English-speaking world (thanks to a large extent to Darwin). With this development, the "mind" was fully within nature, being purely a function of the brain (as the notorious Hobbes had suggested), and was therefore subject to the same prohibition against action at a distance as the rest of nature.

To speak of this late modern worldview, however, is to get ahead of the story; I have yet to explain why the exclusion of action at a distance was so important to thinkers in the second half of the seventeenth century. We should not suppose, as earlier historians of the history of science and philosophy had naively suggested, that this exclusion resulted solely from a disinterested search for truth. Rather, as historians have been documenting in recent decades, strong theological and social factors were involved.

One of the factors making action at a distance such a controversial issue involved the interpretation of "miracles." The authority of the church was to a great extent based on the assumption that God had endorsed Christianity as the One True Religion by the miracles that occurred in New Testament times (and, for Catholics, in the continuing history of the church, especially in and through the lives of the saints). This interpretation was challenged, however, by advocates of Hermetic and other "magical" philosophies, which allowed influence at a distance, including that to and from minds (perhaps through "sympathy"), as a purely natural occurrence. The "miraculous" healings performed by Jesus, accordingly, required no supernatural intervention and, in fact, were no different from healings performed in other traditions. This view threatened not only the authority of the church, but also the stability of the whole social order, insofar as this stability was based on the close relation between church and state.[19] It was in this context that Father Marin Mersenne, Descartes's predecessor, worked to establish the mechanical philosophy in French scientific circles. As shown by Robert Lenoble in his study on "Mersenne or the Origin of Mechanism," the fact that the mechanical philosophy entailed that causal influence at a distance could *not* naturally occur was one of Mersenne's chief motivations for advocating it. The extraordinary events in the New Testament and the ongoing history of the church, accordingly, had to be regarded as genuine miracles, involving supernatural intervention.[20] (Those extraordinary events that occur in non-Christian contexts were said to be due to the "preternatural" power of Satan, which could simulate true miracles.)

The issue of action at a distance was also important because of the "witch craze" of the sixteenth and seventeenth centuries, considered by some historians to have been the major social problem of the era.[21] The accusations of witchcraft presupposed that the human mind (with Satan's help, to be sure) could cause direct harm to people and their possessions. The mechanistic philosophy, by discrediting the idea of causal influence at a distance, was used to undermine the thought-world in which the witch craze had flourished.[22]

Yet another reason for denying the possibility of action at a distance as a natural capacity involved the proper interpretation of gravitation. Newton himself used his denial that gravity is innate to matter, quoted earlier, to provide a proof for the existence of God. Because the apparent force between things cannot be due to matter, he argued, it points to the existence of "immaterial agency," by which he meant, ultimately, God.[23]

Still other theological-social considerations lay behind the adoption of the mechanical philosophy in the late seventeenth and early eighteenth centuries. For example, the idea that the physical world is composed of things that are totally inert, devoid of any capacity for self-motion, was used to support the immortality of the soul (against mortalists who were saying that, although the body is composed of self-moving things, it decays at death) and the existence of God as the First Mover of the universe (against atheists and pantheists who were claiming that the universe, being composed of self-moving things, did not need an external creator).[24] The idea that the physical body, which rather obviously moves, is composed of things that are inherently inert was used to support a dualistic view of the human being as whole, according to which one has a soul that, by virtue of its self-motion, is essentially different from the body and can thereby be presumed not to share its fate at bodily death. The idea that the physical universe, which is obviously in motion, is comprised of things that are inherently inert was used to argue for the necessity of a First Mover outside the universe. (As Robert Boyle put it: "Since motion does not essentially belong to matter, . . . the motions of all bodies . . . were impressed upon them."[25]) The considerations mentioned in this paragraph did not directly involve the issue of action at a distance, but, by reinforcing the commitment to the mechanical viewpoint in general, they reinforced the judgment that causal influence between noncontiguous things is not possible.

That is, the contention was that this influence is not *naturally* possible. The idea that the kinds of events in question actually happen was not rejected by most of these thinkers. It was, in fact, important to them that they *did* happen. They were concerned only to stress that they happened because of supernatural agency. The desire to support this supernaturalistic view of God was, in fact, evidently (along with the desire to defend the immortality of the soul) the primary motivation behind the adoption of the mechanical philosophy in the first version of the modern worldview.

In the *late* modern worldview, by contrast, the kinds of events in question simply cannot happen. Insofar as the dualism of the early modern worldview, by placing the human mind somewhat outside of (mechanical) nature, provided at least a window of opportunity for paranormal events, this window was closed by the transmutation of dualism into the materialism of the late modern worldview, in which the mind is merely a function of the brain. Even more important, the supernaturalistic theism of early modernism transmuted into the atheistic naturalism of late modernism. Accordingly, the mechanical philosophy's implication that events not understandable in terms of action by contact cannot happen *naturally* came to mean that they cannot happen *at all*.

Critical reflection upon the paranormal is so difficult in our culture because these two versions of the modern worldview are still dominant. The worldview of conservative-to-fundamentalist Christians is, for the most part, a continuation of the early modern worldview. Although in our culture at large, this dualistic supernaturalism is at least as influential as the late modern worldview, it is primarily the latter that serves to rule out the paranormal as a topic for critical reflection within the academy. For this reason, in speaking in this essay of "the modern worldview" without a qualifier, I mean primarily the second version of it—the *late* modern worldview—unless I indicate otherwise. I will conclude this section with a couple of illustrations of how effectively this worldview, functioning as a paradigm, is doing its job.

Jane Duran belongs to the tiny minority of philosophers who have published anything whatsoever about the paranormal. However, her acceptance of the modern worldview evidently forestalls any open-minded examination of the evidence. Duran approaches the subject in terms of C. D. Broad's "basic limiting principles," which paranormal events appear to violate.[26] Most crucial for Duran is the principle that "any event that is said to cause another event (the second event being referred to as an 'effect') must be related to the effect through some causal chain." This principle appears to be violated by telepathy, clairvoyance, and psychokinesis. Now, Broad himself believed the evidence for these phenomena, at least the first two, to be strong enough that this principle should be revised.[27] Duran's view, however, is that

> the absence of a specifiable and recognizably causal chain seems to constitute a difficult, if not insurmountable, objection to our giving a coherent account of what it means to make such a claim. As long, at least, as our ordinary notions of causality remain intact, there seem to be strong philosophical reasons for concluding that telepathy, clairvoyance . . . are not possible.[28]

Duran presents a clear example of the belief that action at a distance is impossible. Indeed, she seems to consider the very idea *incoherent*.

Another philosopher who is remarkable for even mentioning the paranormal is Keith Campbell. His dismissal, however, is even more preemptory. While reflecting on the fact that if the occurrence of paranormal events were verified, the philosophical implications would be enormous, he uses the standard Humean argument against all reported evidence for paranormal relations:

> The problem of fraud is that we know men can, and do, cheat and dissemble, but we do not know that they have paranormal capacities. On the contrary, the great weight of our fully attested knowledge of man's origin and constitution makes paranormal capacities extremely unlikely. So . . . the explanation by fraud is the more rational one.[29]

Such an a priori rejection may not seem unreasonable in the abstract, given the widespread impression that the only people who have given testimony to the genuineness of paranormal events are "kooks" or at least third-rate minds. As William James pointed out, furthermore, psychical research is "a field in which the sources of deception are extremely numerous."[30]

As James also said in this connection, however, it takes only one white crow to prove that not all crows are black.[31] In other words, we need only one case of alleged paranormal influence in which fraud, error, and other "normal" explanations are ruled out to cast doubt on the principle that there is no causal influence at a distance. (James spoke specifically of the sensationist principle that nothing appears in the mind that did not derive from the physical senses.)

When one looks at those who have given testimony to the reality of the paranormal, furthermore, one finds, besides the kooks and third-rate minds, people such as James himself, Sigmund Freud, Thomas Edison, Arthur Eddington, Henry Margenau, Henry Sidgwick, C. J. Ducasse, Michael Scriven, H. H. Price, C. D. Broad, and several Nobel-winning scientists, such as Alexis Carrel, Charles Richet, and Brian Josephson. Is it really "more rational" to believe that all of these people, plus many more otherwise trustworthy souls, have been guilty of either engaging in, or being repeatedly taken in by, deception than to assume that paranormal relations really occur?

Campbell's a priori dismissal of the belief in paranormal causal relations on the grounds that such a belief is not "rational," incidentally, is especially interesting in the light of his willingness to countenance other beliefs about causal relations that he admits are irrational. That is, he had at one time rejected psychophysical dualism because of the impossibility of understanding how spirit and matter could interact. Now, however, having decided that materialism is inadequate to our obviously nonmaterial experiences, he affirms epiphenomenalism. This view holds that the brain, as a byproduct of its functioning, produces a spiritual mind, but that this mind cannot act back upon the brain. Campbell affirms this view even though it faces, he admits, the same "equally embarrassing" questions as did dualism. What is worse, he further admits, it includes an arbitrariness that dualism did not, because it affirms "the action of the material on the spiritual" while denying "the action of spirit on matter."[32] Campbell's response to these difficulties is that

> one who holds to the theory must just grit his teeth and assert that a fundamental, anomalous, causal connection relates some bodily processes to some nonmaterial processes. He must insist that this is a brute fact we must learn to live with, however inconvenient it might be for our tidy world-schemes.[33]

Campbell is *not*, however, willing to "just grit his teeth" and admit that paranormal causal processes occur. It appears that what is wrong with causal influence at a distance is not simply that it is anomalous, and not simply that to affirm it would be irrational, but that it is *taboo*. Better to assume that otherwise honorable and circumspect fellow human beings, such as William James, have been involved in fraud than to affirm *this* kind of anomalous causal relation, or to revise one's views so as to remove its anomalous character.

The extreme example of the power of the modern paradigm with respect to the paranormal is provided by the aforementioned Committee for the Scientific Investigation of Claims of the Paranormal

(CSICOP). Its publications refer to those who accept the paranormal as "believers" while referring to its own members as "skeptics." Skepticism in the true sense of the term, however, refers to an attitude of doubt toward all ideas, *especially* those dominant in one's own society. Members of CSICOP, however, show little skepticism about the late modern worldview: With regard to it, they are true believers.

II. THE INTERACTION OF WORLDVIEW, EVIDENCE, AND WISHFUL THINKING

I have thus far suggested that critical thinking about the paranormal is difficult in our culture because the occurrence of paranormal events is ruled out by the modern worldview, especially, in the academy, in its late modern guise. Some people, nevertheless, *are* able to reflect critically about the reality and possible implications of ostensibly paranormal happenings, even though they too have been educated in this same culture. To be adequate, an analysis obviously must be more complex than that suggested thus far.

There are, I suggest, three factors involved in the formation of opinions about controversial matters such as the paranormal. Besides the two factors already discussed—one's worldview, which guides one's view of what is possible and impossible, and one's awareness of empirical data, which guides one's view of what is actual—there is also wishful thinking: Our ideas about what is possible and what is actual are also influenced by what we *hope* to be true. Freud used this dynamic to explain (away) belief in an omnipotent God. The influence of wishful thinking is, however, much more pervasive, being evident, for example, even in the formation of Freud's own worldview. The pervasiveness of wishful thinking becomes all the more evident when we realize that it can be negative as well as positive, as our thoughts about philosophical possibility, and our interpretations of empirical data, are guided by what we hope is *not* true. This side of the dynamic can be called "fearful thinking."[34] The complete dynamic should, accordingly, be called wishful-and-fearful thinking. To avoid this cumbersome locution, however, I will employ one term or the other, using "wishful" as the generic term and "fearful" when that side of the dynamic is especially in view.

Although all three of these factors play a role in everyone's thought processes, we can think in terms of three basic types of people: paradigmatic thinkers, data-led thinkers, and wishful thinkers.

Paradigmatic thinkers, or rationalists, are ones for whom the primary consideration is what they consider, on the basis of their general paradigm or worldview, possible and impossible. Their interpretation of, even their interest in, empirical data is largely determined by their prior judgment of what is possible. If their worldview or paradigm says that some alleged phenomenon, such as telepathy, is impossible, no amount of empirical data will change their minds. William James commented: "I believe there is no source of deception in the investigation of nature which can compare with a fixed belief that certain kinds of phenomenon are *impossible*."[35] This is, of course, the dynamic I discussed in the prior section. An example, notorious in parapsychological circles, is provided by Herman von Helmholtz, one of the great scientists of the nineteenth century. He reportedly said to Sir William F. Barrett—another great scientist (a Fellow of the Royal Society), but one who was open to paranormal events—in a conversation about telepathy:

> I cannot believe it. Neither the testimony of all the Fellows of the Royal Society, nor even the evidence of my own senses would lead me to believe in the transmission of thought from one person to another independently of the recognized channels of sensation. It is clearly impossible.[36]

More in line with the ideal of the scientific or philosophic mind is the fact that the *wishes* of paradigmatic thinkers also take a back seat to their view of possibility. This may mean that they believe things in spite of wishing the truth were otherwise. For example, a materialist may be unhappy about the conclusion that there will be no life after death for him and his loved ones, but will persist in his unsatisfying view of life to the end. Another way, however, for one's wishes to play only a minor role is for them to be brought into line with one's philosophical beliefs: A necessity is turned into a virtue. For example, after deciding that there is no God, one may decide that atheism, besides being true, also has more beneficial consequences than theism. One may decide, perhaps, that belief in God serves as a social opiate, or that it keeps people in an infantile relationship to the universe.

Data-led thinkers, or empiricists, by contrast, wear their paradigms lightly, being ready to change them as soon as the data suggest their inadequacy. For such thinkers, what is possible is settled by what is actual, not vice versa; and, as with paradigmatic thinkers, wishful thinking plays little role in the determination of belief. This account agrees, of course, with the traditional picture of "the scientist," and some thinkers do approximate it. For example, Alfred North Whitehead said of William James: "His intellectual life was one protest against the dismissal of experience in the interest of system."[37] James advocated and practiced an empirical, data-led approach not only in general, furthermore, but also with regard to the paranormal in particular, as shown by his white-crow comment, cited earlier, and his statement that "whether supernormal powers of cognition in certain persons may occur is a matter to be decided by evidence."[38] We should, however, not exaggerate: James could be "empirical" about extrasensory perception partly because of the fact that, having a Swedenborgian father, he had grown up with a worldview that allowed for it.

On the basis of this distinction between paradigmatic and data-led minds, we can provide a fuller answer as to why critical reflection on the paranormal is so difficult. By critical reflection, it will be recalled, I mean both open-minded examination of the evidence and theoretical reflection about what modifications in the modern worldview this evidence, if found persuasive, would require. Now, on the one hand, those who are prone to engage in this type of theoretical thinking are likely to be paradigmatic thinkers; and, having been educated in the modern world, their worldview is likely to make them far from open-minded about the evidence for the paranormal. On the other hand, data-led minds, who are more likely to be open to the evidence, are, even if they find the evidence persuasive, unlikely to engage in theoretical thinking about the worldview implications of the paranormal. That there has been little critical reflection on the paranormal in the modern world is, accordingly, not surprising.

The difficulties become even more manifest once we bring in the third type of mind, the wishful-and-fearful thinker. For this type, "the wish (or the fear) is the father of the thought." This dynamic can apply to the question of possibility: Such thinkers may construct, or adopt, a philosophical worldview guided primarily by their hopes and fears. For example, they may adopt a philosophical position primarily because it shows life after death to be possible, or—if they intensely fear the prospect of life after death, or think the belief in it harmful—impossible. This dynamic can also apply to their attitude toward available empirical data, and thus to their view of what actually occurs—or at least to what they are willing publicly to admit. Many who have a strong will to believe in life after death are extremely credulous with respect to purported evidence for it, not only accepting the evidence uncritically, but also ignoring other possible interpretations of the events in question.

The reasons why many people, especially outside the academy, want to believe in the paranormal are fairly obvious. Negatively, for those who dislike the so-called scientific worldview (meaning the atheistic materialism that has become associated with science since about the middle of the nineteenth century), the paranormal provides the best evidence that this worldview is false. Positively, the paranormal provides, especially for people estranged from institutional religion, support for the wish that the universe be meaningful, including support for the wish that there be life after death.

By contrast, conservative-to-fundamentalist Christians tend to find purported evidence for the paranormal frightening. Many of the reasons operative in the seventeenth century are still relevant today. For example, the category of the paranormal provides a naturalistic alternative to the category of the miraculous, thereby undermining the supernatural attestation to Christianity as the One True Religion. For many Christians, this more than cancels out any positive value psychical research has in providing evidence for life after death. In fact, many evangelical Christians are even *hostile* to this purported evidence, insofar as it suggests that life after death is a natural capacity rather than a supernatural gift of God. Positive near-death experiences, especially if had by non- or lapsed Christians, are often regarded as the devil's deceit.

Thinkers who see the world in terms of the late modern paradigm, who are our primary concern here, also have reasons for fearing evidence for the paranormal. For some, the victory of "enlightenment" over superstition in our civilization is very precarious, and acceptance of any form of paranormal influence could open the floodgates to "the black mud-tide of occultism" (as Freud reportedly once put it, prior to his own acceptance of telepathy).[39] An example of another common fear is provided in a remark relayed by William James. In answer to his own question—"Why do so few 'scientists' even look at the evidence for telepathy, so-called?"—James reported that a leading biologist had once told him:

> Even if such a thing were true, scientists ought to band together to keep it suppressed and concealed. It would undo the uniformity of Nature and all sorts of other things without which scientists cannot carry on their pursuits.[40]

This fear, of course, reflects the common belief that science is uniquely related to the worldview with which it has been associated in recent times. A closely related fear is connected with cultural prestige and power. Given the materialistic, reductionistic worldview, with its assumption that all causal forces are lodged in atoms and subatomic particles, natural scientists, especially physicists, have the greatest social status in the academy, while those in the humanities have the least, and theologians and philosophers of religion least of all—except for parapsychologists, who are generally considered "beyond the pale." Evidence for the paranormal, which includes evidence not only for non-physical forms of causation (at least given the usual understanding of "physical") but also for downward causation from mind to matter, is seen—probably rightly—as a threat by some intellectuals with a vested interest in the status quo.[41]

More generally, the paranormal is emotionally threatening to those who are strongly attached to the modern worldview simply because the paranormal suggests the need for more or less radical revision. Most human beings find challenges to their beliefs threatening. This is especially the case with worldview beliefs, because one's very sense of identity is involved. It has been suggested that religious beliefs should be called *convictions* to bring out the intensity, and oft-times tenacity, with which they are held.[42] This same dynamic occurs as well with worldview beliefs that we do not readily characterize as religious, and may in fact call *anti*religious, such as atheistic materialism: The discussion of "paradigms" in recent decades has brought out the similarity between religious worldviews and worldviews in general in this respect. This dynamic occurs especially in those whose professional identity is closely bound up with their worldview, such as philosophers, theologians, and the ideological leaders of the scientific community.

Besides these paradigm-related reasons for finding the paranormal threatening, there are also more personal, psychological reasons. Many people find it threatening to think that others might be able to "read their minds." Even more threatening, of course, is the idea of psychokinesis, as it reopens the specter of "black magic" or "witchcraft." If, in particular, there can be large-scale psychokinesis, then—I have heard this fear expressed more than once—airplanes could be brought down simply by the power of thought. Many people intensely want the world to be free from this kind of danger, and this wishing affects their beliefs about the way the world actually is. Psychoanalyst Jule Eisenbad, who has been called parapsychology's "premier theoretician," has, in fact, suggested that much of Western religious, philosophical, and scientific thought has been motivated, in part, by the desire to rule out the possibility that human thoughts can have direct effects.[43]

This third variable, wishful thinking, complicates enormously the possibilities for critical reflection on the paranormal. Many philosophers who appear, even to themselves, to be rationalists may actually be wishful thinkers. The attempt to change their minds about the paranormal by means of rational argument will, accordingly, be frustrating, because the primary reasons for the positions they are maintaining will not be addressed. Likewise, many apparent empiricists may be closet wishful thinkers, so that no amount of evidence, however impressive to the presenter, will make a difference.

The situation, furthermore, is even more complicated than I have suggested thus far. We do not simply have three basic kinds of thinkers, plus the confusion as to which kind a particular person really is. In some individuals, two of the three factors share dominance. For example, paradigmatic and empirical concerns may predominate, with little deflection from wishes. The "rational empiricist" is nowadays widely considered the ideal in scientific and philosophical circles. At least equally present in those populations, however, are individuals with the other combinations: There are "wishful empiricists," who base their opinions primarily upon their wishes and the relevant data, with little consideration for questions of philosophical possibility, and there are "wishful rationalists," whose worldview is primarily a product of their wishes and their views as to what is possible, being little affected by attention to empirical evidence. The fields of philosophy and theology seem to attract wishful rationalists to a disproportionate extent, which, if true, would help explain why thinkers in these fields have been especially closed to the paranormal (even though one might suspect, apart from these considerations, that they would be the most open).

A particularly poignant instance is provided by John G. Taylor, a mathematical physicist at the University of London. His encounter with Uri Geller on a television show led him to explore the phenomenon of metal bending. Besides becoming convinced that Geller's feats were authentic cases of psychokinesis, Taylor also came into contact with several boys and girls, some as young as ten years old, who evidently could bend things by thought almost as effectively as Geller. On the basis of his adventures, Taylor wrote a book called *Superminds*,[44] complete with dozens of pictures, in which he assured his readers that the phenomenon was genuine, that there was no possibility that he was duped. For one thing, he argued, whatever one's suspicions might be about Geller, who had been a stage magician, it is impossible to believe that these young boys and girls could have mastered the extremely complicated tricks it would take to create those effects by fraud under controlled circumstances. Taylor also assured his readers that it would be possible to explain this phenomenon on the basis of the principles of physics. Fully accepting the reductionism of the late modern worldview, Taylor explained that there are only four possible forces that could account for PK: gravitation, the weak force, the strong force, and electromagnetism. Then, having ruled out the first three forces, he explained that so-called psychokinesis must be explainable in terms of electromagnetism. Taylor then set out to do this, in preparation for his next book.

Taylor soon learned, however, that this issue had been discussed for several decades by parapsychologists, and that most had long since come to the conclusion that something other than the four forces of physics had to be operating. In particular, some Russian parapsychologists, given their Marxian materialistic orthodoxy, had devised experiments explicitly designed to show ESP and PK to be electromagnetic phenomena. Their experiments suggested otherwise. The presence of barriers that cut the subjects off from most of the electromagnetic spectrum either had no effect or else actually improved the psi performance. On the basis of these and other considerations, Taylor came to the conclusion that PK simply could not be reconciled with modern physics. Maintaining his position that to accept things physics could not explain would be to accept irrational, supernatural beliefs, he entitled his next book *Science and the Supernatural*. In it he declared that all reports of ESP and PK must be due to hallucination, trickery, credulity, the fear of death, and the like. "Such an explanation," he said, "is the only one which seems to fit in with a scientific view of the world."[45] He did not, however, explain how those ten-year-old boys and girls had duped him. (Nor did he, as far as I know, turn back the royalties he had earned from his first book.)

This account could make Taylor appear to be a pure example of the paradigmatic mind. The role played by wishful-and-fearful thinking, however, is made clear by Taylor himself. Having said that he could not see how fraud could have been involved in Geller's demonstration of key-bending right in front of him and the television cameras, Taylor then added:

But this made my faith in science even more at risk, for I just could not see how there could be even a glimmer of a scientific explanation for these phenomena. The scientific framework with which I had viewed the world up till then was crumbling about my ears.[46]

Although Taylor at one place says that he began his investigations with an open mind,[47] he elsewhere admitted that openmindedness is not easy "if the facts that are staring you in the face will totally destroy your understanding of the world."[48]

That wishful-and-fearful thinking plays an important role in seemingly paradigmatic thinkers does not, however, reduce the importance of the paradigm, or worldview, out of which they work. As Taylor's example shows, his wishful-and-fearful thinking was oriented primarily around the late modern worldview, with which he had equated scientific rationality itself, and in relation to which his own sense of professional identity had been shaped.

In sum, critical reflection on the paranormal is so difficult not only because the modern worldview rules it out as impossible, but also because intellectuals, like other people, are influenced in their judgments by what they wish to be the case, and there are powerful reasons, both professional and personal, leading modern individuals to want the paranormal to be a null category. On the other side, positive wishes about the paranormal often make critical reflection about it, as distinct from credulous acceptance, difficult. The primary problem within the academy, however, has been excessive credulity not toward the paranormal, but toward the modern.

III. HOW ACCEPTANCE OF THE PARANORMAL WOULD BE IMPORTANT

Critical reflection on the paranormal, as characterized in this essay, involves two things: (1) open-minded consideration of evidence for the reality of the paranormal and (2) careful consideration of what the paranormal, if real, would suggest, especially for revisions of the late modern worldview. Having discussed factors relevant to the difficulty of the first of these in the previous sections, I turn now to a brief discussion of the second. I organize this discussion in terms of ways an acceptance of the paranormal would be important for the philosophy of religion, including the relation between science and religion.

The acceptance of the paranormal would be important, I have suggested, precisely for the reason that open-minded consideration of evidence for it is so difficult: It suggests the need for a more or less drastic revision in the late modern worldview. The first issue to consider is how drastic this revision would need to be for the new worldview to be adequate to the various forms of paranormality. My view is that the revisions would need to be significant—significant enough to speak of a "postmodern worldview"—but not revolutionary.

The most general point of a postmodern worldview that would be relevant to all the forms of paranormality would be the complete acceptance of action at a distance. It would be regarded as a type of causation that is as natural as causation between contiguous things. More particularly, nonsensory perception would be accepted (perhaps as a form of perception even more basic than sensory perception). Likewise, minds would be understood to be distinct from their brains and to be capable

of acting upon other parts of the body and the outer world not only
indirectly, by means of their action on their brains, but also directly,
with a type of causal influence that, as it were, bypasses the brain. (This
point would involve acceptance of "downward causation" alongside
the horizontal and upward causation recognized by the reductionist
worldview.)

While the changes needed to accommodate paranormal data
would be significant, they would not need to be revolutionary. One
reason is that there is no need to suppose that the new worldview
would involve a rejection of rational coherence as an ideal (although
devotees of the late modern worldview, equating it with "the scientific
worldview," have tended to identify it with rationality itself). William
James, for example, having said that for him science, so far as it denies
paranormal occurrences, "lies prostrate in the dust," added: "the most
urgent intellectual need which I feel at present is that science be built up
again in a form in which such things may have a positive place."[49] C. D.
Broad suggested how to go about this: We need to "revise . . . fundamental concepts and basic limiting principles in such a way as to
include the old and new facts in a single coherent system."[50] (For example, I suggest, we might suppose that each event exerts two forms of
efficient causation: one that is exerted exclusively [at least generally[51]] on
contiguous events, and another, much weaker, form, which can be
exerted on noncontiguous as well as contiguous events.) In other words,
increased adequacy to the facts would not necessarily be at the expense
of rational coherence.

The new worldview might, in fact, be *more* coherent. A
widespread assumption—one that lies behind much of the resistance to
the paranormal—is that the late modern worldview, with its materialistic ontology and sensationist theory of perception, works quite well for
virtually everything except paranormal data.[52] That assumption, however, is far from true. For example, the late modern worldview is real-
istic, presupposing the reality of physical things, but its sensationist
theory of perception (as phenomenalists since Hume have pointed out)
provides no knowledge of an "external world" beyond the perceiver.
This worldview presupposes the reality of time, and yet its sensationism
provides no basis for knowledge that there has been a past or will be a
future (as George Santayana pointed out, speaking of "solipsism of the
present moment"). Scientists and philosophers who advocate this
worldview clearly act on the basis of purposes, presupposing that they
and their colleagues have some degree of freedom to choose among
alternative courses of action, and yet this worldview implies that final
causes play no role in the world and that the human mind is simply a

by-product of the brain's mechanistic workings. A worldview that includes nonsensory perception and an agential mind could well be more coherent.[53]

The main reason the acceptance of the paranormal is often thought to entail revolutionary changes in worldview involves the implications of so-called precognition for the nature of time. The term *precognition*, taken literally and accepted as the best term for the phenomena in question, implies that one *knows* an event prior to its occurrence. To *know* that an event is going to happen entails that the event *will* happen, and, indeed, that it is in some sense already real. Having knowledge of an event generally means that the event has exerted causal influence upon the knower, whether directly or indirectly. To speak, therefore, of precognition implies that the event in question, which is in the future, has exerted causal influence back upon the present knower. Precognition thus implies backward causation, in which the cause comes *after* its effect,[54] or else it implies that time is not really real—that all events, including all those events that we ordinarily think of as future, coexist tenselessly, eternally. Acceptance of either of these ideas would indeed involve a revolutionary change in worldview. Some wishful-thinking advocates of the paranormal, in fact, give special emphasis to precognition, precisely because its acceptance would entail the most drastic revision of the hated "modern scientific worldview."

Acceptance of the paranormal, however, need not have any implications for the nature of time. Paranormal events that are commonly interpreted as precognitive can be interpreted in ways that do not involve backward causation or the unreality of time. For example, what is usually called precognition is often better understood as knowledge of *probable* consequences—probable *if* the present course of events is not altered. Many "fortune tellers," in fact, understand their visions of the future in this way, reporting them perhaps as warnings. Another example: When a vision in a dream is followed by an event in which the dream "came true," one could assume that the causal relation ran from the dream to the future event, rather than vice versa. This "psychokinetic interpretation" of apparent precognition is, in fact, offered by many theoreticians of the paranormal.[55] Many other possible "real-time" interpretations of ostensible precognitive occurrences exist as well. Having strong paradigmatic tendencies, and holding a philosophical position that makes true precognition impossible, I have elsewhere offered eleven more possible alternative interpretations, beyond the two mentioned above.[56]

Yet another implication commonly thought to follow from acceptance of the paranormal is a return to the early modern ontological dualism between mind and matter. The fear that the acceptance of the paranormal would require this return is evidently one of the major reasons among philosophers and scientists for prejudice against it. This return to mind-matter dualism might seem to follow from the above endorsement of the view that acceptance of the paranormal implies that the mind is distinct from the brain. The numerical distinctness of mind and brain, however, need not imply an ontological difference between mind and matter. It would imply this only if one had already, in line with the modern worldview, accepted the idea that "matter," such as the "gray matter" made of brain cells, is completely devoid of experience and spontaneity, thereby different in kind from our own experience. There is no good reason, however, to accept that assumption, which has been rejected by some of the leading philosophers and scientists of the twentieth century, such as Charles Peirce, William James, Henri Bergson, Alfred North Whitehead, Charles Hartshorne, Sewell Wright, David Bohm, and Ilya Prigogine. Besides the fact that the resulting "panpsychist" (or, as I prefer to call it, "panexperientialist") position allows for an intelligible view of the interaction between brain and mind (because the mind is different only in degree [albeit greatly] from the brain cells, not different in kind), it also solves several other problems faced by dualism and materialism[57] and is also more adequate to the range of paranormal phenomena.[58]

Having mentioned three implications that the acceptance of the paranormal, contrary to widespread opinion, need not have—it need not imply irrationality, backward causation (or an atemporal universe), and Cartesian dualism—I return now to the question of how it *would* be important. I indicated above some ways in which the currently dominant worldview would need to be revised to be adequate to the paranormal. I look now specifically—all too briefly, given the complexity of the issues—at some implications these revisions could have for the philosophy of religion and Christian theology.

One such implication was implicit in the above discussion of the idea of miracles. The reality of paranormal influence, especially psychokinesis, would mean a third way of regarding those events that have traditionally been regarded as "miraculous"—a third way beyond the customary alternatives of either accepting the extraordinary events reported in the New Testament (and, for Catholics, in later church history) as reflecting supernatural intervention, or rejecting them as nonhistorical fabrications. One could assume, instead, that those kinds of events did happen (although not necessarily exactly as reported), without assuming that the events involved any supernatural intervention, meaning divine causation different in kind from the divine causation in other events. (Although I am writing in reference to Christianity, the point would apply, of course, to any other religions that have used miracles to support their privileged status.)

This attitude toward so-called miracles also has implications for prayer, especially prayer for healing. Given the supernaturalistic view, according to which extraordinary healings are brought about unilaterally by God, prayer for healing and the actual healings that sometimes followed had problematic theological implications. To implore God to heal someone implied that the person praying had greater knowledge, or perhaps greater compassion, than God, and the fact that the prayers were sometimes followed by healing, but more often not, suggested divine arbitrariness. By thinking instead of extraordinary healing as necessarily always involving the co-operation of divine power and the psychokinetic power of one or more human minds, one can avoid those problems.

Psychokinesis is theologically relevant in another way. The notion of divine activity is presupposed in the biblically based religious traditions in general (as well as many other religious traditions), and in most of the doctrines of Christianity in particular (such as creation, inspiration, revelation, providence, prevenient grace, and incarnation). This notion, however, has been extremely difficult for modern philosophers of religion and theologians, especially in the late modern period.[59] One of the main reasons for this difficulty is that the idea that the human mind is impotent, being merely an epiphenomenal by-product of the brain (if not strictly identical with it), left no analogical basis for thinking of divine activity in the world. The idea of downward causation, especially as supported by psychokinesis, provides the needed analogue. One of the more interesting and controversial forms of psychokinesis, materialization, even provides an analogue for the idea of divine creation.

The idea of religious experience, in the sense of a direct experience of a Divine Reality, has also been difficult for modern thinkers. This difficulty has been created primarily by the sensationist doctrine of perception, according to which we can perceive only those things that can excite the physical sensory organs—namely, physical things. The resulting assumption that there can be no genuine experience of a Cosmic Mind lies behind the various reductionistic theories of religion, such as those of Feuerbach, Marx, Comte, Durkheim, and Freud.[60] The impossibility of authentic religious experience has been widely accepted even in theological circles, and the idea of "mysticism" has often been treated with contempt. If we were, however, to accept the reality of telepathy, which involves the direct perceptual experience of one mind by another,

then we have an analogue for thinking of the direct perceptual experience of a Divine Mind of the universe.

Closely related has been the difficulty of speaking of any experience of those nonphysical things called *values*, such as truth, beauty,
goodness, and justice. This difficulty, combined with the atheistic
assumption that there is no place for such values to exist, has led to
what Max Weber called the "disenchantment of the world," meaning
the view that values do not exist objectively in the nature of things but
only as purely "subjective" preferences of human beings. This assumption has, in turn, been closely related to so-called political realism
(*Realpolitik*), or power politics (*Machtpolitik*), according to which politics,
especially in international relations, has nothing to do with consensual
norms, such as fairness, but is based entirely upon coercive power.[61]
The acceptance of extrasensory perception would overcome the primary reason for this development. We could perhaps recover the idea
that values exist in the mind of God, and that one dimension of the
constant experience of God is our experience of values (which would
explain why we all *in practice*, in spite of what we may espouse in theory, presuppose knowledge of various values, such as truth).

Through the acceptance of paranormal experiences, furthermore,
belief in life after death might even be recovered in intellectual circles.
The idea that the mind is distinct from the brain and has power of its
own provides one of the necessary presuppositions (given the rejection
of a supernaturalistic worldview in which the literal resurrection of the
body can be assumed). Extrasensory perception, if real, answers the
question of whether the mind or soul, even if it could somehow exist
apart from its physical body, could perceive anything. Psychokinesis
would answer the question as to whether such a psyche would be able
to *do* anything to express its thoughts, feelings, and desires. Near-death
experiences and other out-of-body experiences can be interpreted as
evidence that the mind or soul really can exist, perceive, and act apart
from its body. Veridical apparitions of the dead, communications
through mediums, reincarnation-type cases, and various other phenomena provide data that can be interpreted as evidence that persons
actually do continue living past bodily death. Alternative explanations
of all these phenomena are, to be sure, available; but many circumspect
students of the paranormal have found the evidence persuasive. A general return within the intellectual portion of our culture to belief in life
after death would not be philosophically revolutionary in the sense that
an acceptance of true precognition would be; but, given the pervasive
nihilism created by the late modern worldview, it would be of great
significance.

Beyond all these particular points, the acceptance of the paranormal, if generally regarded as involving the changes in worldview discussed above, would mean a general reconciliation between science and religion. This development would be of utmost significance, especially if, as Whitehead believed, religion and science are "the two strongest general forces (apart from the mere impulse of the various senses) which influence [human beings]," so that "the future course of history depends upon . . . the relations between them."[62] Science and religion in the modern period came increasingly in conflict with each other, especially since the middle of the nineteenth century. The movement toward a postmodern worldview has recently brought about the beginnings of a rapprochement. If critical reflection on the paranormal were, by playing a decisive role in moving our culture to a postmodern worldview, to overcome the conflict between the "scientific worldview" and our religious and ethical intuitions, this would be its most important consequence.

NOTES

1. William James, "What Psychical Research Has Accomplished," in *William James on Psychical Research*, ed. Gardner Murphy and Robert Ballou (Clifton, N.J.: Augustus M. Kelley, 1973), 39.

2. Ibid., 26.

3. The term *parapsychology* was originally employed to refer only to that portion of psychical research that involves controlled experimentation. It has become common practice, however, to use the terms interchangeably.

4. Psychical research (or parapsychology) has often been defined simply as the scientific study of paranormal occurrences. This definition implies, however, that parapsychologists necessarily believe in paranormal occurrences, whereas they may not. That definition also leads skeptics to suspect that parapsychology may well be a subject without a subject matter. Both of these problems are solved by the insertion of the qualifier "ostensible," as suggested by John Palmer in "Progressive Skepticism: A Critical Approach to the Psi Controversy," *Journal of Parapsychology* 50 (1986), 29–42.

5. Brian Mackenzie and Lynne S. Mackenzie, "Whence the Enchanted Boundary? Sources and Significance of the Parapsychological Tradition," *Journal of Parapsychology* 44 (1980), at 143, 153, 135. My agreement with the Mackenzies, however, is only partial. See note 7, below.

6. J. R. Ravetz, "The Varieties of Scientific Experience," in *The Sciences and Theology in the Twentieth Century*, ed. Arthur Peacocke (Notre Dame: University of Notre Dame Press, 1981), 200–201.

7. George Price, "Science and the Supernatural," in *Philosophy and Parapsychology*, ed. Jan Ludwig (Buffalo, N.Y.: Prometheus, 1978), 173. Originally published in *Science* 122 (1955): 359–67. Incidentally, although the Mackenzies quote this statement, they do not make causality at a distance central to their own characterization of the paranormal. (For Price's retraction, see "Apology to Rhine and Soal," *Science* 175 [1972], 359.)

8. Mary Hesse, *Forces and Fields: The Concept of Action at a Distance in the History of Physics* (Totowa, N.J.: Littlefield, Adams, and Co., 1965), 118, 125, 291.

9. Richard Westfall, *Never at Rest: A Biography of Isaac Newton* (New York: Cambridge University Press, 1980), 15–16.

10. Ibid., 381.

11. Brian Easlea, *Witch Hunting, Magic and the New Philosophy: An Introduction to the Debates of the Scientific Revolution 1450–1750* (Atlantic Highlands, N.J.: Humanities Press, 1980), 93–95, 108–15, 121, 132, 135.

12. Westfall, *Never at Rest*, 390.

13. Ibid., 464.

14. Ibid.

15. Ibid., 505.

16. Robert E. Schofield, *Mechanism and Materialism: British Natural Philosophy in an Age of Reason* (Princeton: Princeton University Press, 1970), 115–24.

17. Westfall, *Never at Rest*, 644.

18. Keith Thomas, *Religion and the Decline of Magic* (New York: Charles Scribner's Sons, 1971), 577–78; Hugh Trevor-Roper, *The European Witch Craze of the Sixteenth and Seventeenth Centuries and Other Essays* (New York: Harper and Row, 1969), 132–33; Moody Prior, "Joseph Glanvill, Witchcraft and Seventeenth-Century Science," *Modern Philosophy* 30 (1932–33): 167–93.

19. Easlea, *Witch Hunting*, 94–95, 108–15, 138, 158, 210; James Jacob, *Robert Boyle and the English Revolution* (New York: Franklin, Burt, 1978), 162–76.

20. Robert Lenoble, *Mersenne ou la naissance du méchanisme* (Paris: Librairie Philosophique J. Vrin, 1943), 133, 157–58, 210, 375, 381.

21. Alan Kors and Edward Peters, *Witchcraft in Europe 1100–1700* (Philadelphia: University of Pennsylvania Press, 1972).

22. Trevor-Roper, *European Witch Craze*; Easlea, *Witch Hunting*; Lenoble, *Mersenne*, 18, 89–96.

23. Eugene Klaaren, *Religious Origins of Modern Science: Belief in Creation in Seventeenth-Century Thought* (Grand Rapids, Mich.: William B. Eerdmans, 1977), 173–77; Alexandre Koyré, *From the Closed World to the Infinite Universe* (Baltimore: The Johns Hopkins Press, 1968), 178–84, 210–13.

24. Jacob, *Robert Boyle*, 172; Easlea, *Witch Hunting*, 113, 234–35; Klaaren, *Religious Origins*, 173–77; Koyré, *From the Closed World*, 178–84, 210–13.

25. Robert Boyle, *The Notion of Nature*, vol. 4 of *The Works of the Honorable Robert Boyle* (London: Miller, 1744), 363.

26. C. D. Broad, *Religion, Philosophy and Psychical Research* (New York: Humanities Press, 1969), 7–26.

27. Ibid., 9.

28. Jane Duran, "Philosophical Difficulties with Paranormal Knowledge Claims," *Philosophy of Science and the Occult*, ed. Patrick Grim (Albany: State University of New York Press, 1982), 202.

29. Keith Campbell, *Body and Mind*, 2d ed. (Notre Dame: University of Notre Dame Press, 1984), 55.

30. John J. McDermott, ed., *The Writings of William James* (New York: Random House, 1967), 787.

31. William James, "What Psychical Research Has Accomplished," 40–41.

32. Campbell, *Body and Mind*, 135, 131.

33. Ibid., 132.

34. I owe this term to Susan Haack, "Double-Aspect Foundherentism: A New Theory of Empirical Justification," *Philosophy and Phenomenological Research* 53, no. 1 (March, 1993), 116 n. 8.

35. McDermott, *The Writings of William James*, 787; quoted by Marcus P. Ford, "William James," in *Founders of Constructive Postmodern Philosophy: Peirce, James, Bergson, Whitehead, and Hartshorne*, by David Ray Griffin, John B. Cobb Jr., Marcus Ford, Pete A. Y. Gunter, and Peter Ochs (Albany: State University of New York Press, 1992), 107.

36. Quoted in W. F. Barrett, "Address by the President," *Proceedings of the Society for Psychical Research* 18 (1904): 323.

37. Alfred North Whitehead, *Modes of Thought* (New York: Free Press, 1968), 3.

38. Eugene Taylor, ed., *William James on Exceptional Mental States* (Amherst: University of Massachusetts Press, 1984), 109; quoted in Ford, "William James," 91–92.

39. See Carl G. Jung, *Memories, Dreams, Reflections,* recorded and edited by Aniela Jaffe, rev. ed. (New York: Vintage, 1965), 50.

40. William James, *The Will to Believe* (Cambridge: Harvard University Press, 1979), 19; quoted in Ford, "William James," 107.

41. Colin A. Russell has suggested that "Scientific Naturalism—the view that nature's activity can be interpreted without recourse to God, spirits, etc."— was advanced by some to help the scientific community achieve cultural hegemony (*Science and Social Change 1700–1900* [London: Macmillan, 1983], 256, 258).

42. See James W. McClendon Jr., and James M. Smith *Understanding Religious Convictions* (Notre Dame: University of Notre Dame Press, 1975).

43. See Jule Eisenbud, *The World of Ted Serios* (New York: Morrow, 1967) and *Parapsychology and the Unconscious* (Berkeley: North Atlantic Books, 1983).

44. John G. Taylor, *Superminds: An Enquiry into the Paranormal* (New York: Viking, 1975).

45. Taylor, *Science and the Supernatural* (New York: Dutton, 1980), 164.

46. Ibid., 6.

47. Ibid., 165.

48. Ibid., 4.

49. James, *The Will to Believe,* 236; quoted in Ford, "William James," 111.

50. C. D. Broad, *Religion, Philosophy and Psychical Research,* 9.

51. The idea that the regularity of nature is absolute derives from the early modern worldview, according to which God in creating the world imposed absolute laws of motion on it. This notion of absolute regularity was retained in the late modern worldview even though the rejection of early modernity's supernaturalism left the notion with no rationale. Part of the postmodern view of science, suggested by Charles Sanders Peirce, William James, Alfred North Whitehead, and Charles Hartshorne (see note 35, above), is the idea that the so-called laws of nature are to be understood as widespread habits, with statistical rather than absolute regularity—an idea, of course, that has been supported by quantum physics.

52. A few philosophers who have expressed this view are D. M. Armstrong, *A Materialist Theory of Mind* (London: Routledge and Kegan Paul, 1968), 364; Herbert Feigl, "Mind-Body, *Not* a Pseudoproblem," in *Dimensions of Mind,* ed. Sydney Hook (New York: New York University Press, 1960), 28–29; and Keith Campbell, *Body and Mind,* 33, 91–96.

53. I have argued this case at length in *Unsnarling the World-Knot: Consciousness, Freedom, and the Mind-Body Problem* (forthcoming).

54. This interpretation of precognition is given by, for example, J. G. Pratt, *Parapsychology: An Insider's View of ESP* (New York: Doubleday, 1964), 167, and Bob Brier, *Precognition and the Philosophy of Science* (New York: Humanities Press, 1974), 174.

55. See Jule Eisenbud, *Paranormal Foreknowledge: Problems and Perplexities* (New York: Human Sciences Press, 1982), and *Parapsychology and the Unconscious*, 44–46, 87–98, 137–45; W. G. Roll, "The Problem of Precognition," *Journal of the Society for Psychical Research* 41 (1961), 115–28; and Stephen E. Braude, *The Limits of Influence: Psychokinesis and the Philosophy of Science* (New York: Routledge and Kegan Paul, 1986), 256–77.

56. David Ray Griffin, "Parapsychology and Philosophy: A Whiteheadian Postmodern Perspective," *Journal of the American Society for Psychical Research* 87, no. 3 (July, 1993), 270–75.

57. See David Ray Griffin, "The Restless Universe: A Postmodern Vision," *The Restless Earth: Nobel Conference 24*, ed. Keith J. Carlson (San Francisco: Harper and Row, 1990), 59–111; and *Unsnarling the World-Knot.*

58. See Griffin, "Parapsychology and Philosophy."

59. See Owen C. Thomas, *God's Activity in the World: The Contemporary Problem* (Chico, Calif.: Scholars Press, 1983).

60. See John Bowker, *The Sense of God: Sociological, Anthropological and Psychological Approaches to the Origin of the Sense of God* (Oxford: Clarendon, 1973). Freud, incidentally, had developed his reductionistic view of religion long before he came to accept telepathy.

61. See Stephen P. L. Turner and Regis A. Factor, *Max Weber and the Dispute Over Reason and Value: A Study in Philosophy, Ethics, and Politics* (London: Routledge and Kegan Paul, 1984); and the introduction to David Ray Griffin, ed., *Spirituality and Society: Postmodern Visions* (Albany: State University of New York Press, 1988), 5, 24 n. 9.

62. Alfred North Whitehead, *Science and the Modern World* (New York: Free Press, 1967), 181.

5

REFLECTIONS ON INCORPOREAL AGENCY*

Terence Penelhum

Reports of paranormal phenomena have aroused the interest (and the hostility) that they have largely because it has been widely supposed that if they are genuine they make it more likely that our world is affected by the agency of spirits, or even by divine agency. It is not clear that, even if they are genuine, they make either more likely; nor are the two necessarily connected. One can believe in spirit agency without being a theist, and one can believe in the agency of God without believing that there are other spirits who act in the world or beyond it. The writers of the New Testament believed in both, and portrayed Jesus as someone who exercised dominion over the spirits who had taken possession of many of those whom he healed. Contemporary Christians are sometimes reluctant to interpret the stories of his healings in the same way the New Testament writers did. Although most of them would still insist that God acts in the world, they have not, for the most part, been anxious to look for support for this belief in parapsychological phenomena, although there are conspicuous exceptions to this.[1] Their reticence has not made the skeptics about the paranormal any more easy about admitting the possibility of such phenomena, however. The fear of returning to a worldview that is even slightly like that of the first century is very deep.

I want in this chapter to look at some aspects of the suggestion that there are spirits who act in (or on) the world. I want also to look at

* This chapter is a development and expansion of some arguments I included in an essay entitled "Divine Action and Human Action" which was published in *Antropologia e Filosofia della Religione* (Perugia: Benucci, 1982). I am grateful to the volume's editor, Professor Albino Babolin, for kind permission to include material from that essay.

⌐ me of the apparent implications of what I have to say about this for the much more important belief that there is a God who acts in the world. I shall not try to say much about what a spirit is, in general. I shall merely assume that a spirit is a personal being that has no body. And my later comments about divine agency will be comments about the implications of the assumption that God also is incorporeal.

I. TWO MODELS OF SPIRIT AGENCY

Let us suppose we are at a séance, or are playing a foolish parlor game, in which questions are addressed to spirits while we sit around a table on which there is an inverted tumbler, which in "answer" to our questions is expected to move about between points on the table where letters are printed. Let us suppose that at some moment the tumbler does move, while none of us is touching it, and we want to say that a spirit has moved it. What is the difference between saying merely that the tumbler moved and saying that a spirit moved it?

Of course this question is notoriously hard to answer even when the agent to whom one ascribes an object's movement is a normal, that is a corporeal, agent. I wish if possible to avoid commitment on how it is to be answered in these normal cases, as I am only interested in how our options are affected if we accept the supposed agent's bodiless-ness.

To see the sort of difference this makes I will, however, start with a gross version of a Cartesian account of normal, corporeal, human agency. By calling it "Cartesian" I do not wish to try to blame Descartes for it; I have in mind merely the position ascribed to him and attacked and ridiculed in Ryle's *The Concept of Mind*.[2]

A traditional Cartesian account of a corporeal agent's moving the tumbler would presumably list three stages in a causal process: first, a mental stage comprising or issuing in something called a choice or a judgment or an intention or a volition, or some combination of these; second, a stage internal to the body of the agent, within which there would be a sequence of neural or muscular movements, of which the last ones would, in the present case, be movements of the agent's fingers; and, third, the movement of the tumbler itself. There are a multitude of objections to such a story, but I do not think it is necessary to try to list them. For someone who would accept this account of corporeal agency, the question of accounting for spirit agency would be a question of how to bridge the causal gap that would be left if the second of these three stages were lifted out.

For such a theorist, there would only seem to be two possibilities. One would be to suggest that the alleged processes of choice or resolution that comprise the first stage might somehow have direct effects on the movements of physical objects in some circumstances. We might call this the *"psychokinetic* option." The other possibility would be to postulate that the relation between the mind of the agent and the physical object he or she is trying to move is one in which the object stands in the place of the body which embodied agents have. We might call this the *"animation* option."

These two models would seem to exhaust the options for understanding spirit agency, on our amputated Cartesian interpretation of what such agency would be like. For they seem to be the only ways in which this understanding would permit us to include one essential component in the ascription of agency, namely the *efficacy* of the agent's intentions or purposes. There has to be some difference between a spirit that merely observes physical events and has opinions and wishes about them, and one that can do all that and also acts in (or on) the world. And although I cannot prove it, I find it hard to see how there could be any alternative beyond that of locating this difference in the causal efficacy of the mental preambles to the relevant physical events, or that of locating it in the object central to those events having (at least temporarily) the role that the body of a corporeal agent has in normal, corporeal agency.

I would now suggest that however discredited the Cartesian interpretation of normal human action is, we are driven to the same two choices if we try to understand the concept of spirit agency but start from some contemporary alternative to the Cartesian interpretation of normal human action. (More briefly, I wish to suggest that an account of spirit agency has to be neo-Cartesian.) The reason for this is that we have to be able to make sense of a bodiless spirit being responsible for a physical movement in an object that is distinct from that spirit; and this is not merely a matter of the spirit wanting that movement to occur and its occurring immediately or later, but of *the spirit moving the object.* The tale we tell in the case of an incorporeal agent requires us to connect the life of the spirit and the subsequent motion of the object, to provide for the efficacy of the spirit's wishes. A non-Cartesian analysis of normal agency will be one that weakens or denies the distinction between the agent and his or her body; or between the choice or the volition or the intention and the set or movement of the body; or between one or other of these and the bodily dispositions of the agent; or between the mental preambles to the object's movement and events in the agent's brain; and so forth. These can have no counterparts in the analysis of spirit action other than those that are open to us if we try to develop a psychokinetic or animative account of incorporeal agency. The former would perhaps allow us to find some analogue of the corporeal agent's bodily movements in the spirit's mental life, and the latter might allow us to ascribe some of the functions of the corporeal agent's body to the object that the spirit moves.

Neither model is very clear, and of course the concept of a spirit is subject to many difficulties in addition to the ones that will concern us here.[3] I shall now look at the two models more closely, in order to shed a little light upon them, and upon it.

II. THE PSYCHOKINETIC MODEL

To start with, are the two models significantly different from one another? To the extent to which the Cartesian picture of corporeal human action influences us, they will seem to come to much the same. For on that account human action consists of three consecutive causal sequences, causally linked; and in a way it comes to the same thing whether you hold, on the one hand, that by joining up the last item in the first (mental) stage with the first item in the third (moving tumbler) stage, you are giving the mind or spirit direct control over the movements of an outer object, or whether you hold, on the other hand, that by joining the first and third sequences directly in this way you are treating the tumbler as though it had become the locus of the events in the second sequence rather than of those in the third. To use a new metaphor, it seems just a verbal matter whether to say you are eliminating the middleman or turning the middleman into the customer. Perhaps psychokinesis and animation are not merely equivalent in their obscurity, but equivalent in whatever meaning each of them has?

I think this is a mistake. To show why, I would like to turn to a comment I once read (but cannot now trace) about Professor J. B. Rhine's experimental investigations into psychokinesis, or "PK."[4] These included sessions during which subjects were instructed to "will" dice that had been randomly thrown by machines to fall in a particular way, say double-six. It has been claimed that the correlation between willed and actual results has, with some subjects, been statistically significant, and that this makes a case for the existence of a power in some people to exercise purely mental control over the movement of physical objects. The comment that exercises me is this: that there is no good reason for our reluctance to explain these results as due to PK, for this is a common and unproblematic power that we all have and exercise continually.

Each of us regularly manifests this same mental power by effortlessly moving his or her own body about in space. (We might add that a human body is a great deal heavier than a pair of dice.)

I feel there is something deeply wrong with this argument. I suspect most philosophers would feel this also. But I also feel that it is very hard to say exactly what it is that is wrong with it. (It is no good saying that it just manifests the influence of Cartesianism, though no doubt it does.) Whatever the answer is to this puzzle, I want here to use it to help with the lesser question of the options open to us if we try to make sense of the notion of spirit agency.

Most of us would be inclined to say that even if PK exists, there is a big difference between cases where people will dice to fall, or will horses to win races, or will screen cowboys to shoot screen rustlers, on the one hand, and cases where people move their own limbs, on the other; and that whatever the difference consists in, the intimate control that each person has over the movements of one particular body is one of the things that makes that particular body *that person's body*. No one supposes that the dice whose fall I influence by sheer volition (if I ever do) thereby become part of my body.[5] There is also another difference between PK, if it occurs, and the control that I have over my own body and its movements: one of the obstacles to accepting Cartesianism is the fact that when I move my own limbs I may very well not be aware of engaging in any mental process before they move, even though I satisfy all the criteria for moving them deliberately or by choice, whereas in order to obey an experimenter's instruction to influence the dice I must engage in a distinctive mental performance that can be identified separately from the dice's fall—such as a silent command "aimed at" the dice as they start to tumble.

These reflections suggest that if we entertain a hypothesis of spirit agency we have two, and only two, ways of understanding it. One is to construe it on the model of psychokinesis. The other is to suppose it to be like the unmediated sort of control each of us has over his or her own limbs. The psychokinetic model has a clear consequence: if we accept it, we have to postulate in the spirit some separate mental performance that precedes the movement of the object on which the spirit is acting, and which is *a* cause, or *the* cause, of that movement. Attractive or not, this provides in the required way for the efficacy of the spirit's intentions. It does not do this by explaining *how* the fiat of the spirit brings about the object's movement, but it does locate that which fills the gap between the spirit's wishes and the events that the spirit brings about in accordance with them. It locates the spirit's contribution. This is bought at a price. The price is that the spirit can only act on the world by performing a mental act first, just as the allegedly successful

PK subject can only alter the fall of the dice by performing some inner act first. Many philosophers of course would say that an analogous price is paid by corporeal agents: for when I move a tumbler across the table by pushing it, I have to perform one action (moving my fingers) in order to perform the other (moving the tumbler). But in the case of the spirit, the absence of the body, and a fortiori the fingers, makes the distinctness of the two acts obvious.

Let us now look at the alternative model of spirit action, which I have called "animation." It, too, is far from clear, but it is, clearly, different. I want to suggest that it takes us into deeper theoretical perplexities than the PK model does, and that its appearance of greater economy is a deceptive appearance.

III. THE ANIMATION MODEL

We can see the nature of the perplexities as soon as we ask the obvious question: Doesn't the talk about a spirit animating a physical body necessarily compromise the incorporeality of the spirit? That it does this to some degree is obvious. But does it do it to an unacceptable degree? That is, does it lead us into simple self-contradiction?

The animation model seems more natural in some imaginary circumstances than others. The most obvious place for it is in speaking of some cases of trance mediumship, those that C. D. Broad has called cases of *ostensible possession.*[6] Here, for short periods, the medium's body seems to be "taken over" by the spirit with whom the sitters are supposedly communicating. There is an intuitive distinction between these cases and cases of "poltergeist" phenomena, where spirits are alleged to move objects, but are not alleged to inhabit or take over or possess the objects that they are supposed to move. Now if we abandon the PK model of spirit agency, and elect to speak of spirit agency as animative, poltergeist phenomena will also become cases of animation. This may seem less counterintuitive, however, if we reflect that our present concerns require us to maintain a more fundamental distinction than this: that between an object's being moved, even by some mysterious process of animation, by a spirit that is numerically distinct from it, and an object's moving because it has itself, in some occult way, acquired a power of self-movement. Unless we can provide for the distinctness of the spirit, *all* talk of animation will vanish into talk of occult self-movement on the part of natural objects.

Now whatever provides for the separateness of spirits will have to be provided for in wholly mental terms, since the spirit's separate identity can only consist in its mental life. So to ascribe the movement of the object (e.g., the tumbler) to the spirit requires that it is the spirit, conceived distinctly from its temporary occupancy of the object, to which we must ascribe the relevant motives, intentions, purposes, choices, or responsibility. When I say "conceived distinctly" I mean to stress that if the spirit's having of the relevant intention or purpose were a *consequence* of its animating the object, rather than its animating the object being its mode of realizing its prior intentions, then the fact that it animated the object would indeed compromise its incorporeality in an unacceptable way. For, *qua* agent, it would not merely animate the object, but would *have that object as its body.* For animating by the spirit not to be equivalent to the object's moving itself, the body that the spirit animates must not be its own body—since if it is incorporeal it has no such body. So even if, while it animates a body in order to move it, it has a relationship to it that is in detail very like the relationship it would have had to it all the time if that object had been its own body, it must be, outside such incorporated phases, a being that can live a separate incorporeal existence; and it must be as a being capable of such separate mental existence that we ascribe intentions and purposes to it, if the hypothesis of spirit agency by animation is to make sense and still be distinguishable from a hypothesis of self-movement on the part of some physical objects.

This leads to a simple metaphysical conclusion. It is to some degree controversial whether normal intending or choosing or forming purposes are to be understood as consisting in mental acts. If they are, then if spirits move objects, even by animating them, this must take place through the causal efficacy of such acts in the (distinct) mental life of the spirit. If they are not, and the correct ascription of intentions or choices or purposes is a matter of interpreting the behavior and speech that manifest such intentions or choices or purposes, then such manifestations must, for a spirit, be entirely mental in character, and be akin to our inner verbal formulations of our intentions, or our private imaginings of the future acts we plan to perform, or our fears and anxieties about the risks to be faced in executing them, and the like. For an agent with purely mental being, forming intentions or purposes, or making choices, must consist exclusively of such mental performances, since they cannot consist to any degree whatever of the physical manifestations that we encounter in corporeal agents. For these manifestations necessarily involve the corporeal agent's *own body;* and the incorporeal agent has none.

So if we compare the PK model of spirit action with the animation model, we have this result. The PK model appears more complex, because it requires some inner mental act, such as a fiat or volition, that the spirit must perform in order to influence the body that it moves; for without this the efficacy of the spirit's wishes or intentions can find no place. The animation model seems at first to dispense with this requirement, and thus to be more economical. But if we adopt it, we have either to hold the view that there are mental acts of intending or choosing or purposing that the spirit performs, or to hold that the spirit's mental life is filled with mental behavior or mental acts or mental happenings that manifest or actualize its intentions or choices or purposes, for there to be content to the claim that it *has* such intentions or choices or purposes and that they are what explain the movements of the objects on which the spirit is said to act.

Of course, one of the mental expressions of the intentions of the animating agent could be the very sort of fiat or volition that we imagined in the psychokinetic model—although if the two are to stay distinct, this would not here, of itself, be causally efficacious in producing the object's movement. But as soon as we agree that this element in the psychokinetic model can also serve as an expression of the spirit-agent's intention in the animative model, we can see that the PK model provides for such expression as well as for the efficacy of the intention it would express. So it is no longer clear, at all, that the animative model of spirit agency is superior on grounds of economy to the psychokinetic one, in spite of initial appearances; rather the contrary.

A footnote: If one accepts the logical possibility of spirit agency, then whichever way one thinks of it, there is no reason to deny the possibility that spirits would vary in degrees of strength or power. On the PK model, one spirit might be able to shift tumblers by fiat, but fail with tables; another might manage tables, but not bookcases. Their fiats would have different degrees of efficacy. On the animative model, the situation would be more like that of the difference between a slim person who has no problem moving about, and the obese person who can only move with difficulty. There would always be the dubious consolation that the body one was animating on one occasion could be vacated and a less weighty one animated instead; for neither would be one's own.

Which model we preferred would be more likely to be determined by our prior views about the role played by an agent's bodily movements in normal corporeal cases. The more Cartesian we were, the more likely we might be to prefer the PK model, since it would clearly separate the mental and the physical elements in our story. But if the above arguments have any weight, an anti-Cartesian analysis of normal corporeal action would not lend us much comfort with either model if we felt obliged to talk of spirit agency at all.

IV. NON-PSYCHIC ALTERNATIVES

But why, indeed, should we? There are certainly many reasons for philosophers to wish not to. The modes of agency I have been exploring so far are obscure as well as occult. More importantly, such clarification as I may have been able to supply above does nothing at all to address the difficulty of understanding how we are to individuate spirits or interpret their identity through time. It is a common view that our ability to do this with corporeal persons depends on their possession of separate continuing bodies. The difficulties that arise when we try to manage without such corporeal bases for judgments of identity have never, as far as I can see, been answered, or even much addressed.[7] It is therefore sometimes said that however instinctive it is to talk of spirit agency when faced with poltergeist phenomena or ostensible possession, we must ascribe any genuinely paranormal features of such cases to occult powers belonging to the embodied agents who are present: so poltergeist phenomena must be due to psychokinetic activities by disturbed adolescents in the families plagued with them, and apparent possession must be due to telepathic knowledge and self-dramatization on the part of the medium, and the movement of the tumbler in our parlor game must be due to the frivolous exercise of psychokinesis by one of the players.[8] There comes a point, however, where even the most determined may feel obliged to abandon such moves on the ground that the complexities they lead to are too great to accept merely in order to sustain what philosophical reflection tells us *must* be the case or cannot be. It is because I feel that we may already have reached this point in some of the recorded cases that I have tried to explore other aspects of the concept of spirit agency in spite of these perplexities.

V. DIVINE AGENCY

I think the considerations that I have been able to discuss, however, have some bearing on much deeper, theological questions. Whether or not we feel a reluctance to admit the possibility of finite incorporeal agents, it is clear that those who believe in God would maintain that God is both an agent and incorporeal. The suggestion that God has a body would be dismissed by theists as intolerably anthropomorphic.[9] It is worth remarking that some of the reasons for this that come most readily to mind are inadequate. One of these is that God could not have a body because a being with a body would be limited in knowledge or in power. We tend to take it for granted that a corporeal being would be restricted in knowledge to states of affairs near to his or her body, or only have power to affect states of affairs close to that body. But these considerations do not withstand examination. Unless there is some general incoherence in the concepts of clairvoyance or psychokinesis, there is no logical barrier that I can see to ascribing these powers to embodied beings, and these ascriptions are frequently made, for good or bad reasons. And I do not think it self-evident that an omniscient or omnipotent being could not be clairvoyant in knowledge or psychokinetic in power, even if that being had a body.

Another specious argument concerns God's omnipresence. In the chapter entitled "An Omnipresent Spirit" in his book *The Coherence of Theism*,[10] Richard Swinburne seems to assume that omnipresence and corporeality are incompatible; but I think the apparent incompatibility vanishes if one interprets omnipresence as Aquinas did (and as Swinburne also does). Aquinas says, in article 1 of question 8 of the first part of the *Summa Theologiae* ("Whether God is in All Things?") that "God is in all things, not, indeed, as part of their essence, nor as an accident, but as an agent is present to that upon which it acts." In article 2 ("Whether God is Everywhere?") he tells us that "He is in all things as giving them being, power, and operation; so He is in every place as giving it being and locative power. . . . Indeed, He fills every place by the very fact that He gives being to the things that fill all places." Again, in article 3 ("Whether God is Everywhere by Essence, Presence and Power?"): "God is in all things by His power, inasmuch as all things are subject to His power; He is by His presence in all things, inasmuch as all things are bare and open to His eyes; He is in all things by His essence, inasmuch as He is present to all as the cause of their being."[11] These quotations make it clear that Thomas is interpreting God's omnipresence as equivalent to God's power over all things and his knowledge of all things. As far as I can see, if this is what omnipresence is, it is by no means self-evident that it is inconsistent to ascribe it to a being who has a body, provided of course that that being were possessed of unlimited powers of clairvoyance and action at a distance. (If one were to ask how a being, himself located at some remote point in outer space, could nevertheless be thought to be present everywhere else, one would have to give just this sort of answer. In Thomas's case of course, we know that *he* is trying to tell us how a being who does not have that [or any other] bodily position can still be present in all places nevertheless; but what he tells us could well serve as an explanation of how a being who does have bodily position could still be said to be present in places other than the one in which his body is.)

But it is not my purpose to question the orthodox teaching that God is incorporeal—merely to indicate that it does not clearly follow from the teaching that he is omnipresent or omniscient. I return to the theme of divine action. I have been trying to suggest that if we wish to ascribe any events to the action of finite spirits, there are no advantages of economy in thinking of their mode of activity as a form of animation rather than as a form of psychokinesis. When we turn to divine acts, we encounter a distinct difficulty that seems to make it harder to conceive of them as psychokinetic. If psychokinesis ever happens, it seems to require that the agent practicing it must first perform some inner act in order to cause the movement of the body to be shifted. But even if we take it for granted that divine fiats would always be successful in bringing about the physical changes at which they are "aimed," this understanding of divine action looks inconsistent with the *almightiness* of God. We want to say that God's power over his creation is utterly unmediated: he does not have to perform some inner act such as reciting something, like a stage magician, in order to get things to happen. He does not, surely, if he is almighty, have to do one thing in order to achieve another?

If this influences us, we will no doubt look again at the natural and familiar example of unmediated action: the control we exercise over the movement of our limbs, as when we raise our arms or clench our fists. But to use such acts as these as models when thinking of divine agency seems to lead us at once into some form of pantheism. Here, however, we can recall our earlier discussion, and remember that we must so restrict the notion of animation that it does not imply that the body animated is *the body of* the animating spirit. Using the model of animation does, still, compromise the ascription of incorporeality to God; but perhaps it does not do it unacceptably.

Let us explore this. Certainly the relationship I have to the limbs I can move unmediatedly makes the body those limbs are part of, *my* body. For this reason Swinburne, in *The Coherence of Theism*, says that even though God has no body, he is still partially embodied, because of the unmediated power he has over physical things.[12] Let us say that a being that has this power over physical things has, or undergoes, *quasi embodiment*. A being's quasi embodiment will just consist in having this power over those things (in the divine case all things) which that being can unmediatedly control—without those things thereby becoming that being's *own body*. For it is not only this unmediated power of mine over it (or parts of it) that makes that body mine: it is also such things as my feeling changes in it when no one else does; my mental life, and no one else's, being confused when I put alcohol into it; and so forth; and none of these apply, self-evidently, in the divine case.[13]

Let us allow all this. I would still argue that even if we accept that the phenomena we call God's acts are in some manner quasi embodiments of the divine, there has to be more to their being divine acts than that. For God's intending them, or deciding on them, or choosing them, cannot be provided for to any degree in the mere idea of quasi embodiment, any more than a finite spirit's choosing to move an object can be provided for by saying it animates that object. For in neither case can this mental requirement be understood in terms of happenings in the phenomena. This is easy to see: even if we adopt the most behavioristic analysis of choice or intention, such an analysis can only fit fully corporeal beings—that is, beings *whose own bodies* evince the requisite behavior. To analyze my intentions or wishes behavioristically is to analyze them in terms of the behavior of *my body*, and if we are avoiding pantheism we cannot so stretch the idea of quasi embodiment that it allows us to say that the phenomena on which God acts constitute his own body or part of it. So even if we can understand God's actions in or on the world by analogy with our own control over our own limbs, we still have to postulate some additional mental factor in the divine mind that is requisite for his being responsible for the phenomena we call his acts: something to constitute his having, as well as his executing, the intention or purpose these phenomena are thought to carry out in the world. Can we say anything at all about what this could be?

VI. INCORPOREALITY AND ANTHROPOMORPHISM

I have been laboring a simple point that is too easy to overlook: that if some event in the physical world, be it a small one like the movement of a tumbler or a big one like the parting of the seas, is to be judged to be the act of an incorporeal spirit, human or divine, then the spirit said to be responsible for it must be thought to possess an independent mental life of which the event so explained is a product or effect. It is to that mental life that we have to ascribe the purpose or choice or decision that generates the event we are explaining. This is true whatever mode of control the spirit is thought to exercise over the objects it changes.

When the spirit is a finite spirit, particularly if it is thought to be a postmortem human person, there is little reason to suppose that the immaterial expression of the spirit's purpose is much different from what goes on in our minds when we formulate intentions or express wants. But when we are thinking of explaining events as due to divine agency, there are many familiar reasons for thinking that such likenesses cannot hold. God cannot try and fail. God cannot have conflicts of intention. Nor can God form an intention but back away from exercising it. Considerations like this are enough to show that if we think the mental life of the divine agent must include the expression of specific divine intentions, such expression will at most be *analogous* to the expressions of intention that are familiar to us from our own experience.

But analogous it has to be, or so it seems. At least, there would seem to be a logical requirement that there be some feature of the divine mental life that performs the same role or function that inner expressions of intention play in our own case, and in that of finite spirits, if there are any.[14]

In the opening passages of Genesis we find the famous declaration: "And God said 'Let there be light': and there was light." If the arguments above are sound, this cannot be merely a dramatic image, but must be closer than that to a literal truth, however we wish to qualify the notion of saying.

I have not attempted to enter the important controversies about divine eternity or timelessness. It does seem to me, however, that conceiving divinity as necessarily timeless increases the formidable difficulties that already face us if we wish to come closer than I have to an understanding of how divine agency is to be construed.

My concern here has not been with eternity but with incorporeality. When it is said that we must strive to avoid interpreting the idea of God anthropomorphically, this is often illustrated, in my experience, by reference to the doctrine that God is incorporeal. I think, on the contrary, that in one respect the doctrine of divine incorporeality pulls exactly the opposite way: by showing that a God who acts in the world would have to have a mental life that was in some respects rather like ours.

NOTES

1. See, for example, Michael Perry, *The Easter Enigma* (London: Faber, 1959) and *Psychic Studies: A Christian's View* (Wellingborough: Aquarian Press, 1984); and E. Garth Moore, *Believe It or Not: Christianity and Psychical Research* (London: Mowbray, 1977).

2. Gilbert Ryle, *The Concept of Mind* (London: Hutchinson, 1949).

3. For a thorough, classic treatment of these, see Antony Flew, *The Logic of Mortality* (Oxford: Blackwell, 1987). Some earlier reflections of my own are to be found in *Survival and Disembodied Existence*, 2d ed. (London: Routledge, 1980).

4. See J. B. Rhine, *The Reach of the Mind* (New York: Sloane, 1947).

5. On what it is to own a particular body, see Jonathan Harrison, "The Embodiment of Mind, or What Use is Having a Body?" in *Proceedings of the Aristotelian Society*, 74 (1973–74), 33–55; and Richard Swinburne, *The Coherence of Theism* (Oxford: Clarendon, 1977), 102ff.

6. C. D. Broad, *Lectures on Psychical Research* (London: Routledge and Kegan Paul, 1962), 257.

7. See note 3.

8. A famous example of this sort of deflationary diagnosis is Dr. Johnson's explanation of the Cock Lane Ghost. See James Boswell, *The Life of Samuel Johnson*, vol. 1 (London: Dent, 1920), 251–53.

9. In the present essay I am assuming without argument that pantheism is false. There are two recent works that demand consideration I cannot give here. They are Grace M. Jantzen, *God's World, God's Body* (London: Dartman, Longman and Todd, 1984), and Michael P. Levine, *Pantheism* (London: Routledge, 1994).

10. Richard Swinburne, *The Coherence of Theism* (Oxford: Clarendon, 1977), ch. 7; and *The Existence of God* (Oxford: Clarendon, 1979), 49.

11. Quotations from Aquinas are from the revised English Dominican translation of the *Summa* in *Basic Writings of Saint Thomas Aquinas*, ed. Anton C. Pegis (New York: Random House, 1945).

12. See pp. 102–5.

13. The claim that God has, or manifests, quasi embodiment would seem to be promising for those theists who are interested in bridging some of the gaps between Western and Eastern understandings of ultimate reality. See, for example, the discussion of panentheism in J. A. T. Robinson, *Truth is Two-Eyed* (London: SCM Press, 1989).

14. By far the best recent discussion of these issues is, I think, to be found in W. P. Alston, *Divine Nature and Human Language* (Ithaca: Cornell University Press, 1989).

6

SOULS IN PROCESS: A THEORETICAL INQUIRY INTO ANIMAL PSI*

Susan J. Armstrong

This essay brings together three topics: the empirical evidence of animal psi (anpsi), a process philosophy view of animal souls and anpsi, and animal immortality in the Christian tradition. I believe the empirical evidence is compelling enough to require a theoretical account, which can be provided by process philosophy. Such a theoretical account, if satisfactory, enables us to add animal psi to other long-standing arguments for animal immortality.

I. EMPIRICAL EVIDENCE OF ANIMAL PSI

Stephen Braude suggests a useful division of evidence for psi in terms of experimental, semi-experimental, and anecdotal.[1] Semi-experimental investigation (which others term "field investigation") concerns recurrent spontaneous psi phenomena, which occur repeatedly in connection with a certain person or place, outside the laboratory setting. Anecdotal evidence is sometimes termed "sporadic spontaneous psi phenomena."

What weight should be given to these three types of evidence? Led by J. B. Rhine, in the 1930s parapsychology began emphasizing experimental, laboratory work. Recently, however, there has been a reaffirmation of the value of spontaneous reports of psi. For example, Rhea White has argued that while the existence of psi has been ade-

---

* I thank Rhea White for her kind help in finding references.

quately established according to the traditional scientific method, this demonstration has not gotten the field very far. According to White, it is now appropriate to concentrate on spontaneous psi, which she and others classify as part of "exceptional human experiences,"[2] because a study of these unique occurrences can transform our sense of human potential and deepen our sense of the meaning of human life.

Similarly, Braude argues that anecdotal and semi-experimental evidence is "at least as valuable and reliable as the evidence gathered from laboratory experiments, and probably more so."[3] Experimental parapsychology suffers from two weaknesses, according to Braude: the inability to convince skeptics of the reality of psi functioning and the inability to reveal vital facts or data concerning the nature of psi. These limitations spring from the exclusively quantitative nature of laboratory evidence. Such evidence can always (however unreasonably) be dismissed as embodying statistical errors, and can never (due to our ignorance of psi processes) be assumed to be free of psi effects originating from factors not included in the experimental design. In addition, psi functioning may well be determined by the organism's motivations and needs. If this is so, spontaneous occurrences of psi would often provide the best, most representative examples of psi. Psi may in fact be repressed by tightly controlled, sterile, analytic settings. Braude notes that experimental and non-experimental evidence can support each other.

On the other hand, in a thorough review of animal psi as of 1977, Robert L. Morris points to the weaknesses possible in spontaneous cases: distortion in the original perceptions, lack of replicability, the impossibility of assessing the likelihood of coincidence from chance, biases on the part of the investigator, deception by reporter or investigator, sampling biases, and difficulty of comparison due to lack of detail. (Of course, these weaknesses can also occur in experimental work.) Morris finds spontaneous cases useful mainly in providing direction for more precise studies.[4] In summary, investigators and commentators agree that each type of psi evidence has some value.

An interpretative problem unique to animal psi concerns whether or not the psi effects are produced by the animal, by a human being, or by some combination of the two. A number of commentators tend to discount data on the grounds of this uncertainty. Morris for example points out that human influence on animals *per se* would not provide evidence that animals possess psi ability, just as "most of us would not attribute psi ability to dice just because we seem able to influence them."[5] However, in the process view to be discussed below, all psi effects are relational, and hence this distinction is less important.

With these methodological considerations in mind, let us now consider the anecdotal evidence for animal psi. The very abundance of such reports is striking. This abundance can be seen as mitigating the deficiencies in individual reports, along the line of James's observation that "Weak sticks make strong fagots." He adds that "when the stories fall into consistent sorts that point each in a definite direction, one gets a sense of being in the presence of genuinely natural types of phenomena."[6] A number of these stories attribute the psi effects to the animal.[7] I have myself had such an experience. In the late 1970s I had a pet cocker spaniel and two parakeets. My practice was to allow the parakeets to fly freely around the living room, since there had never been any danger to them from the dog. However, one afternoon I stepped outside to do some gardening. While outside I felt an incredibly violent feeling, impossible to put words to. I raced inside and found that my dog had just killed one of the parakeets and was delicately plucking its feathers with her teeth preparatory to eating it. The fact that I was out of the house when the unexpected event occurred, and nevertheless experienced strong emotion at the moment of the parakeet's death, indicates to me that the parakeet was the psi agent.

The work of Penelope Smith deserves special mention in any discussion of the anecdotal evidence for animal psi. Since 1977 she has earned her living as an Animal Communication Specialist. She offers audio and videotapes, two books, a newsletter, and lectures and workshops throughout the United States. She has trained seventeen "Interspecies telepathic communicators" who provide lectures, workshops, healings, and consultation by phone or mail. She has recently spoken to the American Holistic Veterinary Medical Association. Her approach is to quiet her mind and listen to the animal, and to then translate its thoughts and feelings into words for human understanding. According to the videotaped testimony of horse owners, for example, results are evident in distinct behavioral changes or in improvement in health of the animal. Her newsletter includes reports of failures and mistaken communications. When asked in an interview whether she would be willing to work with scientists and scholars, she replied that she would be willing to exhibit and discuss her work, but not in a "sterile, clinical" way.[8]

Another area of evidence for animal psi is that of homing, in which an animal finds its way home over new and strange terrain. Sometimes the trip covers hundreds and even thousands of miles. Much of this material is anecdotal, though there have been field experiments with wild birds and with pigeons. These studies indicate that a number of wild birds are good homers without training in unfamiliar territory.[9]

In the early 1950s Rhine collected case reports of homing dogs and cats and became convinced that the phenomenon indeed occurs and that psi capacity is a legitimate working hypothesis.[10] Homing of turtles and toads over distances of 8–10 miles have been reported.[11] Reports of homing continue to accumulate.[12]

Psi-trailing is Rhine's name for cases in which the animal, left behind when his human companion or family go to a more or less distant location, somehow finds the way to them. As of 1962 Rhine considered these cases to be some of the most promising in terms of providing evidence for animal psi. (Types of cases in addition to psi-trailing and homing included reactions to impending danger to the animal or to its owner; reaction to the death of the owner at a distance; anticipation of the owner's return.[13]) After careful screening, Rhine located fifty-four admissible instances of apparent psi-trailing. The defects of such anecdotal material motivated Rhine to suggest that various semiexperimental tests might be made, using birds. He notes that the greatest difficulty is to avoid running afoul of the animal's side habits, in terms of spatial preferences, etc. Rhine concludes that if these animal cases did indeed occur as reported (and one case concerned a fifteen hundred mile trip), animal psi would seem to be of much greater intensity and consistency than human psi.[14]

Work with dogs and horses has generally been conducted in the semi-experimental or field investigation mode. In her excellent discussion of possible psi in dogs,[15] Rhea White notes that while a number of reports of talking, thinking, or telepathic dogs are found in the records of psychical research, most of the testing was unsystematic. Indeed, the early focus was generally on the "thinking" or "calculating" aspects and not on the possibility of psi. She reviews early reports concerning a number of dogs and provides data from her own work with five.

In 1924 the Russian neurophysiologist W. Bechterev published the first report of controlled psi experiments with animals. He had studied two circus dogs trained by W. Durow. The most impressive results were obtained by a fox terrier named Pikki. After being given a mental suggestion, Pikki was able to execute an action such as to jump on one of the chairs, then to climb on a little round table beside it, and, stretching himself, scratch the big portrait hanging on the wall above the table. Several times Bechterev alone decided on the task and gave the suggestion to Pikki. He made five experiments with this method, changing the task each time. In some variations he stepped outside the room just after the period of willing the task. Bechterev also had Durow cover his eyes with a towel. A further series of experiments replaced Durow as experimenter with two medical doctors, who covered their faces with a wooden, metal, or paraffin screen while Durow was in another room. The screens occasionally, but not always, prevented success. Further successful experiments were carried out without Durow being present or even knowing work was planned.[16]

White, utilizing comments by Vasiliev, comments that placement of targets may have favored the dog's choice of that target, and that in some of the variations the agent first gave the dog the signal to begin while still in its sight, so that possibly when the agent gave the starting signal he also provided a prelearned sensory cue before leaving the room. It seems to me, however, that this latter possibility is not at all likely given that the tasks varied and were unpredictable, having been created by Bechterev or some other person. Unfortunately, further laboratory work by Durow in Moscow in the 1920s with other dogs, while statistically significant, did not sufficiently guard against sensory cuing.

White singles out the best dog case as being that of Chris, a mongrel owned by George Wood. In 1958 Wood collaborated with Cadoret in publishing a report on tests for telepathy and clairvoyance. Some of the tests are best considered as laboratory experiments because of their careful elimination of sensory cues. At least eight people worked successfully with Chris when Wood was not present. Generally at least one person was present who knew the answer to any question, but not always. In one instance Chris indicated the correct score in a baseball game that had just been played, information which presumably no one in his vicinity knew. Pratt tested Chris with the help of the Duke Parapsychology Laboratory, and obtained very significant results in tests of clairvoyant card-calling. Interestingly, when Cadoret observed the tests, Chris performed at significantly below chance.[17]

White discusses in detail some of the difficulties in designing experiments with dogs, difficulties due to the familiarity the dog has with particular modes of response, such as pawing the answer on her or his owner's arm, or with always being near the owner when responding. White stresses the importance of eliminating all possibility of sensory cues in any further investigations. Aural cuing is particularly difficult to eliminate: if the agent knows what the target is before asking the dog to respond, the dog may pick up a hint as to the correct number from nuances in the agent's voice. In addition, it is possible that some of the psi effect may be due to the recorder.

In her own work with five dogs, two of the dogs provided good results under strict conditions, including separation from the agent by a closed wooden door. The results showed the same decline effect which characterizes many psi experiments, whereas the food rewards and possible sensory cues remained constant. White notes also that the barking of the dogs coincided with the scoring: when the dogs were scoring well their barking was rapid and stopped in a definite way; when they were scoring at the chance level only, their barking contained pauses or became hysterical. Also, some of the scores showed displacement (for example, during some trials one dog consistently barked one number higher than the target).

Rhine's well-known study of the horse Lady provides intriguing evidence of human-animal telepathy. Rhine and his wife Louisa made two visits, one in January of 1928 and one in December of 1928. Lady's task was to touch her nose to wooden blocks with letters on them without sensory cues as to which block was desired by the investigator. Rhine determined on the first visit that Lady was not successful unless someone present knew the location of the desired block. He used screens as well as the absence of the trainer to rule out sensory cues. Persons other than the trainer were able to act as telepathic agents, though they were not as successful as the trainer. Lady seemed almost asleep when she was working. Rhine notes that the results indicated telepathy rather than training, because of Lady's extreme fluctuations from perfect to failure. The results were too good to be coincidental and too poor to be the result of training.[18]

By the time of the Rhines' second visit, Lady's telepathic abilities had disappeared in favor of simply being an active horse responsive to obvious sensory cues. Rhine notes, however, that if during his first visit Lady had also been guided solely by sensory cues, her abilities should have improved, which they did not.[19]

Experimental work with animals in the laboratory began in the 1930s, and reached its quantitative peak to date in the 1960s and 1970s. In a review of laboratory research through 1978, James Davis[20] notes the advances with automated testing systems, beginning with Chauvin (under the published name of Duval) and Montredon in 1968. Their work with mice remains one of the most successful in demonstrating probable precognition in animals, with results in the range of $p < .001$ and with successful replication.[21]

Considered as precognitive, animals are psi receivers. Other experiments in the 1970s studied animals as psi receivers using forced choice, only one option of which leads to either positive reinforcement or punishment. Some of these have produced significant results.[22] However, replication has been sporadic for various reasons, including death of high-scoring animals, changes in apparatus and housing practices, and changes in scoring methods. Some studies have utilized emotional anticipation of future stress, the stress ranging from imminent death in a study of rats to being picked out of the tank in a net in a study of goldfish. Several of these studies produced significant results but in divergent directions.[23] A number of parapsychologists rightly dislike studies requiring the killing of large numbers of animals, and so attempts at replication have been few.

Other experimental designs have studied animals as possible psi agents. In experiments by Schmidt, the animal had an opportunity to modify the distribution of outputs from a random number generator (RNG)[24] to make the environment more favorable to it. The experimenter then determined whether or not this distribution differed significantly from chance. Schmidt's cockroach experiment (1970) involved shock as the negative reinforcement, as did the experiments of Duval and Montredon. These experiments yielded statistically significant evidence of psi and have been replicated. However, ethical objections to the use of shock, together with legal and practical difficulties, have resulted in an abandonment of such negative reinforcement. In addition, comparison of experiments is difficult because experimenters have used different definitions of RBT (random behavior trial).

Other experiments that studied animals as psi agents used positive reinforcement and yielded statistically significant results. Schmidt (1970) worked with a heat lamp and a cat; Braud (1976) tested tropical fish for PK, using a mirror image as a reward; and a series of experiments by Watkins (1971) with lizards using a random generator controlling a heat source found significant deviations from chance. However, Davis notes that overall the scoring rates in these experiments are quite low, ranging between 52 and 55 percent in the studies by Braud and Watkins. Such studies require many trials, which invite decline effects, require long periods of time, and don't answer questions as to how PK works. These studies also are not designed to separate experimenter from animal psi.

Overall, Davis's view is that as of 1978 only minimal progress had been made in establishing the existence of animal psi effects independent of human psi, though he does note that these experiments do establish that there are important individual differences among animals with regard to psi ability and that some animals are fairly reliable in their scoring. Similarly, Morris assesses the experimental data for psi in animals as encouraging but still weak.

Mundle is more positive, concluding that Schmidt's method "seems to have provided unambiguous evidence that animals can influence Schmidt RNGs."[25] He adds that results which do not conform to the experimenter's expectations are more likely to be anpsi and that the existence of anpsi is made more probable by the fact that experimenters who study animal psi seem to have more success than those who study human psi, on the assumption that animals in general are more predictable than human beings.[26] Pratt notes that experiments such as those with the dog Chris, in which under strictly controlled conditions results were significant with two different people working with Chris, indicate that the dog may well have been responsible for the results.[27] Instances such as that of Schmidt's cat, in which psi effects stop when conditions become unfavorable from the animal's point of view, indicate that the animal may have been the psi agent.[28]

Several authors note characteristics of both human and animal psi in experimental settings: psi fluctuates, is unpredictable, and shows a chronological decline. High scorers are rare; results are better with fewer trials per day, and there is occasional evidence of psi-missing or displacement.[29]

More recent experiments have been few and far between. Mark Johnson has been unable to replicate Peoch's (1988) highly significant results on PK in chicks, though Johnson's experimental design was somewhat different.[30] Schmidt has continued his work with PK and notes that two different speculative mechanisms for PK with prerecorded random events have been proposed. One possibility is that the subject's PK effort acts backward in time towards the moment when the random events were generated and recorded. The other is that PK works because the event is decided only when observed. In this case "reality" is what the experimenter observes: consciousness "collapses the state vector."[31] If this second possibility is in fact correct, preobservation of the outcome should block any PK effect by a later observer. One such study by Schmidt indicated that preobservation did block subsequent PK success, though dog and goldfish observers were less effective than human observers. However, in a 1989 test, preobservation by goldfish did not weaken the PK success.[32] Schmidt notes that experimenter expectations could have distorted the results, as well as the small number of trials.

An experiment with rabbits from the same litter has provided results indicative of telepathy, though only two rabbits were studied. The investigators studied coincidences (within less than 5 seconds) between the outsets of physiological reactions characteristic of stress, the stress being small stimulae such as the sound of a bell as well as isolation through distance and by means of elecromagnetic and sensorial isolation boxes. Two out of four series of experiments gave significant results ($p < .001$).[33]

Some experiments have concerned animals as receivers of paranormal healing. Watkins and Watkins have studied the resuscitation of anesthetized mice and found that there was significantly faster awakening for the mouse on which the human subject concentrated. The subjects had earlier demonstrated PK ability. Other experiments using nontalented subjects showed no effect. In another experiment anesthesized mice were placed on a table while a healer attempted to shorten the mice's recovery time according to whether or not the mice were on an assigned target side (right or left) of the table. This experiment seemed to indicate a significant "linger effect" related to the side of the table on which the healer had focussed in the previous trial.[34] An experiment with gentling and handling of normal and sick mice by non-healers indicated either that the survival time or weight gain of mice do not respond to handling and gentling or that paranormal healers are required for such effects to occur.[35] Healy suggests that there may be a link between theta rhythm and psi phenomena: theta rhythms coordinate with rat whisker twitching, inhalations, and novel environments.[36]

In my view, the anecdotal observations and semi-experimental and experimental studies cited above provide ample evidence that individual animals of many species exhibit some degree of psi functioning. Let us now turn to the question of how this psi functioning can be understood. The approach I find most congenial is that of David Griffin,[37] who utilizes the philosophy of Alfred North Whitehead (1861–1947).

II. A PROCESS PHILOSOPHY ACCOUNT OF ANIMAL PSI

Griffin identifies the most distinctive feature of psi events as being that of causal influence at a spatial or temporal distance. He suggests the terms *receptive psi* and *expressive psi,* the former to encompass being a telepathic receiver or recipient of clairvoyant information, and the latter to encompass PK, telepathic agency, psychic healing, and psychic stimulation of plant growth.[38] According to this terminology, life after death, out-of-body, and near-death experiences would involve both receptive and expressive psi.[39]

However, Griffin's schema will not accomodate precognition, on the grounds that time in Whitehead's system is constituted by means of efficient causation, which occurs only from past to present occasions of experience. Griffin argues that since every occasion has at least some degree of mentality and self-creativity, future occasions are not fully determinate. There is no perspective from which time can be transcended because the future does not yet exist: the character of future events depends upon the free decisions of intervening events.[40] Griffin attempts to account for the many reports of apparent precognition by means of an assortment of thirteen explanations, based either on coincidence, PK, or a source of information from which a future event can be logically inferred.

However, in an article commenting on Griffin's, the parapsychologist John Palmer describes a new interpretation of RNG–PK experiments, the "IDS" (intuitive dating sorting) model, which Palmer believes would if verified provide "a strong empirical case for true precognition."[41] My own view is that the door should be kept open to true precognition, in harmony with Whitehead's own empiricist approach. For while the indeterminateness of future events is indeed central to his system, Whitehead considered metaphysical concepts to be "tentative formulations."[42] There is of course no uninterpreted, "pure" experience to appeal to, but whether or not true precognition occurs must nevertheless be decided on the basis of experience, rather than on any one set of philosophic categories.

Ultimate reality for Whitehead is made up of momentary events, which he terms "actual occasions." Enduring entities such as subatomic particles, living cells, and psyches are constituted by a series of occasions of experience which inherit a "defining characteristic." The differences between enduring entities are due to variations in the complexities of the actual occasions making up the enduring entity. And in turn the complexities of experience which an occasion enjoys depend upon the organization of its actual world. Each actual occasion arises from a different actual world or situation: the network of actual occasions which that occasion must incorporate into its self-formation. An actual occasion comes into being by "prehending" (taking account of or feeling) objectified actual occasions in its past. In a simple physical feeling the past actual occasion is felt by means of its own "ex-feeling" of prior occasions in its actual world. In a hybrid physical feeling the past actual occasion is felt by means of its own "ex-feeling" of an "eternal object," Whitehead's term for potentials for the process of becoming which provide actuality with definiteness or form. Feelings of eternal objects are termed "conceptual feelings" by Whitehead.

There are two fundamental ways in which enduring entities can form spatiotemporal societies (material bodies) with many contemporary members. One way is to form an aggregate, a society without a dominant member. For example, rocks and machines are aggregates, without a unity of response in relation to their environment. Inorganic societies have no "telos," no unified aim. Griffin follows Whitehead in considering plants to be organic aggregates, without a soul or organizing center above and beyond their individual cells.[43]

The second way in which enduring entities form spatiotemporal societies is by means of a dominant member which integrates many subordinate societies, including subordinate enduring entities, into a temporal society of higher occasions of experience. The soul or psyche or mind is such a "dominant occasion," which unifies the experiences of many hierarchies of societies within societies into one momentary experience. Dominant occasions can be of many degrees of complexity, and thus Whitehead can say: "It is not a mere question of having a soul or of not having a soul. The question is, How much, if any?"[44] Animal life ranges from the relative lack of central organization found in a worm or jellyfish, to the conscious, personal experience of vertebrates.[45]

The perceptive experience of an actual occasion can be either in the nonsensory *mode of causal efficacy*, or in the sensory *mode of presentational immediacy*. Presentational immediacy, what is commonly called "sense perception," is based on chains of contiguous events. It is generally clear and distinct, and is much more likely to become conscious than is perception in the mode of causal efficacy. Perception in the mode of causal efficacy includes the subjective form, the "feel" of past experiences: it is an intuitive and feelingful sense of connection with the surrounding world as well as with the actual occasion's immediate past experience. According to Whitehead it is much more trustworthy in its disclosure of the nature of things than are quantified sense data.

Griffin notes that Whitehead's doctrine of two-fold perception is of great help in understanding both how psi occurs and why it is generally unconscious.[46] Extrasensory perception can be understood as the nonsensory perception of remote events. How can this be understood in process terms? Whitehead postulates that telepathic influence can be understood as resulting from hybrid physical prehension, in which the past occasion is felt by means of one of its own conceptual feelings.[47] The mental feeling of an earlier occasion is felt by the later occasion without other actual occasions in between: the transmission is "immediate" and as complete as is possible given the fact that the later occasion has its own character. Such conceptual or mental prehensions are not bound by the space-time continuum, since they involve eternal forms, which are atemporal. We should note that Whitehead considers not only telepathy but the immediate sense of a feeling-tone in everyday social interactions to be explainable by such immediate mental feelings of the surrounding world.

However, Whitehead adds that since prehensions are integrated in the formation of an actual occasion (including an actual occasion which attains consciousness), any immediate conceptual prehension will be reinforced or hindered by being mixed with chains of mediate physical prehensions of the actual world. Thus, in general any immediate hybrid prehension will be unconscious. Only in rare cases will there be conscious telepathic experience.

This mediated nature of psi is a reason to rule out the hypothesis of "superpsi," the hypothesis that psi phenomena can be of any magnitude. Another reason to rule out superpsi is its theoretical unhelpfulness: the hypothesis of superpsi make the experimenter "helpless in the face of his [or her] own omniscience."[48]

According to the process view of psi, all psi events are relational between partially self-determining subjects. Thus, it is to some extent arbitrary as to which subject is the agent and which the percipient or receiver. Griffin suggests that the agent in conscious psi would be the subject who made an attempt to read a mind, move a rock, heal a plant, etc., and that the attempt would essentially be to persuade by means of what he terms "hybrid physical causation."[49]

Griffin notes that human beings seem to have much greater power to exert expressive psi (materialization, teleportation, poltergeists, telepathic agency) than do animals.[50] He explains this difference by joining Cobb in arguing that the human psyche has sufficient energy to enable the psychic life to become its own end. The human psyche is proportionally less absorbed in bodily maintenance.[51]

It seems to me, however, that a more fruitful way of understanding the differences between the human and animal psyche is that the human psyche is less closely bound to the moment, so that its experience is freer, more creative, allowing more choice and more generality of thought. The animal psyche is more closely bound to the immediate situation—to what is going on in that place and at that time.[52] J. Allen Boone extols "the great dog art of living abundantly and happily in the present tense."[53] The mental pole of animal consciousness is more closely tied to the physical pole. This characterization of animal experience allows us to make sense of two suggestions and observations of animal behavior.

The first such suggestion is that proportionally more of the animal's experience may be conscious, as opposed to human experience. This suggestion is made by the cognitive ethologist Donald Griffin, based on the observation that the central nervous system of the animal (or insect) has a smaller storage capacity than that of a human being.[54] Fewer of the animal's adaptations to a changing environment can be stored as nonconsciously governed behavior. In addition to a capacious central nervous system (CNS), each human being is constituted within a culture, which provides a large array of traditional modes of response.[55] Thus, human beings do not need to devote their conscious experience to figuring out each response they make to a changing environment. But animals, lacking culture and a large CNS, may need to do so. Conscious mental imagery, explicit anticipation of probable outcomes, and simple thoughts about probable outcomes are likely to be more effective than thoughtless, "instinctive" reaction.

The second consequence of animals being more situational than human beings is that we would expect animals to excel in receptive psi. Rhine suggests that if psi had an early evolutionary origin it might be much more potent in lower animals than in human beings. Since psi is unconscious in human beings, whereas sensory perception is conscious, Rhine suggests we should expect to find psi in nonhuman beings as a presensory mode of orientation.[56] For example, as Rhine notes, psi trailing requires far greater psi powers than have ever been exhibited by human beings.[57]

We can put Rhine's suggestion together with David Griffin's observation that human beings have much greater success with expressive psi than do animals. Human beings do seem much more able to affect their environment through PK, telepathic agency, psychic healing, and so forth.[58] But on the other hand, we would expect that animals would strongly exhibit receptive psi, because of its use in orientation. And this does seem to be the case: psi-trailing, homing, unusual migration—all concern orientation. Precognition can also be an aid to adaptation: note that the precognitions exhibited by rodents in laboratory experiments as well as the anecdotal reports of dogs and cats who warn of imminent danger or who sense an imminent arrival are all of the very near future. Likewise, the telepathy exhibited by dogs such as Chris and the horse Lady is dependent all or most of the time upon interaction with persons involved in the immediate situation.

III. AN AFTERLIFE FOR ANIMALS?

So far we have considered how process philosophy makes sense of psi associated with living animals, such as telepathy, psi-based orientation, and precognition. Can process philosophy also make sense of a possible afterlife? One obstacle to a process view of survival of either human beings or animals is that Whitehead denies the existence of "entirely living societies," living societies which survive without the presence of inorganic occasions. In taking this position he assumes that the novelty created in the living occasions renders social tradition and stability impossible.[59] A living society requires the protection of subservient inorganic societies, enduring in accord with inherited tradition (efficient causation). "Life" cannot be a defining characteristic of a society because it is a name for originality and not for tradition. Whitehead states that we have no knowledge of a living society without its "subservient apparatus of inorganic societies." However, nothing in his system rules out entirely living societies in which there would be a highly complex inheritance by the dominant concresence from living societies whose lowest-grade occasions, while still dominantly physical in the sense of being governed by efficient causation, would not be completely inorganic.[60] Such a dominant concrescence would have to be able to unify into one experience the many intense experiences of its "body." Thus, perhaps only human beings and higher animals are capable of existing without bodies containing inorganic societies.

Griffin addresses a different aspect of survival: whether or not the prehensions experienced by a discarnate psyche would provide "sufficient nourishment to the soul" to allow for perceptions which are conscious on a relatively consistent basis. He points out that while for an incarnate psyche most nonsensory perceptions are nonconscious, memory is regularly conscious. In memory "the mind's present occasion of experience directly prehends some of its prior occasions of experience."[61] Perceptions of our bodily sensory systems are also both nonsensory and regularly conscious. Griffin concludes that the absence of sensory data in the discarnate state might allow much greater consciousness of nonsensuously prehended data and that selective agency might be similarly enhanced.

Griffin argues that despite Whitehead's nondualistic, evolutionary philosophy, only the human psyche is capable of survival. The difference in degree has become a difference in kind. As in his discussion of expressive psi, Griffin cites John Cobb's view that the human soul is basically independent of the body in that its interests lie in its own intensely rich experience.[62] Discarnate life is possible because the human mind has developed an "emergent power to survive in a new environment." The animal soul has a continuity of experience, but few purposes aside from the well-being of the body. For Griffin and perhaps for Cobb, even cetaceans and primates, while enjoying "more soul," lack sufficient development of the mental poles of their prior dominant occasion to enable discarnate survival.

Cobb and Griffin both note that this power of the human psyche to operate without much attention to the organism and environment which supports it is not without danger. Such autonomy can in fact lead to the neglect or destruction of the body and environment. Whitehead himself notes that the abstraction and generality of conception that is possible for a human psyche cannot only be dangerous but can actually be less valuable than the achievements of an animal psyche:

> Without doubt the higher animals entertain notions, hopes, and fears. And yet they lack civilization by reason of the deficient gen-

erality of their mental functioning. Their love, their devotion, their beauty of performance, rightly claim our love and our tenderness in return. Civilization is more than all these; *and in moral worth it can be less than all these.*[63]

It seems to me that Griffin is persuasive in his affirmation of the possibility of human discarnate survival but not in his limitation of discarnate experience to human psyches. One reason for my position is that Whitehead's only direct discussion of the issue questions both the "orthodox" belief that all and only human beings are immortal, and that a purely spiritual being would be immortal. He describes his philosophy as neutral on the question of immortality and adds that "there is no reason why such a question should not be decided on more special evidence, religious or otherwise, provided that it is trustworthy."[64]

A second reason for my affirmation of animal immortality is the evidence of animal psi ability (perhaps some of the "special evidence" mentioned by Whitehead), which indicates that animal psyches are able to obtain information and orient the organism by use of receptive psi. Psi indicates that the animal psyche engages in sufficient hybrid physical prehension to have a distinct mentality. This, combined with an indefinitely large number of observations concerning the individuality of animal psyches, indicates that animal psyches, while simpler than human psyches, might be able to survive the death of the animal body.

Evidence for animal survival is provided by the many reports of observations of animal apparitions or ghosts, and of living animals reacting to the site of a haunt or other paranormal occurrences.[65] The only experimental work I know of on this topic is a study by Robert Morris of animal detection of an out-of-body projection by a human being. Morris found that one kitten was significantly less active during an out-of-body experimental period.[66] There are anecdotal reports of deceased animals (generally dogs, cats, and horses) being seen or heard by several human observers. Sometimes feelings of bodily weight and warmth are included. In one case the panting and wheezing of a deceased dog was heard by two women and by a living dog, who went to investigate.[67] Bayless recounts the sighting by two women of what appeared to be their deceased cat walking with a distinctive gait and appearance across their lawn a month after burial. A servant saw the creature about half an hour later and attempted to give it milk. The gardener was required to dig up the cat's body to prove that she was actually dead. Bayless concludes that while many animal apparitions are undoubtedly telepathic in origin, some seem to possess a degree of objectivity.[68]

IV. CHRISTIAN ARGUMENTS FOR ANIMAL IMMORTALITY

The question of the immortality of animal souls has long been recognized as an important one in Christian theology. Sanford points out that early Christians did not reject the view that animals had souls, but saw animal souls as different from human souls. With regard to immortality, this difference was construed in two different ways. The first view is exemplified by Origen's (185–254 C.E.) doctrine of the Universal Salvation, according to which all souls would eventually be saved.[69] Origen refers to Ps. 36:6: "You save humans and animals alike, O Lord" (New Oxford Bible). Aquinas is representative of the second, anthropocentric position, according to which the lack of a rational soul means that animals have no intrinsic spiritual or moral value: human beings have no duty even to be charitable to animals.[70]

Historically the second view of animals as of only instrumental value has dominated Christianity. However, the first view has never been without partisans. Certainly ordinary Christians have often loved animals, have considered them to be within the covenant, and hoped to associate with them in the afterlife.[71] Martin Luther assured a little girl that the beauties of heaven will include little dogs,[72] and a number of seventeenth-century reformers as well as orthodox clergy considered the issue of animal immortality to be an open question.[73] However, not until the mid–eighteenth century in Great Britain do we find formal theological arguments for either the rights of animals or their immortality. This eighteenth-century concern for animals seems to have been motivated by scientific discoveries of the similarity between living things and by the emergence of an industrial order in which animals had become increasingly marginal to the process of production.[74]

In 1722 the Spy Club at Harvard debated "Whether the Souls of Brutes are Immortal." Bishop Butler and John Wesley concurred, as did other less well known theologians.[75] John Hildrop published a book in 1742 in which he argued that since animals preexisted Adam's sin, which presumably brought death into the world, animals must be immortal and intended for God's glory.[76] David Hartley argued that the similarity of species makes strict boundary lines arbitrary between those God will and will not redeem. Soame Jenyns maintained that animal immortality is required by divine justice, in order to recompense them for their present suffering at human hands: "What! one being created under the *foreseen* certainty of its being made *miserable* solely for the use or pleasure of another." Richard Dean added that a soul having a capacity for life, understanding, and activity has a capacity for endless duration of existence.[77]

At roughly the same time on the Continent, Locke's disciple Charles Bonnet offered at least five arguments for the immortality of animal souls. First, animal souls are perfectible by Divine Goodness and can gradually become capable of moral goodness. Second, even if they are not moral beings, animals are capable of happiness. Third, if an animal soul had a human brain it would be capable of having universal ideas. Fourth, there can be differences between souls just as there are among bodies. Fifth, the mere fact that animal souls are not human is insufficient reason to deny them immortality; the argument is analogous to arguing that human souls are mortal because human beings are not angels.[78]

A few years later John Wesley in his famous sermon "The General Deliverance" (1788) repeated Hildrop's argument that a just God will not allow those who suffer to go uncompensated. In Wesley's view the only real difference between human beings and animals is that human beings can have a relationship with God; animals relate to humankind. The animal world fell with the human, and will be "delivered therefrom into the liberty of the children of God." In that new life "no creature will kill, or hurt, or give pain to any other."[79] And the Calvinist clergyman Augustus Toplady maintained in the 1770s that any argument against the immortality of animals could equally apply against the immortality of human beings.[80]

Given these earlier arguments for animal immortality, where does the issue stand in the late twentieth century? Andrew Linzey, a contemporary Anglican theologian, strongly argues for a world-embracing redemption, in which "we affirm the hope of future life for animals as we affirm that the Spirit is the basis of their breath."[81] Linzey argues that the biblical view is that both animals and human beings are similarly created and blessed by God. In fact human beings may not be the epitome of every spiritual gift: "All living creatures should be seen as participating in spiritual becoming, spiritual communion and awaiting spiritual consummation."[82] He cites Keith Ward's view that an adequate theodicy must affirm the immortality of animals on the grounds that each sentient being must have the possibility of achieving redemption.[83] Daniel Dombrowski characterizes Hartshorne's process view in a similar way: animals contribute to God's undying, inclusive life; all creaturely experiences are immortalized in the divine life.[84]

The official teachings of the Roman Catholic communion have held to Aquinas's views.[85] Recently, however, Pope John Paul II has reaffirmed the early Christian doctrine that animals have souls. In a homily at the Vatican in 1989 the Pope quoted Ps. 104, in which animals are said to have the breath of life from God, and called for "solidarity with our smaller brethren."[86] The Roman Catholic theologian Jeffrey

Sobosan describes Aquinas's views on animal life as of "dubious" value. Sobosan affirms animal immortality, so that "all that ever existed will be raised to new life, touching, communicating, enjoying a peace with each other that will not end because there is no more death."[87]

In summary, those Christian thinkers who have affirmed the immortality of animal souls have largely relied on three arguments during the last four centuries:

1. Divine Justice. The suffering of animals requires their survival in order for justice to be done. Suffering of innocents must be recompensed.
2. Universal Spirituality. Spirituality is not limited to human rationality. Sentient beings were created able to experience happiness, and no nonarbitrary reason can be given to exclude them from its eventual experience. There is no nonspeciesist reason to confine spiritual worth to human reason, and in any case animals are capable of a degree of rationality.[88]
3. Universal Deliverance. All creation will be transformed and saved.[89]

William James adds a fourth reason to affirm animal immortality: God's inexhaustible capacity for love, the divine delight in diversity, which is not limited by human prejudices against seemingly grotesque or alien lives. Each life is "animated by an inner joy of living as hot or hotter than that which you feel beating in your private breast."[90] This theme is implicit in the Christian doctrine of God the Creator delighting in the goodness of everything (Genesis 1:31). It is also consonant with Whitehead's doctrine of the ultimate value of self-enjoyment in which "the temporal occasions are completed by their everlasting union with their transformed selves."[91]

What can we conclude about the mutual relevance of animal psi, the process view of animal psi, and the Christian affirmation of animal immortality? Animals do manifest psi, particularly receptive psi. Using process philosophy, we can make sense of how animal psi works: animal psi is evidence of the presence in animals of a distinct mentality, which might be able to survive the death of the animal body. Thus, as a result of our inquiry, perhaps we can now add animal psi as a fifth reason to affirm that animals are and will be partakers of the saving power of God.

NOTES

1. Stephen E. Braude, *The Limits of Influence: Psychokinesis and the Philosophy of Science* (New York: Routledge and Kegan Paul, 1986), 1ff.

2. Rhea White, "EHEs as Vehicles of Grace: Parapsychology, Faith and the Outlier Mentality," *The Academy of Religion and Psychical Research: 1993 Annual Conference Proceedings* (Bloomfield, Conn.: The Academy of Religion and Psychical Research, 1993), 46–55.

3. Braude, *Limits of Influence*, 3.

4. Robert L. Morris, "Parapsychology, Biology, and ANPSI," in *Handbook of Parapsychology*, ed. Benjamin B. Wolman (New York: Van Nostrand Reinhold, 1977), 687–715. Morris provides an extensive bibliography of experimental work from 1929–1977.

5. Ibid., 703.

6. William James, "Final Impressions of a Psychical Researcher," in *The Writing of William James: A Comprehensive Edition*, ed. John J. McDermott (Chicago: University of Chicago Press, 1977), 796.

7. Joseph Edward Wylder, *Psychic Pets: The Secret Life of Animals* (New York: Stonehill, 1978); Berthold E. Schwarz, "Human-Animal Events: The Anecdotal Evidence," in *Extrasensory Ecology: Parapsychology and Anthropology*, ed. Joseph K. Long (Metuchen, N.J.: Scarecrow, 1977), 193–210 (see editor's comment, on pages 207–8); Dennis Bardens, *Psychic Animals: A Fascinating Investigation of Paranormal Behavior)* (New York: Henry Holt, 1987), especially 53, 77; Barbara Ivanova, *The Golden Chalice*, ed. Maria Mir and Larissa Vilenskaya (San Francisco: H.S. Dakin, 1986), especially 137–41. Maurice Maeterlinck, in *The Unknown Guest*, trans. Alexander DeMattos (New York: Dodd, Mead, 1915), refers to a collection of sixty-nine cases made by Bozzano in 1905 in which the principal actors were thought to be cats, dogs, and horses (324–25). I have been unable to trace the reference. Braude recounts a well-attested telepathic dream in which a dog seems to have been the agent (Braude, *Limits of Influence*, 177–80). Raymond Bayless judiciously discusses many reports of animal psi in *Animal Ghosts* (New York: University Books, 1970) including animals as telepathic agents (41–48).

8. Penelope Smith, Pegasus Publications, P.O. Box 1060, Point Reyes, Calif. 94956. Interview quote from "Understanding and Healing Animals," *Psi Research* (1986, March/June), 208–213.

9. J. Gaither Pratt, *Parapsychology: An Insider's View of ESP* (New York: E.P. Dutton, 1966), ch. 9.

10. J. B. Rhine, "The Present Outlook on the Question of Psi in Animals," *Journal of Parapsychology* 15 (1951), 230–51.

11. Vincent Gaddis and Margaret Gaddis, *The Strange World of Animals and Pets* (New York: Cowles, 1970), ch. 9. In general the book is valuable though uncritical.

12. For example, in 1973 my male cat Leo returned after three months from a new owner located about twelve miles away from my home. Needless to

say, I did not attempt to give him away again. More recently, according to Italian newspaper reports a cat found its way home over 125 miles of mountainous terrain over twenty months, having mistakenly jumped aboard a moving van. Unfortunately the cat died of exhaustion follwing a veterinarian's examination (*The San Francisco Chronicle*, 26 February 1994, B7.)

13. For stories of cats and dogs apparently precognizing bomb impacts, their own death, and the deaths of masters, see Gaddis and Gaddis, *Strange World*, chs. 10 and 13.

14. J. B. Rhine, "The Study of Cases of 'Psi-Trailing' in Animals," *The Journal of Parapsychology* 26 (1962), 1–22; Gaddis and Gaddis, *Strange World*, 130–37, and ch. 11.

15. Rhea A. White, "The Investigation of Behavior Suggestive of ESP in Dogs," *Journal of the American Society for Psychical Research* 58 (1964), 250–79. See also the anecdotal accout of "Jim," a Llewellyn English Setter (1925–1937), who seemed to perform both telepathically and precognitively according to Clarence Dewey Mitchell in *Jim the Wonder Dog* (Marshall, Mo.: Red Cross Pharmacy, 1983).

16. W. Bechterev, "'Direct Influence' Of a Person Upon the Behavior of Animals," *The Journal of Parapsychology* 13 (1949), 166–76. Ehrenwald finds Bechterev's (and White's) work persuasive; see Jan Ehrenwald, "Psi Phenomena and Brain Research," in *Handbook of Parapsychology*, ed. Benjamin B. Wolman (New York: Van Nostrand Reinhold, 1977), 716–29.

17. George H. Wood and Remi J. Cadoret, "Tests of Clairvoyance in a Man-Dog Relationship," *The Journal of Parapsychology* 22(1958), 29–39; Pratt, *Parapsychology*, 223–35.

18. J. B. Rhine, "An Investigation of a 'Mind-Reading' Horse," *Journal of Abnormal and Social Psychology* 23 (1929): 449–66. Marthe Kiley-Worthington, an ethologist, states in *The Behaviour of Horses in Relation to Management and Training* (London: J. A. Allen, 1987) that horses may be telepathic, and notes their large convoluted cerebral hemispheres (88–89).

19. J. B. Rhine and Louisa E. Rhine, "Second Report on Lady, the 'Mind-Reading' Horse," *Journal of Abnormal and Social Psychology* 24 (1929), 287–92. Another complex case is that of the Elberfeld horses, which cannot, I believe, be quickly dismissed in all its details.

20. James W. Davis, "Psi in Animals: A Review of Laboratory Research," *Parapsychology Review* 10, no. 2 (1979), 1–10.

21. C. W. K. Mundle, "On the 'Psychic' Powers of Nonhuman Animals," in *Philosophy and Psychical Research*, ed. Shivesh Thakur (London: George Allen and Unwin, 1976), 167–72.

22. See the articles by Davis, Mundle, and Morris for detailed discussion and references.

23. Morris, "Parapsychology, Biology," 698–99.

24. An RNG is an electronic device capable of producing a random sequence of outputs for use as targets in psi testing. Schmidt's instrument was based on emission of electrons from a very weak radioactive source. For a precise description see Mundle, "On the 'Psychic,'" 163–64.

25. Ibid., 171.

26. Ibid., 175. Whether or not there are proportionally more successful anpsi experimenters than human-psi experimenters is an empirical question to which I do not know the answer.

27. Pratt, *Parapsychology*, 210–35.

28. Psi effects stopped in Schmidt's 1970 experiment when the cat seemed to take a dislike to the heatlamp. Helmut Schmidt, "PK Experiments with Animals as Subjects," *The Journal of Parapsychology* 34, no. 4 (1970), 355–61.

29. Carroll B. Nash, "Characteristics of Psi Communication," *Parapsychology Review* 11, no. 4 (1980), 17–22; Morris, "Parapsychology, Biology," 694; J. B. Rhine, "The Present Outlook on the Question of Psi in Animals," *Journal of Parapsychology* 15 (1951), 230–51.

30. R. Peoch, "Chicken Imprinting and the Tychoscope: An Anpsi experiment," *Journal of the Society for Psychical Research* 55 (1989), 1–9; Mark H. Johnson, "Imprinting and Anpsi: An Attempt to Replicate Peoch," *Journal of the Society for Psychical Research* 55 (1989), 417–19.

31. Helmut Schmidt, "PK Effect on Pre-Recorded Targets," *Journal of the American Society for Psychical Research* 70 (1976), 267–91; and "Comparison of a Teleological Model with a Quantum Collapse Model of Psi," *The Journal of Parapsychology* 48, no. 4 (1984), 261–76. "State vectors" are discussed in the 1984 article.

32. Helmut Schmidt, "PK Tests with and without Preobservation by Animals," in *Research in Parapsychology 1989*, ed. Linda A. Henkel and John Palmer (Metuchen, N.J.: Scarecrow, 1990), 15–19.

33. Bernard Thouvenin, "A Study of Telepathic Phenomena among Rabbits," *Revue Francaise de Psychotronique* 1, no. 2 (1988), 15–37. I thank Kathrin Burleson for help with translation.

34. Graham K. Watkins, Anita M. Watkins, and Roger A. Wells, "Further Studies on the Resuscitation of Anesthetized Mice," *Research in Parapsychology 1972*, ed. Wm. G. Roll, Robert L. Morris, and Joanna D. Morris (Metuchen, N.J.: Scarecrow, 1973), 157–59; Roger Wells and Graham K. Watkins, "Linger Effects

in Several PK Experiments," *Research in Parapsychology 1973*, ed. Wm. G. Roll, Robert L. Morris, and Joanna D. Morris (Metuchen, N.J.: Scarecrow, 1974), 143–47. A very strong "linger effect" lasting thirty minutes was demonstrated in a somewhat informal study by a human subject on a compass needle.

35. F. W. J. J. Snel and P. C. v. d. Sijde, "Handling and Gentling as Functions of Paranormal Healing with Normal and Sick Animals by Non-Healers," *European Journal of Parapsychology* 7 (1988–89), 215–36.

36. Joan Healy, "Hippocampal Kindling, Theta Resonance, and Psi," *Journal of the Society for Psychical Research* 53 (1986), 486–500.

37. David Ray Griffin, "Parapsychology and Philosophy: A Whiteheadian Postmodern Perspective," *Journal of the American Society for Psychical Research* 87, no. 3 (1993), 217–88.

38. I agree with Griffin that *expressive psi* is an improvement over *PK*, but prefer to retain the term *telepathic agency* rather than to adopt *thought transference*.

39. Because of his characterization of psi experience as involving action at a distance, Griffin preferred in his 1993 paper not to consider afterlife, near-death, and out-of-body experiences as paranormal, but as experiences occurring without the aid of a physical body. However, Griffin admits that one could argue that the experiences of a discarnate mind would probably involve influence at a spatial distance. Also, he grants that the *evidence* of life after death is clearly paranormal. (See Griffin, "Parapsychology and Philosophy," 228–30). In a more recent paper ("Dualism, Materialism, Idealism, and Psi: A Reply to John Palmer," *Journal of the American Society for Psychical Research* 88, no. 1 [1994], 23–39), Griffin affirms that survival as such is a form of psi.

40. Griffin, "Parapsychology and Philosophy," 271. See also David Griffin, "Why Critical Reflection on the Paranormal is So Important—and So Difficult," section III, in this volume—editors.

41. John Palmer, "Psi in the Context of Ultimate Reality: A Critical Appreciation of Griffin's Paper," *Journal of the American Society for Psychical Research* 87, no. 4 (1993), 309–27. In his 1994 paper, cited above, Griffin replies that non-precognitive explanations of the experimental data would still be viable. See also Schmidt, "PK Effect" and "PK Tests." Braude argues that the alternative to true (retrocausal) precognition is super ESP and PK (Braude, *Limits of Influence*, 256–77).

42. Alfred North Whitehead, *Process and Reality: An Essay in Cosmology*, corrected ed., ed. David R. Griffin and Donald W. Sherburne (New York: Free Press, 1978), 8.

43. While I disagree with this position, space does not permit any discussion.

44. Whitehead, *Adventures of Ideas* (New York: Macmillan, 1933), 267.

45. Ibid., 264.

46. Griffin, "Parapsychology and Philosophy," 255–57. Palmer notes that available evidence indicates that unconscious (human) psi is not any stronger or more reliable than conscious psi (Palmer, "Psi in the Context," 319–20).

47. Whitehead, *Process and Reality*, 308.

48. Davis, "Psi in Animals," 7.

49. Griffin, "Parapsychology and Philosophy," 265–66.

50. Some of the more dramatic instances might involve pure physical causation at a distance (Griffin, "Parapsychology and Philosophy," 267–68).

51. Griffin, "Parapsychology and Philosophy," 261–62. In *A Christian Natural Theology* (Philadelphia: Westminster, 1965), John Cobb emphasizes the animal absorption in the present, as distinguished from the importance of the inheritance from past occasions in the human soul (56–63).

52. For a fuller discussion see Susan Armstrong-Buck, "Nonhuman Experience: A Whiteheadian Analysis," *Process Studies* 18, no. 1 (1989), 1–18.

53. J. Allen Boone, *Kinship with All Life* (New York: Harper and Row, 1954), 58.

54. Donald Griffin, *Animal Thinking* (Cambridge: Harvard University Press, 1984), 41.

55. I thank Whitney W. Buck for pointing out the importance of culture in this respect. For a suggestion that dolphin schools may have existed in the same location for thousands of years and that the information communicated between generations may constitute cetacean traditions, see Joan McIntyre, "Mind in the Waters," in *Mind in the Waters* (New York: Charles Scribner's Sons, 1974), 218.

56. Rhine, "Present Outlook." Edmund Selous has noted the sudden collective impulses governing the flight, sport, or play of birds in *Thought-Transference (or What?) in Birds* (London: Constable, 1931). Shivesh Thakur agrees with Rhine that telepathy may be of evolutionary origin. ("Telepathy, Evolution and Dualism" in Thakur, *Philosophy and Psychical Research*, 205.) Maeterlinck postulates that subliminal psychic faculties may be keener in animals because our conscious, individualized life may atrophy such faculties (*The Unknown Guest*, 327–28).

57. Rhine, "Psi Trailing," 21.

58. Michael Murphy, *The Future of the Body: Explorations into the Further Evolution of Human Nature* (Los Angeles: Jeremy P. Tarcher, 1992), especially chs. 11–23.

59. Whitehead, *Process and Reality*, 157.

60. Susan B. Armstrong, "The Rights of Nonhuman Beings: A Whiteheadian Study," Ph.D. Dissertation, Bryn Mawr College (University Microfilms: 1976), 84–85.

61. Griffin, "Parapsychology and Philosophy," 278.

62. John B. Cobb Jr., *The Structure of Christian Existence* (Philadelphia: Westminster, 1967), 8–9.

63. Whitehead, *Modes of Thought*, 5 (emphasis added).

64. Whitehead, *Religion in the Making* (Cleveland: World, 1964), 107.

65. Gary A. Kowalski provides some reports of dogs exhibiting fear of the uncanny in *The Souls of Animals* (Walpole, N.H.: Stillpoint, 1991).

66. Robert L. Morris, "The Use of Detectors for Out-of-Body Experiences," *Research in Parapsychology 1973*, ed. Wm. G. Roll, Robert L. Morris, and Joanna D. Morris (Metuchen, N.J.: 1974), 114–16. A few reports are recounted in Bayless, *Animal Ghosts*, 163–64.

67. Gaddis, *Strange World*, ch. 15.

68. Bayless, *Animal Ghosts*, ch. 11 and pp. 176–77.

69. John Sanford, *Soul Journey: A Jungian Analyst Looks at Reincarnation* (New York: Crossroad, 1991), 50–55.

70. Thomas Aquinas, "On Killing Living Things and the Duty to Love Irrational Creatures," in *Animal Rights and Human Obligations*, ed. Tom Regan and Peter Singer (Englewood Cliffs: Prentice-Hall, 1976), 118–121.

71. Keith Thomas, *Man and the Natural World: A History of the Modern Sensibility* (New York: Pantheon, 1983), 137.

72. Martin Luther, *Notes and Queries* 8.2.233, quoted in Dix Harwood, *Love for Animals and How it Developed in Great Britain* (New York, 1928), 145–46.

73. Harwood, *Love for Animals*, 138–40.

74. Thomas, *Man and the Natural World*, 181.

75. James Turner, *Reckoning with the Beast: Animals, Pain, and Humanity in the Victorian Mind* (Baltimore: Johns Hopkins University Press, 1980), 8. Turner demonstrates why compassion for animals was so socially significant in the nineteenth century. He also exhibits the beginnings of the ecological ethic in the 1870s.

76. John Hildrop, *Free Thoughts on the Brute Creation*, 2 vols. (London, 1742–43), 1:214.

77. David Hartley, *Observations on Man* (1749), 2.223; Soame Jenyns, *Works: A Free Inquiry into the Nature and Origin of Evil* (Dublin, 1790–91), 3.59–60; Richard Dean, *On the Future Life of Brutes*, 2 vols. (Manchester, 1767), 1:109.

78. Charles Bonnet, *Oeuvres d'histoire naturelle et de philosophie* (Neuchatel: Fauche, 1783), 8 vols.; "Essai de Psychologie," 8.106–7. I have relied on a translation by Dr. Frank Wood, Emeritus Professor of French, Humboldt State University. Bonnet is discussed in Hester Hastings, *Man and Beast in French Thought of the Eighteenth Century* (Baltimore: Johns Hopkins Press, 1936; New York: Johnson Reprint Corp., 1973), 55–57.

79. "The General Deliverance" and "The New Creation," *The Works of John Wesley*, vol. 6 (Grand Rapids, Mich.: Zondervan).

80. Thomas, *Man and the Natural World*, 140.

81. Andrew Linzey, *Christianity and the Rights of Animals* (New York: Crossroad, 1989), 37–38. Linzey presents a persuasive and well-documented argument for animal rights.

82. Ibid., 65–66.

83. Keith Ward, *Rational Theology and the Creativity of God* (New York: Pilgrim Press, 1992), 201–2.

84. Daniel Dombrowski, *Hartshorne and the Metaphysics of Animal Rights* (Albany : State University of New York Press, 1988), 84–85.

85. Linzey, *Christianity and the Rights of Animals*, 54–55.

86. *Gentre Magazine* and *Man/Nature/Animal*, trans. Piera Smith (January 1990).

87. Jeffrey G. Sobosan, *Bless the Beasts: A Spirituality of Animal Care* (New York: Crossroad, 1991), 63, 142.

88. See Armstrong, "Nonhuman Experience," for examples of the ability of some animals to use language, to deceive, to act virtuously, and to experience self-consciousness.

89. C. S. Lewis affirms not "mere compensation" but a new creation which will embrace at least some animals (those he considers to be conscious). However, animals can be immortal only through their association with human beings: only the domesticated animal is fully natural (C. S. Lewis, *The Problem of Pain* [New York: Macmillan, 1967], ch. 9). In a commentary on Lewis, Don Jennings suggests that animals could have a relation to God independently of human beings (Don Jennings, "Why Animal Pain?: Considerations in Theodicies," *Between the Species* 7, no. 4 (1991), 217–21.)

90. William James, "Human Immortality," in *The Will to Believe and Other Essays in Popular Philosophy* (New York: Dover, 1956), 39. In a recent essay on the death of a baby beluga whale, Brenda Peter describes her intuitive sense that the afterlife contains all species, that the "spirit-ark" carries all of us (Brenda Peters, "Beluga Baby," *New Age Journal*, April 1993, 84–7, 124–8).

91. Whitehead, *Process and Reality*, 347.

7

MEDICO-SCIENTIFIC ASSUMPTIONS REGARDING PARADEATH PHENOMENA: EXPLANATION OR OBFUSCATION?

Heather Botting

In a well-lit room in the terminal ward of a large hospital, an elderly man lies dying. His middle-aged daughter keeps vigil, sitting quietly at his side hour after hour, comforted by the look of serenity on his face. As she watches she yearns to communicate with her father, to feel what he feels. Gradually she becomes aware of faint wisps of mistiness which seem to emanate from her dying father's body. The mist rises in two faint columns, one from his solar plexus, the other from the back of his head. As she watches, the mist spreads to form a luminous cloud above his prone body, then gradually stretches out until it lies a meter above him. Slowly it takes on a recognizable form: the shape of her father's body.

The resident physician enters the room, at first an unwelcome presence. The woman asks if he, too, can see the misty image of her father suspended above his physical body. After a cursory glance, the doctor assures her that he can, and that the mist is not at all unusual. He has seen it before. It's just gas escaping from the dying body—nothing more.[1]

Several storeys down, in the hectic atmosphere of the emergency ward of the same hospital, lies a young woman who has just arrived by ambulance after being pulled, unconscious, from a nearby lake. Her breathing had been restored through the efforts of a fellow swimmer before the ambulance had even arrived to pick her up, but she is only now regaining consciousness. Apparently annoyed by trivial questions aimed at determining what caused her near-drowning, she brushes aside all such enquiries and tries desperately to tell the attendant medical staff about the wonderful experience upon which she had embarked at the very moment she had abandoned the struggle to escape the lake's cold depths. She speaks of being sucked down a warm, dark tunnel, then entering a bright light in which there was only peace, trust, and an unconditional love that words simply cannot express.[2] First her doctor, then the nurses assure her it was nothing. With conviction they tell her she was either dreaming or hallucinating. One nurse in particular seems upset by the young woman's account and, when no one else can hear, brusquely tells her to shut up. She then turns on her heel and stalks out of the room.

As the nurse, Mary, heads back to her station she recalls the humiliation she suffered less than two weeks ago when another patient had regained consciousness, eager to describe in detail not only the warm, loving light she had entered while comatose, but also the rather complicated medical procedures the staff had performed upon her to save her life. When the staff persisted in telling her she had been hallucinating, she snapped back: "I *saw* what happened! And one thing that happened was disgusting. That nurse—Mary, according to her name tag—the one with the dark bun and black rimmed glasses, took my urine-soaked clothes away while you were working on me, and threw them into a dryer without washing them first. Ask her, if you don't believe me!"[3]

They asked, and even as she drops her clipboard back on the desk, Mary blushes crimson and wonders once more how her comatose patient could possibly have known about the clothes. She'd said she'd *seen* it, but that was impossible. Then again, it was also impossible for her to have *seen* as she claimed she had, the various medical procedures the staff had performed in the process of resuscitating her. It was especially impossible that she could have seen the whole series of events from a vantage point well above the stretcher upon which she lay throughout. She couldn't have *seen* anything. The woman had been out cold the whole time, and was never near the laundry room!

When the parents of the victim of the near-drowning arrive, Mary escorts them to their daughter's room for a visit, then leaves quickly, determined not to hear as the young woman, in a mood of great excitement, begins to retell for her parents' benefit her tale of tunnels, bright lights, and love.

The young woman is determined that her parents should not only listen, but understand. The peace and the love she felt in the presence of a preternatural light were *not* dreams or hallucinations, she insists. They were more real than anything she has ever encountered in normal, waking life. Worried, her parents discuss the matter with their own family physician. He tells them that their daughter has come very close to death, and that when human beings come that close to death some purely physiological function in the brain is automatically activated to eliminate the fear of death. He explains that anoxia—a lack of oxygen to the brain—can cause temporal lobe disturbance in the brain. This disturbance in turn may trigger the release of large amounts of endorphins into the bloodstream.[4] An excess of endorphins in the body creates a sensation of extreme pleasure or euphoria. In short, the brain helps to ease the fear of death by causing the patient to hallucinate a sense of well-being which makes the process of death *seem* to be pleasant.

Later that evening, a man who has suffered cardiac and respiratory arrest emerges from his near-death experience in a state of throat-binding terror. Panic-stricken, he grasps his doctor's arm as he tries to explain that even though the doctor thought him to be unconscious during the heart attack, he wasn't. In fact, he was painfully aware of being trapped in a dark, barren landscape inhabited by horrifying zombie-like creatures from whom he sensed only a malignant hostility and imminent danger.[5] His doctor assures him that he has been near death, and in such circumstances it is not uncommon for anoxia—lack of oxygen to the brain—to generate frightening hallucinations. The doctor tells him not to worry.

But the patient does worry. Once, in his younger years, he did experience hallucinations while suffering from a very high fever. In his own mind, he is convinced—*knows*, in fact—that what he experienced at death's door was not an hallucination at all. It was starkly *real*. He begins to wonder: Perhaps the fever of years ago damaged his brain? Perhaps he is losing his sanity? Worse yet, what if there is a hell? What will happen when he *does* die . . . ?

By the time this man's wife is finally allowed to see him he has already determined never to speak of his experience to her or to anyone else ever again. He will keep to himself forever the horror of the moments he spent in another terrifying world while the medical staff worked to bring him back to the more familiar world of common sense and rationality.[6]

The decision to keep her experience to herself comes for the near-drowning victim only later that night after her parents have informed her bluntly that if she persists in talking about tunnels and lights and preternatural love, they will have her committed.[7]

Long after the near-drowning victim and the cardiac-arrest patient have fallen into their prescribed, drug-induced, hospital sleep, a woman in her nineties lies upstairs in the terminal ward surrounded by her surviving children, three of her grandchildren, and four of her great-grandchildren. She has been in a light coma for several days now, but in the last hour a rosy glow has suffused her pallid face, and she has regained full, lucid consciousness. After a brief chat with her youngest son, Andrew, she suddenly looks up and stares out over the heads of the family members gathered at the foot of her bed. The euphoric state she seems to have entered is almost palpable in the room when she smiles and exclaims:

"Oh, look Andrew! Your father has come for me!"
As one, the entire family follows her gaze outward and upward. They see nothing.
"And there's your Aunt Margaret, and your Uncle George." Her face softens and she smiles. "David's here, too," she whispers. Tears of joy form in her eyes as she apparently stares at the apparition of the son who died in his teens at Ypres during the fury of the First World War. "And young Kathy's with him!" she declares with a new burst of enthusiasm.

With this final comment the family members exchange several puzzled glances. An elderly woman might very well imagine seeing her *deceased* relatives, but why should she think she is seeing Kathy among the dead? They all know that Kathy, the dying woman's favorite great-grand daughter, is in the peak of health and very much alive. Just last week they had had a party to mark the end of her vacation, then bade her farewell at the airport as she left to resume her studies in Europe. Andrew wonders if his usually bright mother has finally succumbed to senility.

After reporting that several other family members or close friends who are known to be dead are waiting to escort her into the next world, the old woman sinks back onto her pillow, slowly closes her eyes, and dies—her face still etched with the ecstasy of her last moments.[8]

After the death certificate has been signed, Andrew quietly asks his mother's doctor about the events of those last, strange moments he spent by his mother's side. He explains that all the people she reported seeing were family members or friends who had died years before, except for Kathy, his young great-niece, who is alive and well and living in Paris. The doctor nods sagely at the mention of Kathy, then authoritatively dismisses the entire matter. Dying people often hallucinate, he assures the bereaved man. No doubt his elderly patient was having an hallucination about some long-hoped-for afterlife generated by her own wishful thinking and by her deeply held religious convictions. In her confusion she imagined that some of the living would be there to greet her as well. "Forget it," the doctor gently advises. "Go home and try to get some sleep."

As Andrew walks down the hall, he frowns. His mother was hardly a religious woman. She hadn't set foot in a church for years unless there was a wedding or funeral to attend. What's more, he'd never heard her express either hope or desire for being reunited with anyone in some imagined afterlife. And that business about Kathy . . . ? Perhaps it was just a confused hallucination as the doctor had assured him. Or had his mother been senile for some time? If so, had he himself been remiss as a son in not detecting her mental decline earlier . . . ?

Andrew has no way of knowing as he leaves the hospital that when he steps into his own apartment the telephone will be ringing. Soon he will be mourning the deaths of two loved ones, for when he lifts the receiver his distraught sister-in-law will inform him that earlier that day, while on her way to visit friends in Paris, Kathy lost control of her car and was killed in a head-on collision.[9]

The slice-of-life (or -death) scenes presented above are representative of several commonly reported paradeath experiences, in which I include the near-death experience reported by the living and the pre-death experience reported by the dying. The explanations offered by the respective doctors in each case are also representative of beliefs which circulate as common currency among medical staff and are passed on to patients and concerned families as either scientific fact or as scientifically plausible theory for which fact has yet to be clinically established. In each of the incidents described, medical authorities made assumptions that seemed to provide rational explanations for events which are normally considered to be beyond the expertise and the philosophical underpinnings of modern medicine; yet when considered in concert, such answers demonstrate a willful ignorance of such phenomena, and in some instances, a rather shocking lack of concern for basic scientific principles. What man or woman of science, for example, could convince himself or herself that gas escaping from the human body will sort itself out to form a visible, gaseous "replica" of a dying person? And even the most scientifically untutored hospital visitor knows that the back of the head and the solar plexus are hardly the normal routes that egress gas takes when quitting the human body.

The most common assumption evident in the above pericopes, however, is that so-called paranormal events occurring at or near death are products of a disturbed mind—or even more specifically, of a disturbed *brain*—and therefore have no objective, observable basis in what we commonly understand to be reality. "Hallucination," as a term signifying a delusion, a completely unfounded or mistaken impression or notion which is the result of brain dysfunction, provides a convenient and intellectually comfortable "file thirteen" for the reports of those who are dying or have had near-death experiences.

The label is comfortable to medical practitioners precisely because it posits the source of the paradeath experience firmly in the physical brain and thereby obviates any apparent need to consider the possibility suggested by the contents of such reports that the conscious human mind is capable of temporary disembodied existence—that is, not just conscious, but sentient existence outside of the physical body. To resort to "hallucination" as the answer to all reports of journeys to another world told by near-death experiencers allows those who choose to do so to sidestep the very uncomfortable and scientifically unfashionable extension of that notion; namely, that the mind, bereft of the brain, could possibly survive the total death of the brain and the physical body as a whole. Time and again, researchers reporting their findings state that the results of their work should not be interpreted in terms of supporting a belief in an afterlife, but the persistent repetition of the disclaimer speaks for the degree to which such a possible conclusion disturbs them.

Several possible causative factors have been proposed over the years, both to create and to sustain an aura of scientific rationality when dispensing the more scientifically acceptable idea of brain dysfunction as a explanation for paradeath experiences. The very fact that predeath and near-death experiences alike are most commonly associated with profound medical crisis has led to some speculation as to the role drugs, anoxia, anesthetics, disturbances in temporal lobe function, or any combination of these factors might play in the process. Appealing as such explanations initially appear to be (they sustain, after all, the idea of a purely physiological basis for the phenomena), they have over the years been tested and systematically eliminated as contributing factors in either initiating or enhancing paradeath experiences.

Inspired by his own work with dying patients in the 1950s, Karlis Osis conducted a survey in which 10,000 medical staff, including 2,000 general practitioners, 1,000 interns, 1,000 residents, 2,500 general duty nurses and 2,500 private duty nurses, were asked to respond to a questionnaire which focussed on the percentage and content of the experiences of dying patients who remained conscious into the final hour preceding death. Although only 640 of the questionnaires were returned, the results provided data respecting 35,540 patients.[10] As a result of this research, which was published in 1961, Osis determined that the presence of drugs in the dying actually appeared to *inhibit* rather than enhance the occurrence of a predeath experience. From this same body of data, Osis further concluded that high body temperature, a variable often associated with hallucinations, was also counterindicated as a contributing factor in predeath experiences.[11] Sixteen years later, in collaboration with E. Haraldsson, Osis presented additional data which indicated that anoxia, like drugs and body temperature, was a factor which tended to inhibit rather than enhance the likelihood of undergoing a predeath experience.[12] More recent research in the area of near-death studies has shown that fever, drugs, and anoxia are likewise counterindicated as initiators or enhancers of the near-death experience.

Despite the work of Haraldsson and Osis, drugs, fever, and anoxia remain favorite explanations for paradeath experiences. Given the manner in which writers of books published thirty years after Osis's *Deathbed Observations* still resort to such long-discredited answers to paradeath questions, one can speculate that Osis's work is being studiously ignored precisely because it does challenge the more comfortable if insupportable conclusions contemporary scientists in general and medical doctors in particular prefer. Those conclusions do not raise questions about the entire materialistic and mechanistic model upon which western science itself is based.

One of the most fundamental doctrines of Western medicine operative here is the conviction that life is nothing more than an epiphenomenon of purely physical processes. Life begins at conception (or at birth, depending upon personal perspective) and ends with physical death. Any human experience which challenges this notion is swiftly met with what Krister Stendahl has called the "fundamentalism of the unbeliever."[13]

Robert Kastenbaum gives full vent to this emotional form of response in his 1977 article, "Temptations from the Ever After." As a thanatologist with a genuine desire to help both the dying and their loved ones cope with death, Kastenbaum had for years worked to understand the psychological aspects of dying. He questions the significance of the fact that not all people who find themselves in near-death states report having near-death experiences. On its face this may seem to be a reasonable question, but in Kastenbaum's treatment, the issue is drenched in sarcasm. With reference to those who have no near-death tale to tell, he asks:

What? No out-of-body experience? No passage through a long, dark tunnel? No sense of euphoria? No magnificently mystical experience? Not a thing. I just slipped away, faded out—and then slipped back in again. What happened in between, I only know from what people told me. Say, Doc . . . I haven't disappointed you, have I?[14]

It becomes evident that Kastenbaum has at least two separate concerns: first, the common one that apparent near-death reports would seem to support belief in an afterlife (although it is not clear whether Kastenbaum is taking offense from a scientific perspective or a religious one); and second, the possibility that the final passage into death might be accompanied by pleasant experiences is an affront and a threat to his own professional work. He sweepingly accuses all of those associated with near-death studies of trivializing the suffering many people experience as they die. Yet surely, pioneer thanatologist Elisabeth Kübler-Ross and others who work with the dying are as keenly aware of the suffering as Kastenbaum is. Kastenbaum erroneously assumes that statements to the effect that death can be finally painless and pleasant are in some way intended to trivialize the agony many undergo in the months or years prior to death itself. Moreover, it is unclear whether Kastenbaum's greatest underlying concern is the suffering of the dying or the importance of his own role in alleviating that suffering:

> How long has it taken for society to appreciate both the emotional and physical distress of the terminally ill persons! How much effort has gone into promoting a new attitude! How difficult it remains in many situations to ensure that terminal illness does not result in alienation, abandonment and despair! Just at a moment in our culture's reevaluation of life and death that there is some authentic hope for helping the terminally ill person to live well and meaningfully, just at this moment we are blinded and distracted by beatific visions.
> The "happily, happily" theme threatens to draw attention away from the actual situations of the dying persons, their loved ones and their caregivers over the days, weeks and months preceding death.[15]

Although the motives underlying Kastenbaum's article remain unclear, he does manage, however unwittingly, to provide evidence against the theory that near-death experiences are the products of a physiologically based response by means of which the brain makes death seem pleasant. He does more to harm than to help this position when he asks why, if near-death experiences do speak of a life-after-death, everyone returning from a brush with death does not have a pleasant tale to tell. Why do some have either unpleasant experiences or no experience at all? In response, one must ask why, if the contents of near-death experiences really are simple, physiological functions of the brain intended to alleviate the anxiety and suffering of the dying individual, there are reports of visions of "hell" as well as of "heaven"? If the phenomenon is physiological, as in the case of the adrenalin surge which universally prepares the threatened individual for "flight or fight," why isn't the near-death experience universal among those in a near-death state? Why doesn't everyone who has a close encounter with death have not only a near-death experience, but a pleasant one at that? Ultimately, the absence of this kind of experience in 40 percent of near-death patients would appear to vitiate any argument in favor of an innate, physiological cause for the phenomenon in the remainder of the research population.

Moreover, neither brain function nor dysfunction can begin to explain predeath experiences such as that of the elderly woman apparently aware of her great-granddaughter's "crossing to the other side" and yearning to meet her there. In the first place, these kinds of visionary experiences are reported by terminal patients who are in a state of normal waking consciousness at the time of the experience. In particular, these individuals often report seeing dead friends or relatives waiting to receive them when they die. Osis and others have referred to such reported experiences as "peak-in-Darien events" after the final line in Keats' famous sonnet "On First Looking into Chapman's Homer."[16] During these visionary events, the patients are reported to be calm and exhibiting lucid thought patterns. Occasionally, one or more of the dead relatives reportedly appearing to the dying person are presumed by friends or relatives at the deathbed to be living. Upon investigation, however, it is discovered that everyone whom the dying reported "seeing" is indeed dead at the time of the vision.

Elisabeth Kübler-Ross, a pioneer thanatologist, recently added her own research findings on peak-in-Darien events to the growing list. In one of her cases, where the victims of a multiple-casualty traffic accident were taken to different hospitals, one young boy reported that "Mommy and Peter are already waiting for me."[17] The last official report Kübler-Ross and other medical staff had received was that although the boy's mother had in fact died, Peter was alive and being treated in the burn unit of another hospital. According to Kübler-Ross,

Since I was only collecting data, I accepted the boy's information and determined to look in on Peter. It was not necessary, however, because as I passed the nursing station there was a call from the other hospital to inform me that Peter had died a few minutes earlier.[18]

Incidents such as these serve to indicate that even though the individual is involved in the depths of medical crisis, the knowledge he expresses as a part of the content of his experience can in no way in every case be attributed to the side-effects of drugs, wishful thinking, hallucination, anoxia, or other brain dysfunction precipitated by the trauma or illness which brought on the crisis. These cases also clearly demonstrate that simple ESP functioning among the living cannot account for the dying person's knowledge of a death in the family to which no other members of the family in attendance at the deathbed are privy. If an individual in attendance at a deathbed is aware of a death in the family and withholds that information lest he or she upset their loved one, ESP may somehow account for the dying person's knowledge, and this has in fact been offered as a plausible "scientific" explanation for such knowledge. Yet it was not that long ago that the idea of ESP was itself vigorously debunked as the byproduct of pure imagination, wishful thinking, or simple coincidence.

Through the results of their painstaking research, parapsychologists were eventually able to demonstrate to the satisfaction of some scientists that some people in close proximity who were involved in a deliberate attempt to communicate information from mind to mind were able to succeed at a rate beyond that which could be anticipated by chance alone. Perhaps the fact that these experiments obviously involved only living subjects provided a measure of security in making the assumption that the events had a basis in physical reality. But note the incredible leap of apparent faith involved in translating the results of ESP experiments that are conducted under carefully controlled laboratory situations to account for spontaneous ESP events occurring across thousands of miles at moments just prior to the death of the receiving party. The latter-postulated ESP is far greater than the ESP data ever suggested or the most expansive theory of synchronicity ever entertained. To use ESP as a scientific explanation for such paradeath phenomena as peak-in-Darien events is to place it in the same category with the equally unscientific and unsatisfactory theory of the omnipotent, omnipresent ether of Wilhelm Reich. He also claimed that his mysterious, all-causative orgone was physically based and physically discoverable—even if he could never prove it.[19]

The use of terminology which has a scientific ring about it can provide the verbal trappings of scientific authority for the most unlikely candidates in a field of theories, granting them a respectability far beyond what the objective merits of those theories warrant. Technical terms have been coined for use in explaining ESP, describing it thus as a rational, physical process. But the gloss of scientific respectability such jargon affords is whisper-thin. The use of apparently scientific rubrics with respect to ESP, when offering it as an answer to the mysteries of life and death, certainly did little to impress Arthur Koestler. In *The Roots of Coincidence* he tersely commented: "That ESP should be transmitted by electro-magnetic waves is . . . a most unlikely hypothesis; and what a 'personal psi-plasma field' means is anybody's guess."[20] In any case, however ESP is transmitted, resorting to it as an explanation for peak-in-Darien events accomplishes little more than what Raymond Moody has referred to as "substituting one mystery for another."[21]

Clearly, the contemporary scientific community wishes to avoid the taint of mysterious ethers long associated with parlor seances and ectoplasmic extrusions. The desire to avoid such paranormal or pseudo-scientific explanations is almost invariably couched in terms of concern for scientific principles, but at a deeper level the resistance to give serious consideration of any kind to paranormal events is often more a matter of personal belief and expectation than scientific explanation. With reference to the manner in which the scientific community received the evidence for the reality of ESP, for example, Koestler remarked:

> Needless to say, a number of scientists maintain a hostile attitude, though they admit being impressed by the evidence. Perhaps the most bellicose among them is Professor [C. E. M.] Hansel, who recently made a sort of last-ditch stand on the conspiracy of fraud theory. Another psychologist wrote in the American journal *Science* that "not a thousand experiments with ten million trials and by a hundred separate investigators" could make him accept extra-sensory perception. In a similar vein the Professor of Psychology at McGill University, D. O. Hebb, a leading behaviorist, frankly declared that he rejected the evidence for telepathy, strong though it was, "because the idea does not make sense"—admitting that this rejection was "in the literal sense just prejudice." The mathematician Warren Weaver, the founder of modern communication theory, was equally sincere: "I find this [ESP] a subject that is so intellectually uncomfortable as to be almost painful."[22]

Although the disbelief, prejudice, discomfort, and pain expressed in the above quotation express the attitudes of some scientists toward

ESP in particular, they are generally evident in relation to any phenomenon which may be referred to as paranormal. The term *paranormal*, of course, has meaning only in relation to that which is defined as normal, and the definition of *normal* according to the contemporary scientific perspective is deeply rooted in the materialistic and mechanistic paradigm of earlier centuries. The most widely accepted definition of reality offered by normal science within the context of the contemporary, Western worldview rests firmly on the assumption that all reality is physical and, therefore, subject to measurement and objective verification. Paradeath experiences are generally assumed by scientists to be of a totally unobjective nature, and hence real only in the context of brain dysfunction. Yet many of the events common to paradeath experiences would seem to have a basis in objective reality. With reference to apparitions of the dead, Ian Currie noted:

> People do not take such experiences lightly. They are intensely vivid experiences, unforgettable, shocking, even terrifying. And they have happened to literally millions of people. They have been repeatedly studied, in the 1890s, 1930s, 1940s, and 1970s. They are a human universal, a recurring theme in the literature and folklore of all societies, and all ages.[23]

Scientific explanations for sightings of apparitions usually revolve around imagination, hallucination, and wish-fulfillment. But none of these factors can account for reports in which more than one person claims to have independently witnessed an apparition. As Currie succinctly noted, "although such cases are rare, they are important precisely because they cannot be hallucinations."[24] Hallucinations are strictly private events, which by definition cannot be shared. The following multiple-observer case, originally reported in *Proceedings for the Society for Psychical Research*, was quoted by Currie. It involved a terminally ill patient, Harriet Pearson, and three relatives who were caring for her:

> Harriet . . . slept in a large three-windowed bedroom over the drawing-room. The room behind was occupied by Mrs. Coppinger and myself. . . . On the night of December 22nd . . . Mrs. John Pearson was in [Harriet's] room, Mrs. Coppinger and myself in the back room; the house lighted up on the landings and staircases, our door wide open.
> About 1 or 2 a.m. on the morning of December 23rd, both Mrs. Coppinger and myself started up in bed; we were neither of

us sleeping, as we were watching every sound from the next room. We saw someone pass the door, short, wrapped up in an old shawl, a wig with three curls each side and an old black cap. Mrs. Coppinger called out, "Emma, get up, it is . . . Aunt Ann" [Harriet's dead sister]. I said, "So it is." We jumped up and Mrs. John Pearson came rushing out of the room and said, "That was . . . Aunt Ann. Where is she gone to?"[25]

According to the account cited by Currie, "Harriet Pearson died at 6 p.m. that day, but before she did, she too said that she had seen her dead sister, who had come for her."[26] Along with the synchronic, multiple-observer cases, there are a host of diachronic cases in which the same apparition has been seen and reported over a long period of time by individuals who know nothing of previous accounts of such apparent "hauntings."

In addition to the peak-in-Darien and multiple-observer cases of apparitions, one can add the phenomenon of apparitions of an individual the observer believes to be alive, where she learns only later that that individual died at approximately the same time as the appearance of his or her apparition. In these cases wish-fulfillment, imagination, and hallucination all seem to be unlikely causes. Even if they could account for the apparition itself, none of these possible explanations can account for the timing of the event. Given that ESP usually functions in the transfer of thoughts or images within the brain, it too is an unlikely candidate in such cases.

The propensity of many contemporary scientists in general and many medical doctors in particular to evade the issue of the significance of events reported to occur in paradeath experiences by making ambiguous statements about brain function or dysfunction was challenged most directly by Kenneth Ring, a professor of psychology at the University of Connecticut:

In this regard, I would like to advise any neurologically minded researcher interested in investigating this issue of one important constraint: Any adequate neurological explanation would have to be capable of showing how the *entire complex* of phenomena associated with the core experience (that is, the out-of-body state, paranormal knowledge, the tunnel, the golden light, the voice or presence, the appearance of the deceased relatives, beautiful vistas, and so forth) would be expected to occur in subjectively authentic fashion as a consequence of specific neurological events triggered by the approach of death. A neurological interpretation,

to be acceptable, should be able to provide a *comprehensive* explanation of *all* the various aspects of the core experience. Indeed, I
am tempted to argue that the burden of proof has now shifted to
those who wish to explain near-death experiences in this way.[27]

Ring's words apply equally to any investigation of events associated
with or analogous to those surrounding death.

The challenge put forth by Ring involves much more than a new
rigor in the application of the principles of scientific investigations in
research in the areas of paradeath phenomena, however. It may eventually involve the demolition of what Koestler has called "the greatest
superstition of our age—the materialistic clock-work universe of early-
nineteenth-century physics."[28] Commenting on the price paid for our
investment in and commitment to the clockwork universe of the indus-
trialized world, Caitlin Matthews wrote:

> Modern, Western society still carries the legacy of the Age of
> Reason which, aided and abetted by the Industrial Revolution,
> firmly banished all faeries, spirits and "irrational" states into a
> rationalist's oblivion. Most of us have consequently grown up to
> distrust that which we cannot see, to take faery and folk tales with
> a pinch of salt and to treat any personal impressions of comple-
> mentary reality as signs of hallucination, mental breakdown or
> incipient madness.[29]

The emotional quality of the response of the majority of the members of the traditional scientific community to any research in the area of
paranormal events suggests that the existing paradigm is, however,
suffering severe erosion and that we are already embroiled in a classic,
Kuhnian scientific revolution. That the erosion of the clockwork
paradigm has been in progress for some time was attested to by Sir
Cyril Burt in *The Scientist Speculates: An Anthology of Partly Baked Ideas*:

> As a theory of the relation of body and mind, [materialism] rests
> on a glaring inconsistency—In a purely mechanical world of cause
> and effect, ruled by the law of conservation of energy, no "phe-
> nomenon" . . . could possibly appear without some appropriate
> cause. Within the nervous system, therefore, so [it was] . . . sug-
> gested, energy must in some inexplicable fashion be "trans-
> formed" into consciousness. The chemistry of the brain must "gen-
> erate" it, much as the liver generates bile. How the motions of
> material particles could possibly "generate" this "insubstantial

pageant" remained a mystery. Any such process would obviously be, not physical, but psychophysical; so that the perfection of a purely physical universe was already rudely violated.[30]

In the name of explanation, members of the medico-scientific community have all too often resorted to obfuscation. In doing so they forsake the need to account for genuine human experience in order to shore up a model which is structurally unsuited to deal with any problem outside a controlled laboratory setting. Ultimately, however, the existing model cannot be sustained; for as surely as the evidence of a psychophysical process violates the perfection of a purely physical universe, the vision of a purely physical universe which runs according to the clockwork model violates the emotional and psychological well-being of those who have encountered paradeath phenomena. To be told that such events are the products of brain dysfunction leaves these individuals in a state of perpetual anxiety in which they come to fear for their own sanity. It is not only the experiencers who must deal with the labels of pathology, however. The sanity of those few scientists who do undertake serious research in paradeath studies is likewise questioned. Commenting on her own experiences in this regard, Kübler-Ross wrote:

> I have been criticized for "getting involved in spiritual matters," as some people put it, since I was trained in the "science" of medicine. Others, in reacting to a growing spiritual awareness on my part, have dismissed all my work and clearly stated that "Ross has become psychotic; she has seen too many dying children!" . . . I have been labeled, reviled, and otherwise denounced.[31]

Invectives such as those leveled against Kübler-Ross are to be expected when it is understood that the practitioners who work within the bounds of mechanistic theories such as the clockwork model of the universe and its social science handmaiden, the functionalist model of human society, begin with the premise that the master model itself is already essentially perfect. Persons or events who appear as anomalous when assessed against the model interrupt the regularity of the metronomic ticking of contemporary medico-scientific assumptions. The very proposition of such anomalies is an irritant, and naturally enough, any who claim actually to have experienced such phenomena are labeled deviant. If the model does not hold in all cases, it is regarded as being the fault of the deviants rather than that of the model. Since it is assumed that the model cannot be in error, the deviance of those who do not fit the model must be blamed on their own innate physiological defects or pathologies—a conclusion which brings not only blame but shame to those who are held personally responsible for their failure to comply with the model.

Resistance to changing the model is typical of all resistance to intellectual revolutions, once the current model is overwhelmed by perceived anomalies for which it cannot account. Neither the so-called deviants nor the few scientists committed to understanding the experiences of those anomalous individuals will abandon the search for a model which more accurately reflects an apprehended reality too large to fit the confines of the current, clockwork theory of the universe. Despite the obfuscation of members of the traditional scientific community, a new model is likely to emerge which will no longer regard today's "deviants" as pathological, since it will be capable of accommodating with fairness questions concerning dimensions of human experience, the true breadth and depth of which we are only now beginning to rediscover, let alone understand.

NOTES

1. Robert Crookall, *Events on the Threshold of the Afterlife* (Moradabad, India: Darshana International, 1967), 9. Also, Archie Matson, *Afterlife: Reports from the Threshold of Death*, originally published as *The Waiting World* (New York: Harper and Row, 1977), 14.

2. For a description of the "classic" near-death experience, see Raymond Moody, *Life After Life* (New York: Bantam, 1978), 21–23.

3. For the account of a similar incident see Barbara Harris, *Full Circle: The Near-Death Experience and Beyond* (New York: Simon and Schuster, 1990), 27.

4. Kenneth Ring, *Life at Death: A Scientific Investigation of the Near-Death Experience* (New York: Quill, 1982), 215ff.

5. P. M. H. Atwater, *Coming Back to Life: The After-Effects of the Near Death Experience* (New York: Dodd, Mead, 1988), 14. Also, Maurice Rawlings, *Beyond Death's Door . . .* (Nashville: Thomas Nelson, 1978 and London: Sheldon Press, 1979), 18–19.

6. For a lengthy treatment of "negative" near-death experiences see Rawlings, *Beyond Death's Door*. See also Atwater, *Coming Back to Life*.

7. Atwater, *Coming Back to Life*, 103.

8. Karlis Osis, *Deathbed Observations by Physicians and Nurses*, Parapsychological Monograph no. 5 (New York: Parapsychology Foundation, 1961), 16–17.

9. Ibid.

10. Ibid., 18–20.

11. Ibid., 26.

12. Ibid., 16–17.

13. Krister Stendahl, "Immortality," in *The End of Life*, ed. John Roslansky (New York: Fleet Academic Editions, 1973), 75.

14. Robert Kastenbaum, "Temptations from the Ever After," *Human Behavior*, September, 1977, 28.

15. Ibid., 32.

16. The following passage constitutes the final sestet of Keats' poem "On First Looking into Chapman's Homer":

> Then felt I like some watcher of the skies
> When a new planet swims into his ken;
> Or like stout Cortes when with eagle eyes
> He star'd at the Pacific—and all his men
> Look'd at each other with a wild surmise—
> Silent, upon a peak in Darien.

(*John Keats: Selected Poems and Letters*, ed. Douglas Bush [Boston: The Riverside Press; Cambridge: Houghton Mifflin, 1959], 18.)

Osis's explanation of the adoption of Keats's phrase to describe certain predeath experiences is outlined in *Deathbed Observations*, 16–17. On page 16, he explains that "Peak-in-Darien" was borrowed from Keats's sonnet in referring to the otherworldly visions of those in an antedeath state by earlier psychic researchers including Cobbe, Hyslop, Barrett, and Hart. He wrote: "This concept is based upon the belief that the spirits of dead relatives come to aid the dying and 'take them away to another world.' According to this view, the dying patients 'see' the spirits as apparitions in their sickrooms. These patients are not delirious, so the apparitions cannot be explained in this way. The 'Peak-in-Darien' explanation implies that dying persons 'see' only the dead. This belief that dead relatives come to take dying patients away is quite widespread and some patients may expect such an eventuality" (64).

17. Elisabeth Kübler-Ross, *On Children and Death* (New York: Macmillan, 1983), 210.

18. Ibid.

19. Richard Grossinger, *Planet Medicine: From Stone Age Shamanism to Post-Industrial Healing* (Berkeley, Calif.: North Atlantic Books, 1990), 283–89.

20. Arthur Koestler, *The Roots of Coincidence* (London: Picador, 1974), 18, originally published by Hutchison, 1972.

21. Moody, *Life After Life*, 174.

22. Koestler, *Roots of Coincidence*, 19.

23. Ian Currie, *You Cannot Die: The Incredible Findings of Research on Death* (New York: Hamlyn, 1978), 17.

24. Ibid., 119.

25. Ibid., 120. Originally presented in *Proceedings of the Society for Psychical Research* (1889), 6, 20.

26. Ibid.

27. Ring, *Life at Death*, 216.

28. Koestler, *Roots of Coincidence*, 79.

29. Caitlin Matthews, *The Celtic Book of the Dead* (Toronto: Stewart House, 1992), 10.

30. Sir Cyril Burt, *The Scientist Speculates: An Anthology of Partly Baked Ideas*, ed. I. J. Good (London, 1962), 34–35.

31. Kübler-Ross, *On Children and Death*, 206.

8

POSTMORTEM SURVIVAL: THE STATE OF THE DEBATE

Stephen E. Braude

INTRODUCTION

For more than two thousand years philosophers have speculated on the possibility and nature of postmortem survival, and for the most part they have recognized that the issue is not entirely empirical. In order to determine whether people (or other animals) survive bodily death, one must tackle notoriously difficult issues about personal identity and the very *concept* of survival. One must also confront difficult issues concerning the nature of explanation, because the best rival hypotheses may all be inherently (or at least practically) unfalsifiable, according to at least certain (and perhaps needlessly) strong criteria of falsifiability.

Nevertheless, research into postmortem survival has managed to progress. Since the founding of the (British) Society for Psychical Research in 1882, parapsychologists have compiled a massive body of data suggesting some form of personal survival. The case material covers ostensible apparitions of the dead and various haunting phenomena, as well as impressive reports of mediumistic communications and cases suggesting reincarnation. Many of these have been scrupulously investigated, and it is fair to say that we now have a substantial body of cases for which the hypotheses of malobservation, misreporting, and fraud are highly improbable and for which some sort of paranormal explanation seems unavoidable. In fact, there are now so many good cases that the main task for survival research is primarily one of interpretation. What needs to be done now is to choose among the best competing explanations of the evidence.

Unfortunately, that area of survival research has not been as successful as the gathering of interesting data. Quite apart from the venerable philosophical debates about the nature of identity and the concept of a person (which I will be unable to address here), survival researchers have stumbled over a different set of obstacles in their attempts to account for the evidence suggesting survival. I have discussed some of these in other writings, and accordingly I shall only summarize those points here. But because my earlier writings have provoked some interesting published responses, it might prove useful to examine the current state of the debate, as least as I see it.

I. WHAT'S WRONG WITH THE LITERATURE ON SURVIVAL

In my view, the literature on survival suffers from four outstanding defects. The first concerns the inadequate appraisals of alternate explanations in terms of psychic functioning (or *psi*) among the living. These have traditionally been called "super-psi" explanations, because in many cases one would have to posit psychic functioning that is apparently far more refined or extensive than what one ostensibly finds in controlled laboratory studies. Now I am not happy with the term *super-psi*, and it is likely that some of the problems plaguing the literature on survival can be traced to that unfortunate bit of terminology. For one thing, it is not clear that the psychic functioning required to counter survivalist hypotheses is any more impressive than what has been well documented *outside* the lab (Braude, 1986, 1989). For another, the term *super* is unclear and inappropriately evaluative. In fact, the term (perhaps unjustifiably) suggests that the degree of psychic functioning required is antecedently implausible. Hence, to many it suggests—right from the start—that the super-psi hypothesis should not be taken seriously. Despite these problems, however, I shall adhere to tradition and speak of the super-psi hypothesis as an alternative to explanations in terms of postmortem agency. I ask only that the reader keep the aforementioned caveats in mind.

The reason I have been underwhelmed by most discussions of the super-psi hypothesis is that, generally speaking, they underestimate the subtlety and force of that hypothesis. All too often, they set up a straw man by considering the hypothesis in an unacceptably weak or implausible form. For example, writers often rely on the indefensible assumption that if super-psi occurs, it will always be clearly identifiable and it will not simply blend in with or be masked by the extensive network of surrounding normal events. This is what is frequently behind the charge that there is no evidence for super-psi. But of course, there need be no *observable* difference between paranormally produced events and normal events (for example, a plane crash caused psychokineti-cally and one caused by normal engine failure). They may differ only with respect to their unobservable causal histories. Furthermore, we must be careful not to suppose that psychic functioning occurs in total isolation from the full range of ordinary human needs and organic capacities. It is more reasonable to suppose that psi plays some role in life, that it may be driven by our deepest needs and fears (rather than those of which we are immediately or consciously aware), and that it does not occur only when parapsychologists set out to look for it.

Moreover, the super-psi hypothesis in its strongest form is really a *motivated*-psi hypothesis; that is, it posits the operation of psychic abili-ties in the services of some agent's genuine or perceived real-life needs and interests. But in that case, we must also accept the possibility that our psychological interests may be best served when our psychic activ-ities remain covert, especially if our influence is extensive or if it raises intimidating issues of responsibility. Hence, in order to take the super-psi hypothesis seriously, one must accept (whether one likes it or not) that deeply motivated psychic functioning might be sneaky and naughty, and that its manifestations (like those of other organic capac-ities) could range from the dramatic and conspicuous to the mundane and inconspicuous. (See Braude [1989] for a more thorough discussion of this topic. And see Braude [1992a, 1992b] for a detailed discussion of super-psi explanations of survival.)

These sorts of issues have led some to complain that "nothing could count for the nonexistence of super-psi" (Almeder, 1992, 53), and hence that the hypothesis is empirically meaningless. I would agree only that super-psi explanations fail strict Popperian tests of falsifia-bility. But that is not the same as saying that nothing can count against those explanations. In this respect, super-psi explanations are like hum-drum—and perfectly acceptable—explanations of people's behavior in terms of needs, interests, motivations, etc., which likewise cannot be strictly falsified, but whose viability rests on a variety of pragmatic con-siderations. That is how we might properly prefer to explain Jones's behavior as an expression of his insecurity, rather than his unfriendli-ness or arrogance.

A related problem with discussions of the super-psi hypothesis, and in particular the charge that there is no evidence for either highly refined or wide-ranging psi, is the questionable assumption that such psychic functioning would be radically different from any for which we have good evidence. Usually, that assumption is linked to an inde-fensibly parochial attitude toward the evidence in parapsychology gen-erally, according to which the only evidence worth mentioning comes from laboratory studies. Nevertheless, I sympathize with Almeder's claim that "we need to have some independent empirical evidence . . . for the existence of super-psi in other contexts before we can appeal to it as a way of explaining . . . features of . . . alleged cases of reincarnation [or survival generally]" (Almeder, 1992, 53). But as I have argued at length elsewhere (especially Braude, 1986, 1989), although we may not have direct evidence for the exact phenomenon we are positing, there is a substantial body of direct evidence for what is at least pretty dandy psi (in particular, the evidence from physical mediumship), as well as indirect evidence from ostensible precognition and PK experiments with prerecorded targets. The latter body of evidence can be construed as evidence in favor of super-psi on the grounds that the next most plausible explanation requires positing a phenomenon even more deeply controversial—namely, backwards causation. And the former body of evidence, at the very least, shows that psychic functioning can operate on a level of magnitude and refinement far exceeding anything demonstrated unambiguously in laboratory experiments. That has to weaken the argument that psychic functioning is unlikely to operate at a higher level still. Besides, the evidence from physical mediumship is arguably as super as anything posited to explain the evidence for survival. After all, it is not as if there is a clear standard by which we measure how "super" a psi phenomenon is.

The second problem with the literature on survival concerns a matter of conceptual and empirical priority. Even the most superficial acquaintance with dissociative phenomena such as hypnosis and multiple personality reveals striking similarities to what one encounters in many cases of mediumship (or "channeling"). But all too often, writers on survival have an impoverished grasp of the literature on dissociation generally and multiple personality in particular. As a result, they frequently offer naive opinions about the nature of mediumship and the likelihood of dissociation in those cases as well as in cases of ostensible reincarnation. In a way, this deficiency in the literature on survival is quite surprising. It is simply premature to settle on an explanation of the best evidence for survival without a firm grounding in the experimental and clinical literature on dissociation. Indeed, that seems to be an obvious prerequisite for deciding whether (or in what respect) the behavior of mediums or subjects in reincarnation cases is distinct from other dramatic forms of dissociative behavior.

The third problem with the literature on survival is that it fails to address central issues about the nature and limits of human abilities. These arise, first of all, in connection with the varieties of dissociation, because in cases of hypnosis, multiple personality, and various forms of automatism, it appears that dissociation liberates or permits the development of abilities that would presumably not have manifested in normal waking states. Moreover, and perhaps even more relevantly, studies of savantism and prodigies suggest that people can manifest impressive abilities not only without practice, but even in the absence of other skills and capacities that we would normally expect to occur along side them. The importance of these cases is particularly evident in connection with the literature on responsive xenoglossy, and (more generally) evidence for survival suggesting the persistence of skills or abilities (Braude, 1992a, 1992b, 1993).

The fourth problem with the literature on survival is clearly related to the others, especially the last two. The problem is that authors who personally investigate cases tend not to probe beneath the psychological surface. As a result, subjects and relevant others appear to be mere psychological stick figures, as if they are little more than merely potential emitters of (or vehicles for) psychic functioning. This is a serious obstacle to evaluating any competing explanation (including super-psi explanations) in which needs and motivations play a role. To illustrate the seriousness of this problem, I have recently taken a fresh look at the famous case of Sharada, a case of ostensible reincarnation and responsive xenoglossy (see Akolkar, 1992; Stevenson, 1984). That study revealed that the woman manifesting an apparent previous personality may instead have suffered either a dissociative disorder or else some other serious psychological dysfunction, and that if any psi functioning is required at all to account for certain features of the case, it could plausibly be attributed either to her or to those with whom she was intimately involved (Braude, 1993). This reappraisal of the Sharada case can only strengthen the general suspicion that the more we know about the relevant figures in survival cases, the more feasible it will be to evaluate alternatives to the survival hypothesis. We may not be able to falsify those alternatives any more conclusively than everyday conjectures about beliefs, intentions, motivations, etc. (for which there can be perfectly good reasons to accept or reject). Nevertheless, it would be a significant advance in our study of survival to supplement the usual inquiries with depth-psychological investigations, because in most survival cases the weighing of rival hypotheses rests on a paucity of useful data.

Before examining recent responses to my published complaints about the literature on survival, it might prove useful to supplement those earlier discussions by considering some work I have not already singled out for criticism. The reason for this is not to pick on a specific author (or at least not to do so any more than I have already). Rather, I want to buttress my earlier contention that the preferred methodology in survival research is perniciously superficial. After that, we can consider the merits of recent objections to my views.

II. THE HYPOTHESIS OF PARENTAL INFLUENCE

Virtually all case studies of apparent survival are modeled after the work of Ian Stevenson (see, e.g., Stevenson, 1974a, 1974b, 1975, 1977, 1980, 1983, 1984, 1990). Although in many ways I consider that state of affairs to be unfortunate, the value of Stevenson's massive body of work should not be underestimated. For one thing, from a public relations or political point of view, Stevenson has probably done more than any other investigator to make survival research respectable within the academic community. That is not to say that his work has silenced all objections to the legitimacy of such research. But Stevenson's work has seemed so meticulous, thorough, and level-headed (or perhaps merely conservative) that many open-minded readers have been willing to take seriously what they might otherwise have dismissed both uncritically and disdainfully. Moreover, Stevenson has done much to help rule out what one might regard as the first wave of skeptical counterhypotheses—those positing normal or abnormal processes such as fraud, misreporting, malobservation, and cryptomnesia. Stevenson himself concedes that a second wave of counterhypotheses, positing various subconscious or unconscious motivations along with psi among the living, are more refractory.

It is not surprising, then, that other survival researchers have emulated Stevenson's methods and embraced his (usually tacit) assumptions about which issues matter (see, e.g., Haraldsson, 1991; Keil, 1991; Mills, 1989, 1990a, 1990b; Pasricha, 1990a, 1990b, 1992). I have noted elsewhere the respects in which I consider Stevenson's work to be critically superficial psychologically, even when he attempts to address the topic of his subjects' motivations (Braude, 1992a, 1992b, 1993), and I have very briefly lodged a similar complaint against his protege and occasional collaborator, Pasricha (Braude, 1992c). To illustrate further how profoundly unilluminating this general body of work is, I would like to consider a recent paper by Pasricha, which is characteristic of much of the literature on survival, and which at least appears to address a subtle psychological issue (Pasricha, 1992).

Pasricha proposes to consider the *hypothesis of parental influence*, according to which "parents may assign to, and even impose on a child the personality of a deceased person" (168), or (in other words) that "cases of the reincarnation type occur due to parental guidance of a child to speak or behave like a particular deceased person" (177). This hypothesis has been advanced by those who favor sociopsychological analyses of reincarnation cases over survivalist explanations. And although the hypothesis is not unreasonable, I sympathize with Pasricha's rejection of it. The problem, however, is that Pasricha's arguments are very unconvincing; indeed, they seem to miss the central issues.

On the surface, at least, Pasricha's consideration of the hypothesis of parental influence looks like an attempt to dig beneath the psychological surface of the evidence to address important issues of motivation. After all, if the hypothesis of parental influence is on the right track, the influence in question would presumably involve very subtle forms of manipulation and suggestion, perhaps carried out unconsciously by the parents. Otherwise (that is, if the parents consciously trained their children to act the part of a previous personality), the issue would be one of fraud rather than parental influence. To counter that hypothesis, then, one would have to address various deep issues concerning the motivation of the parents and the intricate and covert processes by which their desires would be conveyed to their children. But Pasricha never addresses these topics. She claims that the hypothesis of parental influence "presumes a detailed knowledge of such [reincarnation] cases and the deceased person on the part of the parents who are providing a model for the child" (168). For her, the two crucial issues to consider are (a) whether the subject's parents "know, or at least know about, the presumed previous personality and/or his family" and (b) whether they "know the details of the features of other cases" (177).

There are several problems with this position. First, even if it is true that the proposed parental influence would require knowledge concerning the deceased person, it is far from obvious that it requires detailed knowledge of other reincarnation cases. In fact, those details may be largely irrelevant to what really matters in such cases—namely, the personal meaning *behind* the detail. To put the point another way, there need be no lawlike connection between the importance to the parents of a reincarnation case in the family and the actual details of the case. In fact, in the absence of two critical pieces of information, we simply have no idea what particular features of a given case are likely to be important. These are (1) *why* the parents might want their child to behave as if he/she is the reincarnation of *some* previous personality or other, and (2) why it would be important for the parents to single out the specific previous personality whom their child appears to be. But

Pasricha and Stevenson apparently seldom (if ever) ask the sorts of questions that would elicit this information. Or, if they do, they apparently do not pursue those matters with the tenacity or attention to detail that characterizes their treatment of peripheral features of the cases. Certainly, these deeper issues fall outside the scope of their surveys.

Revealingly, the features of the cases Pasricha finds relevant and potentially important are likely to be quite trivial from the parents' point of view. These are, for example, the interval between the previous personality's death and the subject's birth, or whether the previous personality died violently or naturally, or the age at which the subject started (or stopped) speaking about a previous life. For that matter, not even the difference in caste level needs to be important to the parent. Although Pasricha recognizes that membership in a higher socioeconomic class provides "at least a motive for linking the subjects' family to that of the previous personality" (177), it is a mistake to think that the lack of evidence for such a link subverts the hypothesis of parental influence. There may simply be other details about a previous personality that matter more than socioeconomic status. Actually, it may be the mere *fact* of reincarnation, rather than any particular details, that matters to the parents. In general, what is most important in evaluating the hypothesis of parental influence is the personal significance attached by the parents to (or the parents' psychological investment in) their child claiming to have lived previously. And that kind of personal meaning may be wildly idiosyncratic from one case to the next.

A further example of the psychological superficiality (or naivete) of Pasricha's study is the following remark: "Another reason why it is unlikely that parents shape and guide the child's statements or behavior, is that in many cases . . . the previous life presented by a child is uncongenial and even annoying to the parents" (178). Apparently, Pasricha is assuming that parents in those cases would not consciously or unconsciously encourage annoying behavior in their children. Now perhaps some parents would never do such a thing. But one does not have to be mental health professional to recognize that this assumption is not true of parents generally. Hence, if Pasricha's argument is to carry any weight, she would have to show why specific parents in specific reincarnation cases have not been doing what most parents probably do at some time or another. Along the same lines, Pasricha counters the hypothesis of parental influence by arguing that "although Hindu parents of northern India almost all believe in reincarnation, most of them believe that a child who remembers a previous life will become ill and even die prematurely" (178). Here, her assumption is that the Hindu parents who have that belief would not want any harm to befall their children; hence, they would not (unconsciously) encourage their children to act as if they were a previous personality. But once again, one does not have to be a mental health professional to see what is wrong with Pasricha's assumption. People's unconscious wishes and actions often run contrary to their conscious desires, and parents *do* sometimes harbor death wishes against their offspring (just as children sometimes harbor death wishes against their parents). Moreover, these are truths about people generally, not rare or unusual individuals.

I must emphasize that my intent is not to single out Pasricha, or anyone in particular, for criticism. Pasricha's paper is characteristic of most of the empirical literature on survival in its psychological superficiality and attention to irrelevant detail. But it is important to grasp what sorts of irrelevant details most authors focus on, how they frequently display an astonishing degree of psychological naivete (especially in cases when the authors are psychologists or psychiatrists), and how they either ignore or simply do not understand the importance of depth-psychological probings into the *meaning* of the phenomena suggesting survival.

I should also emphasize that I direct these criticisms toward the literature on survival generally, not simply studies of ostensible reincarnation. On the whole, case studies of mediumship have likewise only skimmed the psychological surface. In fact, researchers would do well to heed some remarks made more than eighty years ago by Pierre Janet (Janet, 1907). Although Janet was focusing on mediumistic phenomena, his remarks apply, *mutatis mutandis*, to reincarnation cases as well.

> Even the phenomena that are apparently purely physical, incidents like raps or materializations always depend on the presence of a medium. *The investigation of these facts ought always to begin with the study of this particular person*, with an investigation that should exhibit his deceptions, his unconscious mistakes, and the nervous and mental conditions which accompany the phenomena.
>
> . . . we will doubtless find a rich field of psychological information when disentangling the mental condition of a medium, and also the singular mental condition of the believer who watches seances of the kind in an uncritical spirit. (86–87, emphasis added)

III. REPLIES TO CRITICS

In an earlier article (Braude, 1992a), I argued that defenders of survivalist theories have not dealt with super-psi counterhypotheses in sufficiently potent forms. That paper quickly inspired a couple of interesting replies. In one of them, Alexander Imich (1993) concedes that need-based super-psi hypotheses should be taken more seriously, but he counters that in reincarnation cases, the only relevant needs would be those of "the entity that has once lived" (94), not those of the subject, the subject's parents, or other living persons. Imich offers no argument to support this assertion, however, and I would allow only that the most *obvious* presumed needs would be those of the previous personality. My paper had argued for the importance of depth-psychological investigation of survival cases, of the sort begun in the Sharada case. And since that case shows clearly that relevant needs of living persons seem to emerge with a bit of probing, Imich's undefended assertion seems simply to be false. In fact, Imich may not be asking the right question when he wonders, "Who has a need to survive?" A more perspicuous and appropriate question might be, "Whose interests are served by the appearance of ostensible evidence for survival?"

Another interesting criticism was offered by James Deardorff (1992), who challenged defenders of super-psi counterhypotheses to explain "why the subject child's memories are those of a particular person viewed as if he or she were still that person" (291). He argues that propositional knowledge of the previous personality's life could just as well have been obtained paranormally "without simultaneously taking on the previous personality of the deceased person" (291). I agree with Deardorff that this is an interesting and potentially important datum. But in the absence of in-depth investigations into the lives and psychologies of relevant individuals in the case, we cannot assess the plausibility of various super-psi counterhypotheses. For example, if we learned that the parents reaped profound psychological benefits from their child appearing to be reincarnated (or the reincarnation of a specific individual), then we would have to consider the possibility of parental telepathic influence on the child. And before the reader protests that this kind of telepathy is implausible and without precedent, I would point out that such putative influence would presumably be similar to what both survivalists and antisurvivalists have posited to explain mediumistic trance-impersonations. The principal difference between the two explanations is whether the telepathic agents are alive. For example, antisurvivalists might argue that sitters at a seance are the agents, whereas survivalists would contend that the telepathic agents are postmortem surviving personalities.

Deardorff also asks why children in reincarnation cases don't exhibit a series of different personalities rather than just that of the previous personality. But I fail to see a problem here for the super-psi hypothesis. First, in a society believing in reincarnation of individuals *one at a time* and *one to a person*, the phenomena conform to cultural expectations. Possession phenomena, however, might take the form Deardorff suggests. But those phenomena might not fit comfortably into the prevailing belief system. And second, it is not difficult to imagine how a single reincarnated individual in the family might offer different—and possibly more profound—benefits to the family than random visitations by different previous personalities.

Deardorff also asks why the subject is "almost never born before the (past) personality has died" (291). Several points can be made in response to this question. First, as Deardorff admits, in some cases the previous personality has not died prior to that personality's reemergence. Ironically, that could be taken to support a hard-core *anti-*survivalist position, because it would suggest that all the evidence for reincarnation is constructed (presumably unconsciously) by living persons who simply blunder sometimes by selecting as a previous personality an individual who has not yet died. Second, defenders of the super-psi hypothesis are not obligated to give a general explanation of this feature of the evidence. A robust super-psi hypothesis has to be case-specific, tailored to the different psychological idiosyncracies of different cases. The most it can say with respect to the entire corpus of cases is that in the absence of a thorough inquiry into the lives of relevant individuals in a reincarnation case, we have no reason to rule out psi among the living as an explanation of the case's features. In fact, as long as the debate between survival and super-psi hypotheses remains at the level of generality apparently preferred by Deardorff, no solution will be found. That is why an avoidance of case-by-case specifics seems simply to be a refusal to take the super-psi hypothesis seriously.

IV. THE SIGNIFICANCE OF OBEs

Since the founding of the Society for Psychical Research, many have thought that out-of-body experiences (OBEs) might furnish a kind of indirect evidence for survival. The line of reasoning behind this position is roughly the following. Assuming that the evidence for OBEs is persuasive, and assuming that the evidence cannot be explained in terms of "ordinary" ESP, it shows that one's mental activity can literally *be* at locations different from those occupied by one's body. But that tends to support a strong Cartesian dualism, according to which a person's mental activity (or thinking self) is not identified with or causally dependent on bodily activity. And that presumably strengthens the case for survival, because survival requires that one's mental activity is neither identical with nor causally dependent on bodily states.

Recently, this position has been defended by two philosophers, Robert Almeder (Almeder, 1992) and Mark Woodhouse (Woodhouse, 1994). Moreover, they agree that the Osis/McCormick OBE experiment with Alex Tanous strengthens the case for survival (Osis and McCormick, 1980). That experiment had two very intriguing results. First, the subject (Tanous) identified remote targets that could be viewed only from a very specific location; and second, a strain-gauge detected physical perturbations at the spot where the subject's perceptual perspective seemed to be. It seems to me, however, that the case for survival gains very little support from OBEs and that the issues are more complex than Almeder and Woodhouse appreciate. Moreover, Almeder's rejection of the leading paranormal counterhypothesis seems to rest on a serious misconception about the evidence in parapsychology. Let us look, first, at that misconception.

Almeder considers the possibility that the Osis/McCormick data could be explained in terms of a combination of clairvoyance and psychokinesis (PK). Clairvoyance would explain the subject's ability to identify the targets, and PK would allegedly account for the strain-gauge readings. Almeder rejects the appeal to PK because "People do not produce effects consistent with action at a distance (or general PK) unless they have a deliberate intention to do so" (Almeder, 1992, 186). And he asks rhetorically, "what evidence do we have—either in the lab or outside—that this unintentional PK works *in a regular way* consistent with the data in the Osis-McCormick experiment?" (186). Although I commend Almeder for his open-mindedness with regard to the evidence for PK, this line of reasoning unfortunately betrays his unfamiliarity with the data. There is, in fact, an interesting body of evidence for unintentional PK, from both inside and outside the lab. Helmut Schmidt's PK experiments provide numerous examples of unintentional PK in laboratory experiments (see the summary of his work in Braude, 1979), and poltergeist cases as well as some cases of physical mediumship provide evidence from outside the lab (see Braude, 1986).

A deeper problem, however, is the assumption (shared by Almeder and Woodhouse) that the OBE evidence is radically discontinuous with the evidence for ESP generally and that OBEs are not simply a particularly vivid (or imagery-rich) form of veridical ESP. But that position requires more of a defense than those authors seem to realize, and a sober and thorough appraisal of the evidence for ESP suggests that it would be a difficult position to defend. To appreciate why, let us review some relevant theoretical and empirical matters about ESP.

First, assuming that ESP occurs, then whatever the fine details of its full analysis turn out to be, we can safely assert that it would be at least a two-stage process. The first stage would be a stimulus or interaction stage during which the subject interacts with a remote state of affairs, either another mental state (in the case of telepathy) or a physical state of affairs (in the case of clairvoyance). The next stage would be a response or manifestation stage during which the results of the first stage are expressed or experienced by the subject. Most parapsychologists now recognize that it is during this second stage that subjects would be able to impose their idiosyncratic dispositions and characteristics (or psychological "signatures") on the evidence. Their responses to the psychic stimulus would presumably pass through what we could imagine to be a psychological filtering system, consisting of the subjects' general conceptual framework, assumptions, and state of mind at the time. This is clearly analogous to the way in which different people experience the same event differently, according to their own psychological idiosyncracies, prevailing moods, needs, concerns, etc. And it seems to explain why many ESP experiments suggest that subjects filter or symbolically transform psychically acquired information in ways appropriate to their own distinctive needs and histories. For example, in one well-known dream-telepathy experiment, a target picture of an old rabbi was apparently converted by a Protestant subject into Christian or secular imagery (Braude, 1979, 138). In a similar way, subjects might impose distorted perspectives on information that in other respects seems accurate. For example, if the target image is a picture of a man in front of a fence, the subject might have an image of a man behind the fence (or behind bars). Or, if a small detail of the target picture is a coiled rope, images of rope might figure prominently (rather than peripherally) in the subject's experiences. Admittedly, there is a serious problem in free-response ESP tests in distinguishing partial hits from misses. But what seems clear is that ESP experiences, assuming they occur, are likely to be a cognitive cocktail of accurate information and confounding material generated by the subject. And what matters for the present discussion is that the subject's contribution in these cases might be to alter or provide the visual perspective from which the information is presented. Hence, in cases of apparent clairvoyance where no such perspectival distortions or alterations occur, it might look as if the subject was "at" the location experienced clairvoyantly.

Parapsychologists also recognize that some ESP subjects experience more vivid imagery than others and that ESP often seems to occur in the absence of imagery. In many reported cases of telepathy and clairvoyance, subjects seem to experience nothing more than inexplicable or incongruous desires to act (e.g., "I must phone so-and-so"). Hence, it appears that occurrences of ESP would be as idiosyncratically varied as other kinds of mental states, and that (as in the case of memories) some people's psychic experiences are regularly more detailed, vivid, and rich in imagery than others.

Hence, one would think that OBEs could plausibly be interpreted as imagery-rich manifestations of contemporaneous ESP activity, and that for some the information reported is accurate and perspective-specific, just as it seems to be in apparent cases of ESP *not* accompanied by experiences of leaving one's body. In that case, however, it is unclear why *any* case of veridical ESP (or OBE) requires the subject actually to leave the body.

Perhaps the underlying issue here is whether normal and paranormal perspectival forms of information-acquisition have to be formally similar—that is, whether paranormal awareness requires being at an appropriate location in the way normal visual perception does. The data of parapsychology suggest that the similarity does not hold. Consider, for example, the disanalogies between ESP of card faces in a sealed deck and visual perception of those card faces. So long as the deck is sealed, it is physically impossible for one to have a visual perception of (say) the 10th card down. But the absence of a location from which to view the card has apparently never been a barrier to identifying cards correctly in ESP tests. Moreover, although visual perception requires the reflection of light rays from the object perceived, ESP of a card face seems to depend on no analogous form of emanation from the card. In fact, if ESP of an object depended on emanations from that object, it would seem to be impossible to explain how ESP could be selective—for example, how one could identify correctly specific cards in a deck. After all, as C. D. Broad recognized (Broad, 1953), the relevant emanations from the card face would be part of much larger array of emanations: from the back of the card, from all the other cards in the deck, and (one would think) from everything else in the vicinity (and presumably from the whole universe). Similar issues arise in the case of subjects who correctly identify objects in sealed envelopes. Apparently, then, the familiar prerequisites to accurate visual perception do not require counterparts in the case of ESP. But in that case, there is no reason to think that veridical OBEs require a Cartesian dualist explanation. And that, clearly, undermines the significance of OBE reports with respect to the evidence for survival (see Braude, 1994, for further comments on this topic).

V. THE BIRTHMARK DATA

For quite a few years, Ian Stevenson has been collecting an interesting body of data that some think might clinch the case for reincarnation. Stevenson writes:

> Among 895 cases of children who claimed to remember a previous life (or who were thought by adults to have a previous life), birthmarks and/or birth defects attributed to the previous life were reported in 309 (35%) of the subjects. The birthmark or birth defect of the child was said to correspond to a wound (usually fatal) or other mark on the deceased person whose life the child said it remembered. (Stevenson, 1993, 404)

The full presentation of Stevenson's data has not yet appeared in print. Hence, the comments that follow will have to focus only on the tantalizing appetizer published in Stevenson (1993).

There is no doubt that Stevenson's data are interesting and they deserve a close examination. For example, in some cases the subject has birthmarks that correspond to entry and exit bullet wounds on a deceased individual, and the size of the two birthmarks likewise corresponds to the actual (and standard) difference in size between entry and exit wounds. This is not the place to consider whether the evidence is as clean and compelling as Stevenson suggests—for example, whether the correspondences are in fact as close and as unusual as he claims. What is at issue now is which explanation of the best data one should accept, assuming that the data are well authenticated and that they require at least a partially paranormal explanation. Hence, for present purposes, I prefer to focus on other aspects of Stevenson's initial presentation of the evidence. And what I find particularly striking is, first, how Stevenson dismisses super-psi counterexplanations, and second, how psychologically superficial Stevenson's conjectures become when he discusses how best to interpret the evidence.

For example, Stevenson considers, and then rejects, the claim that "reports of the child's statements and unusual behavior . . . [are] a parental fiction intended to account for the birthmark (or birth defect) in terms of culturally accepted belief in reincarnation" (412–13). He writes, "the parents (and other adults concerned in a case) have no need to invent and narrate details of a previous life in order to explain the child's lesion" (413). But one must ask here: What is the justification for this claim? Stevenson has shown no sign in his other investigations of probing beneath the psychological surface, and there is no reason to believe he has done so in these cases either. But then there is no reason to accept his assurances that adults in birthmark cases lack deep and inconspicuous motivations of the sort Stevenson rejects.

Stevenson does offer some brief remarks to support his claim, but they only fuel concern about the psychological superficiality of his investigations. He writes, "Believing in reincarnation, as most of [the parents] do, they are nearly always content to attribute the lesion to *some* event of a previous life without searching for a *particular* life with matching details" (413). Apparently, then, Stevenson believes that because the parents betray no conspicuous interest in identifying their child with a specific previous personality, one can conclude that they have no desire or reason to do so, and therefore that the parents played no role in forging or finding a match between the child and a specific deceased person.

But this position seems far too simplistic. Although the complete presentation of the evidence may indicate otherwise, it would appear that Stevenson does not take seriously the idea that people may be unaware of their motivations, either due to ignorance or self-deception. Clearly, there can be a big difference psychologically between (on the one hand) believing that your child is a reincarnation of *somebody or other* and (on the other) apparently having enough evidence to pick out the previous personality. Because in the latter case the child's odd behavior seems actually to be explained by its connection to a real, but deceased, individual, it suggests strongly—and not simply vaguely— that the ostensible reincarnation is genuine. The child's parents, then, would presumably feel an additional and substantial degree of confidence or conviction from discovering the apparently quite specific connection to a previous personality. But of course, this discovery is maximally compelling only when the parents feel they played no role in actually shaping the case and arranging the data (just as those with a psychological investment in feeling victimized must cultivate ignorance of their role in setting themselves up for being victimized). Hence, if the parents' motivations for identifying their child with a previous personality were either obvious or conscious, the match with the previous personality would be less convincing to them and it would lose much of its psychological utility. This may be especially important if the parent has any latent concerns, guilt, or shame (say, about possible responsibility) for the child's ugly birthmarks or deformities.

Moreover, that kind of concern or guilt may clearly override the relatively superficial worry about the social status or less-than-admirable character of the previous personality. It is disappointing, then, that Stevenson merely offers a relatively common and indefensibly glib observation about the undesirability of identifying oneself or one's child with an individual of a lower social class. He writes, "Few parents would impose an identification with such persons on their children" (413). One should not have to point out, at this relatively advanced stage in the literature on survival, that parents have many (and often conflicting) needs and interests, some of which may be far more important than the apparent identification of their child with someone they would not wish to be themselves.

Then, when discussing the possibility that the children (Stevenson should have added: parents) might have used ESP to obtain information about a previous personality, he offers a rebuttal that he also should know is weak and irrelevant—namely, that the "children subjects of these cases . . . never show paranormal powers of the magnitude required to explain the apparent memories in contexts outside of their seeming memories" (414). But, as many have observed, if psychic functioning is situation-sensitive and need-dependent (as it seems to be and as is plausible to assert in any case), this is presumably just what one would expect. Stevenson simply glosses over what are well-known and quite complex issues about how psychic functioning would actually manifest in real-life contexts.

Still, in the absence of alternative conjectures about how a super-psi explanation might work in the birthmark cases, the above considerations are merely abstract speculations. Let us consider, then, how to formulate a kind of explanation-template for at least some (probably many) of those cases. But I remind the reader that alternative super-psi explanations can best be formulated only on a case-by-case basis, and only after enough psychological probing to allow for an assessment of the conjectured motivations, needs, etc. What follows, then, should not be construed as a genuine explanation of the data. Rather, it is more of a general strategy to follow once more intimate details of the individual cases become known.

There are two general versions of super-psi explanations for the birthmark evidence. The first version looks to the subject's family for the living psi agent, and the second posits an agent in the family of the previous personality. According to the first version, after the subject (S) is born with one or more birthmarks or deformities, some member of S's family psychically finds an individual whose death provides the appropriate correspondences, and the child's subsequent behaviors (apparent memories, etc.) would be explained in terms of telepathic influence. According to the second version, some members of the previous personalty's (PP) family is vitally (though perhaps unconsciously) interested in having PP reincarnated—for example, to reveal the murder

194   STEPHEN E. BRAUDE

that family committed, or to relieve the grief of *PP*'s death. That person psychically finds an infant born with appropriate birthmarks, and the child's subsequent behavior would be explained in terms of telepathic influence.

I realize that many will balk at the apparent magnitude and refinement of psychic functioning posited here. But I remind the reader that the required degree of psychic snooping is no more extreme than what is plausible in many other cases (e.g., ostensible precognition and Schmidt-type experiments with prerecorded targets). Moreover, there is independent evidence for telepathic influence, although perhaps not of the same degree.

VI. CONCLUSION

I think it is safe to conclude at this point that the literature on survival provides additional evidence for paranormal goings-on of some sort, and it also provides a wealth of evidence of extraordinary (but not paranormal) cognitive functioning continuous with the still poorly understood evidence concerning savants, prodigies, and exceptional performances under dissociative and other altered states. But given the unsophisticated and superficial attempts to meet the challenge posed by the super-psi hypothesis, it is simply premature to conclude that even the best cases provide good evidence for postmortem survival. I would suggest that parapsychological investigations of survival cases—and indeed, of cases *not* suggesting survival—be conducted with an eye to discerning as much as possible about underlying psychodynamics, and that this aspect of case investigations be given the same attention currently lavished on questions of authenticity. In order for the super-psi hypothesis to be evaluated properly in cases suggesting survival, investigators need to be clearer about why and to what extent people seem to use their psychic abilities in other cases. The evidence for survival is only part of the total body of evidence in parapsychology, and the parapsychological evidence is but part of the larger tapestry of psychology (and probably of psychopathology).

REFERENCES

Akolkar, V. V. (1992). "Search for Sharada: Report of a Case and Its Investigation." *Journal of the American Society for Psychical Research* 86, 209–247.

Almeder, R. (1992). *Death and Personal Survival*. Lanham, Md.: Rowman and Littlefield.

Braude, S. E. (1979). *ESP and Psychokinesis: A Philosophical Examination*. Philadelphia: Temple University Press.

———. (1986). *The Limits of Influence: Psychokinesis and the Philosophy of Science*. New York: Routledge and Kegan Paul.

———. (1989). "Evaluating the Super-Psi Hypothesis." In G. K. Zollschan, J. F. Schumaker, and G. F. Walsh, eds., *Exploring the Paranormal: Perspectives On Belief and Experience*. Dorset: Prism, 25–38.

———. (1992a). "Survival or Super-Psi?" *Journal of Scientific Exploration* 6, 127–44.

———. (1992b). "Reply to Stevenson." *Journal of Scientific Exploration* 6, 151–56.

———. (1992c). "Review of S. Pasricha, *Claims of Reincarnation: An Empirical Study of Cases in India*." *Journal of Parapsychology* 56, 380–84.

———. (1993). "Dissociation and Survival: A Reappraisal of the Evidence." Paper presented at 40th International Conference of the Parapsychology Foundation, Boston, 6 Nov.

———. (1994). "Does Awareness Require a Location?: A Response to Woodhouse." *New Ideas in Psychology* 12, 17–21.

Broad, C.D. (1953). *Religion, Philosophy and Psychical Research*. London: Routledge and Kegan Paul.

Deardorff, J. (1992). "Comments On Survival or Super-Psi?" *Journal of Scientific Exploration* 6, 291.

Haraldsson, E. (1991). "Children Claiming Past-Life Memories: Four Cases in Sri Lanka." *Journal of Scientific Exploration* 5, 233–61.

Imich, A. (1993). "Super-Psi or Reincarnation?" *Journal of Scientific Exploration* 7, 94–95.

Janet, P. (1907). "Letter of Dr. Pierre Janet." *Journal of the American Society for Psychical Research* 1, 73–93.

Keil, J. (1991). "New Cases in Burma, Thailand, and Turkey: A Limited Field Study Replication of Some Aspects of Ian Stevenson"s Research." *Journal of Scientific Exploration* 5, 27–59.

Mills, A. (1989). "A Replication Study: Three Cases of Children in Northern India Who Are Said to Remember a Previous Life." *Journal of Scientific Exploration* 3, 133–84.

———. (1990a). "Moslem Cases of the Reincarnation Type in Northern India: A Test of the Hypothesis of Imposed Identification Part I: Analysis of 26 Cases." *Journal of Scientific Exploration* 4, 171–88.

————. (1990b). "Moslem Cases of the Reincarnation Type in Northern India: A Test of the Hypothesis of Imposed Identification Part II: Reports of Three Cases." *Journal of Scientific Exploration* 4, 189–202.

Osis, K., and McCormick, D. (1980). "Kinetic Effects At the Ostensible Location of an Out-Of-Body Projection During Perceptual Testing." *Journal of the American Society for Psychical Research* 74, 319–29.

Pasricha, S. (1990a). *Claims of Reincarnation: An Empirical Study of Cases in India.* New Delhi: Harman.

————. (1990b). "Three Conjectured Features of Reincarnation-Type Cases in Northern India." *Journal of the American Society for Psychical Research* 84, 227–33.

————. (1992). "Are Reincarnation Type Cases Shaped By Parental Guidance? An Empirical Study Concerning the Limits of Parents' Influence On Children." *Journal of Scientific Exploration* 6, 167–80.

Stevenson, I. (1974a). *Twenty Cases Suggestive of Reincarnation,* 2d ed. rev. Charlottesville: University Press of Virginia.

————. (1974b). *Xenoglossy: A Review and Report of a Case.* Charlottesville: University Press of Virginia.

————. (1975). *Cases of the Reincarnation Type.* Vol. 1. *Ten Cases in India.* Charlottesville: University Press of Virginia.

————. (1977). *Cases of the Reincarnation Type.* Vol. 2. *Ten Cases in Sri Lanka.* Charlottesville: University Press of Virginia.

————. (1980). *Cases of the Reincarnation Type.* Vol. 3. *Twelve Cases in Lebanon and Turkey.* Charlottesville: University Press of Virginia.

————. (1983). *Cases of the Reincarnation Type.* Vol. 4. *Twelve Cases in Thailand and Burma.* Charlottesville: University Press of Virginia.

————. (1984). *Unlearned Language: New Studies in Xenoglossy.* Charlottesville: University Press of Virginia.

————. (1990). "Phobias in Children Who Claim to Remember Previous Lives." *Journal of Scientific Exploration* 4, 243–54.

————. (1993). "Birthmarks and Birth Defects Corresponding to Wounds On Deceased Persons." *Journal of Scientific Exploration* 7, 403–16.

Woodhouse, M. B. (1994). "Out-Of-Body Experiences and the Mind-Body Problem." *New Ideas in Psychology* 12, 1–16.

9

MORALITY AND PARAPSYCHOLOGY

James R. Horne

This chapter is not about a subdivision of professional ethics, such as medical ethics or business ethics. Instead, it deals with a topic that is preliminary to such studies, the assumption that the activity or profession in question is itself moral. This assumption is usually justified, but we should be aware of it and on occasion should discuss it. There are, after all, activities that cannot be part of the moral life. Aristotle tells us that some actions and passions cannot be done in accordance with a mean.[1] The Buddhist eight-fold path to salvation, with its fifth requirement that one choose the right means of livelihood, accepts that some occupations (such as theft) are so immoral that they must be avoided altogether.[2] In a contemporary version, this theme appears as a question about "practices." Alasdair MacIntyre says: "By a 'practice' I am going to mean any coherent and complex form of socially established cooperative human activity through which goods internal to that form of activity are realized in the course of trying to achieve those standards of excellence which are appropriate to, and partially definitive of, that form of activity, with the result that human powers to achieve excellence, and human conceptions of the ends and goods involved, are systematically extended."[3] Some of his examples are architecture, farming, physics, music, and football, and he specifies that bricklaying and tic-tac-toe (among other activities) are not practices.

There is a certain amount of individual judgment involved in identifying practices (one wonders what bricklayers would think of MacIntyre's categorization of them), but the concept is useful. Practices are activities (often professions) which produce goods, some intrinsic to the activity and some products of it. These goods range from inspiring examples of human achievement (as in sports) to the more concrete products of technologies. A given participant in a practice might fail to produce its goods, but the practice itself would still be such that it should be accepted or even encouraged for the goods that are intrinsic to it. MacIntyre also admits that practices may occasionally produce evils, as when a person passionately devoted to the practice of an art neglects his or her family. In fact, he even entertains the remote possibility that somehow, somewhere, a society could support a practice that was, on balance, evil.[4]

In spite of these concessions, which appear to reflect his resolve not to rule out possibilities with a priori stipulations, MacIntyre clearly intends that for all practical purposes we should think of practices as good activities. They are distinguished from bad conduct, and from more marginal activities whose status as practices (and therefore as moral undertakings) is in question. In our society parapsychology is surely one of the latter activities, and in discussing its status I am not concerned with moral conduct within it, since I assume that it would be very much like responsible conduct in any field of inquiry. The nature of morality is also not an issue in this discussion, in which we assume that morality is known by good people of common sense, ourselves included. With respect to parapsychology these working assumptions are justified by our virtually unanimous agreement in identifying fraud and respectability in both subjects and researchers. Of course some might say that anyone involved in parapsychology is morally suspect, but they would thereby raise this paper's subject, which is whether parapsychology itself is moral. Is it a cooperative human activity that tends to produce and extend human good, or does it tend to do the opposite? Is it or is it not what MacIntyre terms a "practice"?

Many criticisms of it imply that it is not. In addition to misgivings about experimental controls and other technical problems, they often convey a tone of moral disapproval. This has been accepted as part of the literature, but as far as I know the specific nature of the moral suspicions that are enfolded within the technical criticisms, the reasons for them, and whether they are justified, have not been articulated and discussed. Therefore I will attempt to state those moral concerns explicitly, and to suggest some tentative answers to them.

I find that the moral charges against parapsychology are of three distinct kinds. The first states that parapsychology is wrong because it is a waste of human resources. The second says that parapsychologists not only make intellectual errors, but should be morally condemned for doing so. That is, parapsychologists are not only fools, but culpable fools. The third holds that parapsychology is an activity such that one engaging in it as experimenter or subject is exceptionally liable to moral corruption. This third accusation occurs in two variations: a scientific one contending that requirements for success in the field predispose both subjects and experimenters to carelessness or fraud, and a religious variation saying that paranormal powers themselves place subjects and experimenters in grievous moral danger. The religious accusation again branches into a traditional interpretation of the dangers as demonic and a liberal interpretation of them as psychological. Let us consider these accusations in the order stated.

The first is clearly implied in many critical discussions, such as that in which George O. Abell says that (considering fees, books, and so on), "Americans spend billions of dollars each year on astrology. . . . With such enormous stakes at issue, astrology deserves close scrutiny."[5] The same concern for resources is evident in Isaac Asimov's introduction to James Randi's *Flim-Flam*, a book devoted to disproving all claims to paranormal powers. Asimov praises Randi's exposures of "knaves and rascals" because he believes that "folly and fakery" is very dangerous when (in 1982) there is an energy crisis. Such pressing problems can be solved, he says, only by science and technology. We must, as Randi does, expose and condemn those who would have us entertain unscientific beliefs or adopt unrealistic methods. Such people are wasting resources that we cannot afford to lose.[6] The psychologist Edward Girden implies the same thing more temperately in his magisterial assessment of the history and accomplishments of parapsychology. Having summarized parapsychology's theoretical and experimental difficulties, he warns:

> As . . . bad money drives out good money, it would appear that bad science drives out good science. Perhaps it is time that the establishment stop leaning over backward in attempting to demonstrate fairness; additional bends, and the cost to science may be enormous before necessary correctives are introduced.[7]

Such passages imply that parapsychologists are failing to meet two moral obligations. First, they should get on with solving humanity's problems while foregoing impractical hopes and pursuits. Second, they should employ reliable technical and scientific means to maximize results. We can hardly quarrel with these injunctions. Why would we not want to solve human problems using the best means available? Nevertheless, in the vehemence of Asimov in particular there is a crusading tone that is jarring. Perhaps the extreme enthusiasm of such true belief should be resisted a little.

First, a preliminary argument can be interposed. Although Asimov does mention the misuses of science, we can still remark that the methodology that brought us thalidomide and Chernobyl should be treated cautiously. If we blame parapsychology for its lack of results, may we not blame the sciences for certain of their overabundant results? Of course, advocates of science can reply with perfect truth that science's disasters are due to human error and perversity, and not to scientific method. However, parapsychology's defender can then respond with another *tu quoque*, to the effect that if human vice and error are not the fault of science and technology, they are also not the fault of parapsychology. Of course, this argument is embarrassingly trivial, deployed only for the *tu quoque*'s usual purpose of neutralizing an unfair preliminary accusation. Obviously sciences can produce well-defined, concrete goods and evils, often of great magnitude, and just as obviously parapsychology produces goods and evils (such as apparent precognitions, which we do not always want) that are psychological in character and are so ambiguously defined that there is disagreement about their magnitude and their very existence. But knowing these things is not of much use in deciding whether parapsychology is a moral practice.

Asimov's more serious argument is that parapsychology is a waste of time and resources that could be better used in solving pressing human problems. This argument has some force, and it is best answered by considering how much of our time and energy we should devote to obviously practical good works. The best answer is that although we may experience a constant obligation to work for human welfare, quixotic attempts to do so without interruption are, for various practical reasons, less effective than a mixed life. John Stuart Mill himself, discussing whether the Utilitarian standard is "too high for humanity," says that "ninety-nine hundreths" of our actions are (quite properly) not done from duty.[8] As ingredients of the good life he lists simple enjoyments, benevolence, problem-solving of various kinds, and leisurely pursuits, saying, "A cultivated mind . . . finds sources of inexhaustible interest in all that surrounds it: in the objects of nature, the achievements of art, the imaginations of poetry, the incidents of history, the ways of mankind, past and present, and their prospects in the future."[9] This wise prescription would surely allow good persons to satisfy their curiosity by engaging in apparently unproductive investigations of paranormal "ways of mankind," if such investigations were part of a balanced moral life.

Of course, parapsychology can be part of such a life only if it is a respectable activity like farming or football. To decide whether it is, let us turn to the second and third moral criticisms of it, noting that the second focuses on the character of the parapsychologist and the third on parapsychology itself. However, we must first observe that both presuppose a correlation between parapsychology and the incidence of immorality. It is not clear whether critics think that immorality produces parapsychology or parapsychology produces immorality, but we must examine this supposed correlation before we go on to the criticisms themselves.

As a matter of fact the assumed correlation is not as obvious as it seems. The founders of parapsychology in both Britain and America were people of very good character who conducted their investigations conscientiously.[10] We need not exaggerate the goodness of scholars like Henry Sidgwick and his colleagues, but we are justified in judging them to have been responsible and honest. Of course, those qualities are not enough to guarantee that investigators will produce warranted scientific truth. We are properly critical of the methodology of the early Cambridge group, remembering particularly their loosely structured sessions with mediums and their use of anecdotal evidence. Yet we also know that they were willing to accept criticism and worked to improve their investigative techniques. Even the thoroughly skeptical C. E. M. Hansel, who points out experimenter fraud where it has been proven, does not argue that these parapsychologists, or indeed the greater part of their twentieth-century successors, cheated in any way. Rather, he criticizes experimental designs that could have allowed subjects or experimenters to cheat. Hansel's point is that the results of such experiments have to be discarded, regardless of the experimenters' moral rectitude. He is right, of course, although there continues to be dispute about some of the "flaws" he points out.[11]

Still, in spite of the experimenters' good characters, there is a persisting impression that parapsychologists are likely to be frauds, and we wonder why. Why does James E. Alcock, for example, say, "There have been numerous cases of demonstrated fraud in parapsychology"?[12] Is it because the demonstrated frauds were so impressive? Certainly, they do not occur in impressive numbers. The most famous are W. J. Levy, director of Rhine's laboratory, who was caught tampering with his apparatus,[13] and the English parapsychologist S. G. Soal who was judged to have altered target sheets in his most important experiment.[14] These two famous incidents are regularly used to support phrases such as Asimov's "folly and fakery," and Flew's "endemic fraud problems of parapsychology."[15] However, the fact is that most parapsychologists have not been accused of fraud, but rather of designing and conducting experiments that *permit* it. As Alcock explains: "Hansel examined the 'conclusive experiments' upon which the case for ESP seemed to be most solidly based, and in each case found that cheating and trickery were at least *possible* given the experimental set-up."[16]

Thus, Flew's use of "endemic" could not imply that a large proportion of parapsychologists have been proven fraudulent. McDougall, Murphy, Krippner, Rhine, Schmeidler, and others have had their methods and interpretations criticized, but not their personal morality. Also relevant are the rather dull statistical results they report, which are more like those of scientists making honest contributions than of charlatans seeking fame and fortune. For example, Hansel discusses a series of experiments conducted by Pratt and Woodruff at Rhine's Psychology Laboratory, in which 32 subjects attempting to read Zener cards clairvoyantly undertook 2,400 runs of 25 cards each. Their average number of correct readings per run of 25 should have been close to 5, and was in fact 5.204. This result, which might strike a layman as unsurprising, impresses statisticians as far above chance expectation. Yet, one can hardly imagine charlatans using such a figure to attempt to impress people.[17]

Thus, if with fraud in mind we compare parapsychologists with conventional scientists, we find a surprising resemblance. In both communities most experimenters are apparently hardworking, respectable, and honest, although both communities have been embarrassed by striking cases of fraud. In the conventional sciences, for example, there have been the Piltdown Man fraud, Cyril Burt's fabrication of evidence about identical twins, and Gregor Mendel's support of his theory of heredity with highly improbable data. Most interesting, because it included replication, was the "N-Ray Scandal" of 1903, in which René Blandot's spurious "discovery" of rays with peculiar penetrating powers was confirmed by other scientists over a period of two years. (Still, like the recent "cold fusion," N-rays may be a case of error rather than fraud.)

Less spectacular than these famous cases, but perhaps of broader significance, was a "Comment" published in the journal *American Psychologist* in 1962. In it Leroy Wolins reported that a graduate student gathering information for a master's thesis wrote to thirty-seven authors of recent journal articles, asking for their raw data. Thirty-two of them replied, twenty-one saying that they could not find or had accidentally destroyed their data. Two more refused to release it unless they had complete control over its use. Of the remaining nine who sent their data, three were found to have made gross errors in computation or statistical procedures, of such a nature as to render their results worthless.[18]

My intention in citing the foregoing scandals and intimations of cheating or carelessness is not to put established sciences or their achievements in disrepute. Rather, the point is that, human nature being what it is, fraudulent or flawed research is a possibility in any science. Its incidence in parapsychology may not be very different from what goes on in other sciences.

Still, even a sympathetic writer must admit that the strong impression of "an endemic problem of fraud" will not go away. One possible explanation for parapsychology's bad reputation is that investigators in the field have frequently kept bad company. Mediums, fortune tellers, and others whom parapsychologists study do very frequently turn out to be frauds. Furthermore, some of these doubtful characters (ironically termed "miracle men" by Hansel) are popularly identified as parapsychologists, sometimes because they claim to be, and sometimes because critics like Randi expose them in the course of discrediting parapsychologists' research, and thus appear to include them in the company of parapsychologists. (Randi generally characterizes parapsychologists, such as Beloff, Tart, Rhine, and Schmidt, as mistaken rather than dishonest.)[19] However, the close association of parapsychologists and "miracle men" does present the problem of explaining the difference between genuine investigators and their often disreputable subjects. At this point I shall merely suggest that those properly called "parapsychologists" are marked by their efforts to comply with scientific standards, even if their peculiar subject matter does make such compliance difficult. (This further difficulty with parapsychology will be discussed in connection with the third criticism.)

But let us now turn to the second criticism, which blames parapsychologists for intellectual shortcomings. At first it might seem unfair because it amounts to moral condemnation for epistemological errors. We might briefly cavil at such blame, until we recall that we are commonly held responsible for knowing facts and for acting sensibly. Ignorance of facts or rules is not always an acceptable excuse for wrongdoing, and this common moral perception is expressed as a principle in Clifford's "ethics of belief," with its maxim: "It is wrong always, everywhere and for anyone to believe anything upon insufficient evidence."[20] Since all of us make intellectual errors at one time or another, we may find this a stern rule, and may well want to mitigate it. In fact, a plausible qualification could say that it is wrong to believe on insufficient evidence when the belief may, directly or indirectly, cause harm to someone. This would be more consistent with Clifford's salient example, which depicts a careless shipowner ordering a voyage that becomes a tragic catastrophe because he did not bother to learn about the condition of his vessel.[21]

False or unwarranted beliefs can cause harm in many ways, of course. They can lead to hate and injustice, and to unnecessary risks and injuries. As dogmatic rules of conduct they can inhibit self-realization in life, or they can simply be bad examples. Yet we can moderate Clifford's harsh dictum because some false or unwarranted beliefs seem to do no harm at all. (For example, belief in unicorns is not likely to be dangerous). Added to this observation is William James's well-known reply to Clifford, that sometimes believing without sufficient evidence may be beneficial. For example, belief in success can sometimes be a necessary condition for success. Thus, the morality of belief is not as simple as Clifford's maxim would suggest. Nevertheless, it is true that certain beliefs can cause harm, and responsible parapsychologists must seriously consider whether their commitment to unproven beliefs (at least to the extent of entertaining them) renders them culpable in that respect.

Are parapsychologists culpable fools? The most obvious argument that they are at least fools would begin by detailing parapsychology's very limited results since its inception in 1882. This would suggest that the evidence for paranormal abilities is so weak that it should be given no further consideration. Critics note that most experiments have been so loosely designed as to permit either opportunity for fraud or naturalistic explanations of apparent successes, and only a few experiments, such as the Pratt-Woodruff series, have been thought to merit serious scientific consideration at all. Even in those cases critics have found reasons for doubt, and the results have not been spectacular. This paucity of believable results in a period of more than a century is compounded by conceptual problems. For example, paranormal events are defined negatively as not natural, not fraudulent, and not coincidental, which creates the problem of how they are to be explained. Failures to demonstrate paranormal phenomena are often not accepted as falsifications, but are instead explained away by further elaborations of the theories that were to have been proven. The most successful experiments are so designed (involving, for example, attempts to correctly identify cards in a large randomly ordered series, or to influence the fall of large numbers of dice) that the putative paranormal events cannot be isolated for study. Furthermore, the successful experiments cannot be replicated reliably.

Some might see these problems as good reasons for deciding that parapsychology should be abandoned. However, in discussing its morality we must ask whether we have heard clear arguments that belief in paranormal abilities is significantly harmful. We have to answer that the only real harm connected with such beliefs occurs when they are used to defraud people (which has certainly happened). The important point, however, is that although mediums and magicians have perpetrated this kind of fraud, parapsychologists attempting scientific research have not typically done so. Their beliefs may be foolish, but they are not culpably so. One historian's sympathetic characterization of the nineteenth-century pioneers of psychical research also applies to those who came later:

> Even if their findings were illusory, their ideals unattainable, one cannot dismiss their quest as unworthy and lives devoted to it as wholly misspent. And for my part I cannot see in their work any signs of hopeless credulity, or of an overmastering will to believe.[22]

Admittedly, this applies only to the group that is defined so as to exclude mediums, magicians, and other disreputable characters, and admittedly some of the latter have represented themselves as parapsychologists in the scientific sense. Nevertheless, there have been investigators who clearly tried to be scientific and honest, and their work justifies the claim that there is a moral practice of parapsychology, even if it must constantly work to rid itself of disreputable associations. Of course, even the honest, scientific investigators have been subject to severe criticism, much of which conveys the suspicion that their subject-matter may erode their ability to be respectable scientists.

Let us therefore turn to the third accusation, which centers more on the nature of the subject matter. Why does this particular suspicion (that the activity actually corrupts the participants) cling to parapsychology among all the sciences that involve study of human beings? We have suggested one reason, which is that parapsychologists become closely associated with some doubtful characters whom they study. We must now add another, which is that success in experiments may require that the parapsychologists develop empathy with their subjects. This may well involve more than a tentative adoption of their beliefs, and obviously any such move would create the risk that committed researchers could become "true believers," discounting negative evidence and failing to note when experiments were designed or performed carelessly. At the extreme they could falsify data, to "prove" subjectively held certainties which had, unfortunately, not yet been confirmed empirically.

The case of Samuel Soal, mentioned above, may be one in which this happened. This reputable professor of mathematics was a conscientious and reliable experimenter for many years. In the 1930s he attempted to replicate Rhine's results with the Zener cards, faithfully reporting uniformly negative results in massive numbers of experiments. In a famous informal investigation, the Gordon Davis case, he produced persuasive anecdotal evidence that mediums do not contact departed spirits. He was known as a careful and reserved experimenter who avoided sensational claims.

He seems to have changed into a "true believer" when Whately Carrington suggested that he look for a different sort of correlation in his card-guessing data. Doing this, Soal decided that two of his subjects had apparently been demonstrating paranormal abilities after all. One of them appeared to have been guessing the cards that were the next targets at a rate well beyond chance expectation, thus displaying not only telepathy or clairvoyance, but precognition. Soal carried out further tightly controlled experiments with the talented subjects, producing very convincing results. However, some years later a disaffected assistant claimed to have seen him altering target sheets after guesses had been made. There was suspicion that the experimental design would have permitted Soal (provided that he had a prodigious memory) to produce above-chance results by changing 1s to 4s and 5s. The original target sheets were not available for examination, but eventually a computer study of the frequency of relevant numbers in random number tables and in copies of the target sheets revealed a skewed pattern consistent with the cheating strategy that had been alleged. Although the evidence is complex it has generally been judged sufficient to discredit Soal and to suggest that, captured by belief in the paranormal, he doctored the evidence.[23] In Soal's case, as in other cases of fraud in this field, we get the impression that the subject matter itself is seductive, and can lead one to become an unscrupulous advocate of an unproven belief.

This possibility is increased by the fact that parapsychologists deal with subject matter that is very "soft" because it occurs within individual private experiences that are said to be influenced by personal relationships. However, this difficulty is not peculiar to parapychologists. We could legitimately compare their work with that of psychologists of religion. In both cases the subjects studied do not attribute their experiences entirely to natural causes, and they often report unusual experiences that are available only to those who are in private states such as faith. In both fields there is difficulty in producing replicable results and in developing theories that will explain alleged phenomena in ways that skeptics can understand. In both cases the "privacy" of the subjective experiences makes it difficult to verify their presence or absence and to develop experimental procedures for studying them.[24] In both fields there are those who suggest that to fully understand the relevant phenomena one must experience them, and we may well ask whether there can be a viable science with such a requirement.

Certainly, what is required for successful paranormal performances is more than mere intellectual belief. We are told that subjects who achieve high scores report that a peculiar mental state is associated with their performances. It is one of calm and relaxed acceptance, of willingness to believe, combined with alert interest and a basic wish to perform tasks well, without anxiety about results.[25] This general characteristic of successful subjects, combined with the claim that certain subjects are "stars," and with the need for experiments to be imaginatively designed so as to interest participants, and with the fact that in long experimental series successful performance rates decline, indicates that success in parapsychology has to be combined with a mental state that rather resembles that expected of a person engaging in petitionary prayer.

If paranormal phenomena exist, this positive mental state might also be at least necessary for success in producing and detecting them. This is the theory of Gertrude Schmeidler. In a series of ingenious experiments she identified persons likely to be in the appropriate frame of mind and claimed to demonstrate its correlation with paranormal events. This became known as "the sheep-goat effect," the sheep being those in this mental state who can demonstrate the existence of the paranormal, and the goats being doubters who regularly demonstrate its nonexistence. Both subjects and experimenters could be sheep or goats, the attitude of the experimenters being very important, since failure to replicate results is often attributed to their skepticism.

The sheep-goat effect would deserve ridicule, except for its appearance in other disciplines. Patrick Grim reports a similar phenomenon in social psychology, where it is called "the Rosenthal Effect." It amounts to the observation that sympathetic experimenters in even the most controlled experiments have a tendency to get the results they believe in, although the effect does decrease as controls are tightened. Grim has pointed out that parapsychology's sheep-goat effect and social psychology's Rosenthal effect (also known as experimenter bias) are so similar as to be indistinguishable from each other, although the Rosenthal effect is accepted as a real occurrence and the sheep-goat effect is not.[26]

At this point we should again recall that successful experiments in parapsychology are all constructed in environments of random events, such as the order of carefully shuffled cards, the fall of large numbers of dice, and the occurrence of randomly generated electronic signals. This is consistent with the circumstances in which spontaneous paranormal phenomena occur, but it does create additional difficulties. If successful intuitions or volitions occur only in circumstances of this kind, they are hidden in crowds of guesses or events that occur by chance, so that there is no way to identify and isolate the paranormal events for study. (In fact, no one seems to have asked whether there are actually discrete paranormal intuitions and volitions, or whether paranormal powers, if they exist, might serve to improve the subject's chances on every occasion without decisively resolving any given event into one that is normal or paranormal).

However, these are considerations that form the background for our questions about the nature of this putative practice. If success in parapsychology requires the subjective involvement of both subjects and experimenters, and if success occurs only within crowds of chance events, we must continue to ask whether parapsychology is a science at all. Our answer has to be that the "fraud and folly" historically associated with it, plus its curious requirements for success, would surely rule parapsychology out of the sciences, except that it shares these methodological problems with respectable disciplines in the social sciences, including psychology of religion.

However, some might then suggest that all such disciplines are unsound or incomplete as sciences, especially because they can easily encourage experimenters to become involved with the experiences and beliefs of those they study. This would seem to be a breach of scientific propriety, or at least a serious temptation to compromise one's integrity as an experimenter, and to render all these sciences morally suspect. However, I would suggest that this need not always be the case. In one such science, at least, sympathy with the subjects and even adoption of their beliefs has assumed the status of a moral requirement. This interesting entanglement of epistemological and moral requirements has arisen among twentieth-century anthropologists discussing magic in other cultures. Nineteenth-century anthropologists had not recognized that magic served purposes and produced benefits within the cultures that used it, and they had dismissed it as irrational. Thus, they condemned "primitive" magic because it seemed to accomplish none of the things that were considered valuable in the anthropologists' own cultures. This reprehensible reaction occurred only as a brief stage in the history of anthropology, and attitudes toward strange and apparently useless practices soon became much more sympathetic. In fact, some anthropologists eventually argued for the positive values and the rationality of magic.

Of course, they did it in various ways. Some held that magic is rational only in its cultural context. They believed that magic should be supplanted in contemporary life, but they recognized it as a rational means for coping with problems in the context of outdated beliefs.

People might be dissuaded or weaned from its use, but certainly not ridiculed for practising it. However, other anthropologists suggested that magic is an unavoidable part of any life in any culture, including our own. For example, George Gmelch (an anthropologist who had been a professional baseball player) catalogued the rituals of pitchers and batters, and found that they illustrated Malinowski's rule: that magic is used in risky situations, as an effective means for coping with uncertainty.[27] (A. F. C. Wallace advanced a similar argument, holding that religious rituals such as prayer help us to cope with daunting tasks.)[28] Anthropologists also studied other less formal ritualistic practices, such as regimens of exercise and diet, as instances of the same pattern.[29] E. E. Evans-Pritchard expressed acceptance in the extreme when he reported that while studying magic and oracles in the Azande culture he had used the poison oracle, and found it to be a sensible way of conducting one's life.[30]

Some philosophers have also said positive things about magic, mostly to the effect that in certain contexts it may occasion the appearance of aesthetic, psychological, and social benefits.[31] Outstanding among such treatments is that of Collingwood, who advances the theory that magic is an art form that is used to change the quality of experience so that personal and social goods may be realized. Collingwood has in mind the (frequently bad) art that appears in the costumes, symbols, and ceremonies used in military reviews, national celebrations, church services, and even social events like dinner parties.[32] In remarks related to Collingwood's, and invoking some of Wittgenstein's remarks, Iris Murdoch also argues for magic's benefits in transforming our experience of the world.[33]

An additional theme present in sympathetic scholarly evaluations implies complete understanding that magic is not a reliable way of accomplishing practical things. When magic in these ordinary-life senses "works," it is not in the technical sense that every magical ceremony is followed by the literal appearance of what it purposes. It is as if magical "results" appear by chance but in striking coincidences that seem to be beyond chance expectation. Thus, as Malinowski says, magic is practiced mainly in situations where chance is a significant factor. When magic is employed in such situations it works because of the power of imagination, enabling people to act effectively when otherwise they might be frozen by indecision or apprehension. Magical practices enable some people to act so as to take advantage of fortunate chance occurrences or be reconciled to runs of bad luck. Jung's theory of synchronicity could well be interpreted as an endorsement and theoretical elaboration of magic understood in this sense.

At this point, let us review and sum up. This excursus on the rationality of magic has been occasioned by misgivings about the suggestion that successfully understanding and demonstrating paranormal phenomena requires belief in them. That requirement would seem to be a serious breach of scientific propriety and thus of a subdivision of morality. With reference to it I have observed that there are strong parallels and overlaps between the activities of experimenters who are committed to belief in the paranormal, certain kinds of social scientists (especially anthropologists studying magic), and successful users of magic. I now suggest that we must give serious consideration to the hypothesis (partly suggested by Schmeidler's results) that successful parapsychologists are not only studying magic but also, on occasion, participating in its practice. In the modern experimental context all of this may be done unwittingly, and both experimenters and subjects may believe themselves to be involved in a branch of psychology. Yet, they may also be doing magic, even as Alcock's title, *Parapsychology: Science or Magic?* suggests. Edward Girden suggests the same thing, with the same disapproval, at the end of his survey. Trying to explain the continuing interest in parapsychology, he says that "we are dealing with a deep motivational need for magic."[34] However, in invoking this hypothesis I do not intend to follow Girden and suggest that magic is bad and therefore parapsychology is bad. In fact (defining magic as Collingwood does), I am inclined to a careful and qualified endorsement of both magic and parapsychology.

My argument is that the moral criticism of parapsychology that holds that it is a bad or corrupting influence is connected to the felt but barely articulated insight that, however sensible and honest the investigator, any successful display of paranormal powers depends on a certain special mental state, not only in the subjects but quite possibly in the experimenters as well. In the experiments described by Schmeidler and others the technique is clearly that of recognizing and at least tentatively believing in psychological abilities that magic requires, and then capitalizing on certain subjects' possession of them. The abilities in question involve skill in mobilizing imagination, interpretation, and will power for dealing with chance events. However, if this explanation of what is going on in successful experiments in parapsychology be accepted, a question still remains. We may still ask whether the activity itself should be morally condemned, and therefore excluded from the realm of practices.

As we prepare to state our final answer, we should note one more important fact. It is that the experiential and behavioral pattern of magic appears in gamblers. In obvious ways they use their imaginations to

strengthen and integrate their wills so as to be able to make risky decisions and then take advantage of fortunate outcomes or be reconciled to
unfortunate ones. Like successful users of magic, gamblers making haz-
ardous decisions characteristically engage in ritualistic behavior to prepare themselves for their difficult decisions. Like users of magic, they
develop imaginative explanations to account for the irregular appearance of the rewards.

Since we are concerned with the morality of parapsychology and
magic, we should also remember that there are doubts about the morality of gambling, even if governments sometimes organize, administer,
and profit from it. In fact, the doubts about gambling are very similar to
those about parapsychology. Critics argue that a great waste of
resources is involved, and frequently those who can least afford it waste
their money in attempts to become wealthy. Since they are almost certain to lose, and their losing often has bad effects on others, gamblers
could also be charged with being culpable fools. In addition, gambling
is notorious for its association with fraud and crime, both in cheating by
individual gamblers and by those who run the lotteries and other
games. There is also the fact that individual gamblers often become
obsessed with their activity, probably because well-designed games are
arranged so that, although the odds are against the players, there are
intermittent and tantalizing rewards. In their fascination with such
rewards, gamblers can permit their lives to become distorted, neglecting
family and business obligations. They can become unreliable and
unprincipled, and in general can exhibit the form of life that Paul Tillich
(eschewing belief in literal demons) describes as "demonic." What
Tillich means by that term is a form of life that is distorted in its public,
behavioral aspect, and experienced as obsessive in its private, mental
aspect.[35]

I have explicated these criticisms of gambling in obvious parallel
to criticisms of parapsychology because in my opinion both sets of
criticisms are directed at approximately the same thing, and both are
to some extent justified. Magic, gambling, and successful experiments
in parapsychology all feature interesting (even fascinating) rewards
that come by chance to those who have not earned them. These
rewards sometimes obsess the participants, who can thus be cor-
rupted. Therefore we are dealing with a morally marginal set of practices that can have certain benefits, but can also produce distorted
lives. As William James points out, gambling may be necessary, especially when certain decisions are forced upon us in real life. (In addition, of course, it may be enjoyable). On the other hand it may be
morally dangerous. Our society's decision at present seems to be that

its benefits outweigh its dangers, so that it is frequently treated as a permissible activity.

All of this would suggest that suspicions about the morality of magic, gambling, and parapsychology, while not without foundation, are not sufficient to condemn these activities unequivocally. In fact, charges of the first two kinds can be answered satisfactorily and dismissed. We can point out that a portion of any life must be devoted to interests that are merely satisfying and not obviously useful in producing goods and services. Gambling, magic, and prayer may be among the satisfying activities that do not display the focused problem-solving rationality of science and technology. Such activities can be permitted, since they are not always harmful or culpably foolish, and since they may on occasion have good results.

Still, the third accusation, that parapsychology has a tendency to corrupt those who take part in it, is serious. It points to the possibility that successful parapsychology involves magic (as defined by Collingwood and modern anthropologists), and we can plausibly hypothesize that magic (like gambling and religion) can be addictive, obsessing some people who are susceptible to its attractions and allow them to distort their lives. (There are, after all, addictive personalities). This must be taken seriously, although we need not suppose that the experimenters or subjects are in danger of being possessed by demons. Their moral peril can be explained clearly in psychological terms, without invoking an additional hypothesis about supernatural forces.

Our present evaluation must therefore be ambivalent. We no longer totally condemn gambling and no longer fear that people practicing magic can be harmed by supernatural forces. (The "we" in these generalizations obviously refers to the academic community, but even with that group in mind it would not refer to everyone). Therefore, activities which involve strong individual commitment to unverifiable symbolic beliefs and to ritualistic actions in the face of uncertainty can be accepted as options in life in spite of their moral and psychological dangers. This is probably because we now value individual freedom very highly, and accord people the right to take risks in working out their own destinies within the bounds of morality and rationality.[36] The question of whether the nonaddictive person may sometimes risk such activities seems to receive an implicit affirmative answer. Gambling, parapsychology, and religious practices, with their various magical forms, can at least be condoned, even if we continue to be wary of extreme behavior in each of them.

NOTES

1. *Nichomachean Ethics*, 2.6.1107a.9–11, in *The Basic Works of Aristotle*, ed. Richard McKeon (New York: Random House, 1941), 959.

2. John B. Noss, *Man's Religions*, 4th ed. (London: Collier Macmillan, 1969), 138.

3. Alasdair MacIntyre, *After Virtue*, 2d ed. (Notre Dame: University of Notre Dame Press, 1984), 187. Charles Taylor, in *Sources of the Self* (Cambridge: Harvard University Press, 1989), defines *practice* more briefly as "any stable configuration of shared activity, whose shape is defined by a certain pattern of do's and don'ts" (204). His examples, such as child-raising procedures, marketing systems, ways of making political decisions, and polite greetings, indicate that he, too, associates practices with goodness and production of goods.

4. MacIntyre, *After Virtue*, 200.

5. George O. Abell, "Astrology," in *Science and the Paranormal*, ed. George O. Abell and Barry Singer (New York: Charles Scribner's Sons, 1981), 71.

6. Isaac Asimov, "Introduction," in James Randi, *Flim-Flam!* (Buffalo, N.Y.: Prometheus, 1982), xiii.

7. Edward Girden, "Parapsychology," in *Handbook of Perception*, vol. 10, ed. Edward C. Carterette and Morton P. Friedman (New York: Academic Press, 1978), 408–9.

8. John Stuart Mill, *Utilitarianism*, ch. 2, in *Ethical Theories*, 2d ed. with rev., ed. A. I. Melden (Englewood Cliffs, N.J.: Prentice-Hall, 1967), 403.

9. Ibid., 400.

10. The personal integrity (as well as the eccentricity) of the pioneers of SPR is attested everywhere in the literature. See, for example, C. D. Broad, "Henry Sidgwick and Psychical Research," in C. D. Broad, *Religion, Philosophy and Psychical Research* (New York: Humanities Press, 1969), 86–115; and Alan Gauld, *The Founders of Psychical Research* (London: Routledge and Kegan Paul, 1968), 137ff.

11. For Hansel's criteria in examining evidence from experiments, see C. E. M. Hansel, *ESP and Parapsychology: A Critical Reevaluation* (Buffalo, N.Y.: Prometheus Books, 1980), 19–28.

12. James E. Alcock, *Parapsychology: Science or Magic?* (Toronto: Pergamon Press, 1981), 139.

13. Ibid., 139–40.

14. Ibid., 140–41.

15. Flew uses this phrase in his introduction to a selection on fraud in parapsychology in Antony Flew, ed., *Readings in the Philosophical Problems of Parapsychology* (Buffalo, N.Y.: Prometheus Books, 1987), 235.

16. Alcock, *Parapsychology: Science or Magic?* 139.

17. Hansel, *ESP and Parapsychology*, 127.

18. Leroy Wolins, "Responsibility for Raw Data," in the Comment section of *American Psychologist* 17 (1962), 657–58. This incident, as well as accounts of famous frauds in science, can also be found in Ian St. James-Roberts, "Are Researchers Trustworthy?" *New Scientist* 2 (September 1976), 481.

19. Randi, *Flim-Flam!* 150, 233–36, 265, 272.

20. W. K. Clifford, "The Ethics of Belief," quoted in *To Believe or Not to Believe: Readings in the Philosophy of Religion*, ed. E. D. Klemke (Toronto: Harcourt Brace Jovanovich, 1992), 500.

21. For further discussion of this issue see James C. S. Wernham, *James's Will-to-Believe Doctrine* (Kingston and Montreal: McGill–Queen's University Press, 1987), 69–74.

22. Gauld, *The Founders of Psychical Research*, 341.

23. The most important discussions of irregularities in Soal's research can be found in *Proceedings of the SPR* 56 (1974–1978). Note especially the articles by C. Scott and P. Haskell (43ff), and by B. Markwick (250ff).

24. For a discussion of these problems see Gardner Murphy, "The Problem of Repeatability in Psychical Research," in Flew, *Philosophical Problems of Parapsychology*, 254ff. Comparable problems are discussed by David M. Wulff in *Psychology of Religion: Classic and Contemporary Views* (Toronto: John Wiley and Sons, 1991). See especially his sections on the questionnaire method of studying subjective experiences such as faith ("Can Religious Faith Be Meaningfully Measured?" 246–47), and on attempts to measure the effects of prayer ("Early 'Experimental' Approaches," 164–72).

25. Murphy, "The Problem of Repeatability," 258.

26. Patrick Grim, "Psi and the Rosenthal Effect," in Flew, *Philosophical Problems of Parapsychology*, 148.

27. George Gmelch, "Baseball Magic," in *Magic, Witchcraft and Religion*, 2d ed., ed. Arthur C. Lehmann and James E. Meyers (Mountain View, Calif.: Mayfield, 1989), 295–96.

28. A. F. C. Wallace, *Religion* (New York; Random House, 1966), 234.

29. Jill Dubisch, "You Are What You Eat; Religious Aspects of the Health Food Movement," in Lehmann and Meyers, *Magic, Witchcraft and Religion*, 69ff.

30. E. E. Evans–Pritchard, *Witchcraft, Oracles and Magic Among the Azande* (Oxford: Clarendon, 1965), 270 (the first edition was 1937).

31. See especially I. C. Jarvie and Joseph Agassi, "The Problem of the Rationality of Magic," in *Rationality*, ed. Bryan Wilson (Oxford: Basil Blackwell, 1970). In this collection various anthropologists and philosophers advance versions of the belief that magic can bring about personal integrity and social harmony, to the benefit of individuals and society.

32. R. G. Collingwood, "Art As Magic," *The Principles of Art* (Oxford: Clarendon, 1965), 57–77.

33. Iris Murdoch, *Metaphysics as a Guide to Morals* (London: Chatto and Windus, 1992), 421–33.

34. Girden, "Parapsychology," 409.

35. Paul Tillich, "The Demonic," in *The Interpretation of History*, tr. N. A. Basetzki and Elsa L. Talmeya (New York: Charles Scribner's Sons, 1936), 77ff.

36. For a thorough and critical explanation of our contemporary commitment to ideals of freedom, benevolence, and the values of ordinary life, consult Charles Taylor, *Sources of the Self*. Taylor would understand, but would, I suspect, regret this essay's acceptance of magic (explained naturalistically) as part of a morally acceptable life. (See especially his "Conclusions: The Conflicts of Modernity," 495–521).

LIST OF CONTRIBUTORS

Susan J. Armstrong is Professor of Philosophy and Women's Studies at Humboldt State University, Arcata, California. Her previous publications include *Environmental Ethics: Divergence and Convergence* (McGraw Hill, 1993), as well as various journal articles in the areas of environmental ethics and process philosophy, and book chapters on Hegel, Kierkegaard, moral personhood, and contemporary theology.

Heather Botting is an anthropologist who specializes in religious studies. She is coauthor of *The Orwellian World of Jehovah's Witnesses* (University of Toronto Press, 1984). She is currently involved in the administration of a project on religious pluralism in Canada, at the Centre for Studies in Religion and Society at the University of Victoria, Canada.

Stephen E. Braude is Professor of Philosophy at the University of Maryland Baltimore County. His previous publications include *First Person Plural: Mulitiple Personality and the Philosophy of Mind* (Rowman and Littlefield, 1995), *The Limits of Influence: Psychokinesis and the Philosophy of Science* (Routledge, 1991) and *ESP and Psychokinesis: A Philosophical Examination* (Temple University Press, 1979). He is past president of the Parapsychological Association.

Donald Evans is Professor Emeritus of Philosophy at Victoria College, University of Toronto, Canada. His previous publications include *Spirituality and Human Nature* (State University of New York Press, 1993) and *Struggle and Fulfilment: The Inner Dynamics of Religion and Morality* (Collins, 1979; Fortress, 1981). At Toronto he has taught courses in philosophy of mysticism and the paranormal, of social science, and of human nature.

David Ray Griffin is Professor of Philosophy of Religion and Theology at the School of Theology at Claremont and Claremont Graduate School.

His previous publications include *Founders of Constructive Postmodern Philosophy* (State University of New York Press, 1993), *Evil Revisited* (State University of New York Press, 1991), and *God and Religion in the Postmodern World* (State University of New York Press, 1988). Forthcoming is *Parapsychology, Philosophy, and Spirituality*. He is also Executive Director of the Center for Process Studies.

James R. Horne, an Anglican priest, is Professor of Philosophy at University of Waterloo, Canada. His previous publications include *Beyond Mysticism* (Wilfrid Laurier University Press, 1978), *The Moral Mystic* (Wilfred Laurier University Press, 1983), and *Mysticism and Vocation* (Wilfred Laurier University Press, 1996). He is interested in ethics, religious experience, and mysticism, and has taught a popular course in philosophical problems related to parapsychology and magic.

Hugo Meynell is Professor of Religious Studies at the University of Calgary, Canada. His previous publications include *Is Christianity True?* (The Catholic University of America, 1995), *The Nature of Aesthetic Value* (Macmillan, 1986), and *The Intelligible Universe: A Cosmological Argument* (Macmillan, 1982). He is a Fellow of the Royal Society of Canada.

Terence Penelhum is Professor Emeritus of Religious Studies at the University of Calgary, Canada, where he was formerly Professor of Philosophy, Dean of Arts and Science, and Director of the Calgary Institute for the Humanities. His previous publications include *Survival and Disembodied Existence* (Routledge, 1970), *God and Skepticism* (D. Reidel, 1983), and *Reason and Religious Faith* (Westview, 1995). He received the Canada Council Molson Prize for the Humanities in 1988 and is a Fellow of the Royal Society of Canada.

Michael Stoeber is Associate Professor of Philosophy of Religion at the Catholic University of America, Washington, D.C. Previous publications include *Theo-Monistic Mysticism* (Macmillan and University of Toronto Press, 1992) and *Evil and the Mystics' God* (Macmillan and St. Martin's Press, 1994). He was a Social Sciences and Humanities Research Council of Canada Post Doctoral Fellow from 1990–92.

INDEX